Returning to Revolution

Plateaus – New Directions in Deleuze Studies

'It's not a matter of bringing all sorts of things together under a single concept but rather of relating each concept to variables that explain its mutations.'
Gilles Deleuze, *Negotiations*

Series Editors

Ian Buchanan, Cardiff University
Claire Colebrook, Penn State University

Editorial Advisory Board

Titles available in the series

Visit the Plateaus website at www.euppublishing.com/series/plat

RETURNING TO REVOLUTION
Deleuze, Guattari and Zapatismo

Thomas Nail

EDINBURGH
University Press

For the revolution under way

© Thomas Nail, 2012

Edinburgh University Press Ltd
22 George Square, Edinburgh EH9 9LF

www.euppublishing.com

Typeset in Sabon
by Servis Filmsetting Ltd, Stockport, Cheshire, and
printed and bound in Great Britain by
CPI Group (UK) Ltd, Croydon CR0 4YY

A CIP record for this book is available from the British Library

ISBN 978 0 7486 5586 1 (hardback)
ISBN 978 0 7486 5587 8 (webready PDF)
ISBN 978 0 7486 5589 2 (epub)
ISBN 978 0 7486 5588 5 (Amazon ebook)

The right of Thomas Nail
to be identified as author of this work
has been asserted in accordance with
the Copyright, Designs and Patents Act 1988.

Contents

Acknowledgements

I wish to express my sincere appreciation to the following people for all their feedback and support during the writing and editing of this book: Ted Toadvine, Colin Koopman, John Lysaker and Tres Pyle. Over the years I have had many wonderful and fruitful discussions on the topics discussed in this book with many people; I would like to thank in particular: Kieran Aarons, Neal Miller, Daniel Bowman, Daniel W. Smith, Sean Parson, Nicolae Morar, Greg Liggett, Lindsay Naylor and the Theory Group at the University of Oregon Department of English (especially Tristan Sipley, Eric Luttrell, Shane Billings, Josh Magsam and Melissa Sexton). Not only in theory, but in practice, I am also extremely appreciative of all the dedicated activists and collectives I worked with during the writing of this book, who are committed to the difficult labour of direct democracy: the Students' Cooperative Association, Cascadia Forest Defense and No One Is Illegal (Toronto).

Many of the following chapters were theorised and composed in Café Roma, one of those rare cafés where there is no Internet and nothing but classical music. I am very thankful for this space. This book was also made possible in part by the financial and scholarly support of the US Fulbright Program, the University of Toronto and the Wayne Morse Center for Law and Politics, all of which provided me with the means, space and time to work on these chapters.

I am grateful to Carol Macdonald at Edinburgh University Press for her kindness and helpfulness during the final stages of the book's preparation.

I would also like to thank my best reader and wife, Katie Riddle, for her contributions and company during all stages of this book's creation.

A Note on the Text

In-text citations for all works by Gilles Deleuze (including those co-authored with Félix Guattari and Claire Parnet) are listed by their date of English translation. Their page numbers, however, are given first according to the page number(s) of the original French text and then followed by the page number(s) of the translated English text. All other in-text citations are to the extant translations, where such translations exist.

Preface

The year 2011 was one of incredible, worldwide revolutionary activity. Shortly after the completion of this book the largest global occupation movement in history crystallised in October 2011. This occupation movement is the practical and theoretical heir to the political strategies developed by Deleuze, Guattari and the Zapatistas as articulated in the chapters of this book. Inspired by the Arab Spring, the occupations in Wisconsin, the riots against austerity measures in Europe and the UK, and the occupations by the Spanish *indignados* and the Greeks at Syntagma Square, the Occupy movement has spread to over 2,556 cities across eighty-two countries, and over 600 communities in the United States (Occupy Together 2011). The Occupy movement is based on the popular outrage at the growing disparity of wealth and power between individuals and corporations, as well as the failure of political representatives to resolve the problems of increasing unemployment, housing foreclosures, paralysing student debt and the aggressive defunding of social services. But, as some theorists have correctly remarked, the Occupy movement is demonstrably more than a mere protest against greedy bankers and corrupt politicians: it is a sustained movement that is responding to the problems of global capitalism and the institution of political representation itself (Hardt and Negri 2011; Žižek 2011; Graeber 2011).

Rather than proposing a list of formal demands or lobbying political parties for reforms to the system (although such reforms would probably not be unwelcome), the Occupy movement has mostly resisted such negotiations as potential co-optations. If the problem were simply corruption or greed one would expect to hear a unified message for reform and legislation. This message could then be adopted by party politicians and mobilised in the next election. The fact that the Occupy movement has not delivered a clearly unified set of demands indicates a deeper mistrust of the very form of political representation itself that would respond to such demands. Additionally, the method of intervention chosen –

'unlawful occupation' – should also indicate a breakdown of the normal legal channels that are supposed to respond to the will of the people. Instead of demanding reforms from representatives or even trying to create its own representatives or leaders, the Occupy movement has seized public space and tried to create its own form of direct democracy based on consensus decision-making, equality and mutual aid. In societies that have failed to provide many of its members with the basic necessities of life and failed to listen to their demands, the Occupy encampments around the world have decided to provide these things for each other. They have created kitchens, libraries, clinics and media centres open to everyone who needs them. The Occupy movement thus demonstrates that state capitalism itself is the cause of the current crisis. Not only does it express a popular acknowledgement that we do not live in the best of all possible worlds, it also demands that we start creating some alternatives to the current system here and now, and not wait around for political representatives or corporations to fix the problems they created.

The Occupy movement and its strategies did not come out of nowhere. As theorists have already done well to point out, many of the strategies deployed by the Occupy movement have their origins in the alter-globalisation movement (Klein 2011; Hardt and Negri 2011; Graeber 2011). In particular, horizontal and leaderless net-working, consensus decision-making and a multi-fronted struggle equally inclusive of race, class, gender, sexuality and environmental issues are important dimensions of both movements. But where did the alter-globalisation movement get these strategies from in the first place? It is well established in the scholarly literature on this topic that the alter-globalisation movement and one of its main organising groups, Peoples' Global Action, originated most directly from the first and largest global anti-neoliberal gatherings: the Intercontinental *Encuentros* organised by the Zapatistas (Notes from Nowhere 2003; Khasnabish 2008; Curran 2006; Engler 2007). The basic principles of horizontalism were laid out by the Zapatistas at the first *Encuentro*; consensus decision-making was (and still is) used by the indigenous peasants of Chiapas, and their struggle was radically inclusive of all fronts of struggle (race, gender, class, sexual orientation and environment). Given this clearly established lineage and the still-active struggle in Chiapas (one of the more long-standing revolutionary 'occupations' in recent history), it is surprising that no one has yet (as I write this) made this connection explicit or traced its strategic influence on the current struggles.

Similarly, no one has yet explored the theoretical origins of the Occupy movement in any depth. Michael Hardt and Antonio Negri were quick to cast the Occupy movement as an expression of their own concept of '"multitude form" . . . characterised by frequent assemblies and participatory decision-making structures' (Hardt and Negri 2011). But where did Hardt and Negri get this concept from in the first place? Just as the practical origins of Occupy lie deeper than the alter-globalisation movement, so its theoretical origins lie deeper as well. It has already been recognised that Deleuze and Guattari's work holds special promise in the development of a new philosophy of revolution that can revitalise contemporary political thought. Slavoj Žižek, in particular, has gone as far as to say that 'Deleuze more and more serves as the theoretical foundation of today's anti-global Left' (Žižek 2004: xi). But Deleuze and Guattari's work has moved to the centre of the debate primarily due to the success of Hardt and Negri's political trilogy *Empire* (2000), *Multitude* (2004) and *Commonwealth* (2010), which takes Deleuze and Guattari's work as one of its primary philosophical touchstones (2010: 172). It is to Deleuze and Guattari that Hardt and Negri turn for their philosophical account of how the singularities of the multitude can be sustained in a lasting revolutionary movement. Hardt and Negri's books are certainly some of the best-selling works of political philosophy in our time; *Empire* alone sold over 52,000 copies and was translated into ten languages within its first year of publication (Laffey 2002: 109) and Žižek has called it 'the communist manifesto for the twenty-first century'. Hardt and Negri's influence on the academy and activists has been apparent in the increasing number of conferences, anthologies and journal articles devoted to Deleuze's contributions to political thought, and in the growing interest in these ideas among scholars and students.

But Hardt and Negri devote only brief, although numerous, sections and footnotes to what they admit are the clear Deleuzian foundations of their views. In fact, even in their more academic solo works, where one would expect to find a more sustained engagement with Deleuze's political philosophy, Hardt and Negri prefer instead to engage Deleuze more obliquely through readings of common figures in the history of philosophy: Spinoza, Nietzsche and Marx. Meanwhile, none of the current scholarly books on Deleuze and Guattari have taken their concept of revolution as a central theme, nor do any of the currently available books address Deleuze and Guattari's relationship with contemporary revolutionary practice in any detail. This book thus offers the first scholarly investigation of Deleuze and Guattari's concept of revolution treated in Hardt and Negri's bestsellers. By offering a detailed investigation of Deleuze and Guattari's philosophy of revolution that complements the one provided by Hardt and Negri, this book fills a lacuna and provides the missing theoretical link at the heart of contemporary revolutionary struggles like Occupy.

However, while a full exploration of the contemporary revolutionary conjuncture and its origins in the theory and practice of Deleuze, Guattari and the Zapatistas is beyond the scope of this book, one of the strengths of this book is that it is meant to be used as a set of four strategic tools to carry out such a contemporary labour. I must admit I am excited to see, at the end of writing this book, the strategic fruit of Deleuze, Guattari and Zapatismo borne in the global Occupy movement and its continued deployment of the revolutionary strategies outlined in the following chapters. The aim of this book is thus not only to provide a thematic account of the concept of revolution in the work of Gilles Deleuze and Félix Guattari and its relationship to the contemporary revolutionary struggle of Zapatismo, but to be used in the present as a diagnostic and guide to understanding the current return to revolution.

Introduction

> We have to try and think a little about the meaning of revolution. This term is now so broken and worn out, and has been dragged through so many places, that it's necessary to go back to a basic, albeit elementary, definition. A revolution is something of the nature of a process, a change that makes it impossible to go back to the same point . . . a repetition that changes something, a repetition that brings about the irreversible. A process that produces history, taking us away from a repetition of the same attitudes and the same significances. Therefore, by definition, a revolution cannot be programmed, because what is programmed is always the *déjà-là*. Revolutions, like history, always bring surprises. By nature they are always unpredictable. That doesn't prevent one from working for revolution, as long as one understands 'working for revolution' as working for the unpredictable.
>
> (Guattari 2008: 258)

We are witnessing today the return of a new theory and practice of revolution. This return, however, takes none of the traditional forms: the capture of the state, the political representation of the party, the centrality of the proletariat, or the leadership of the vanguard. Rather, given the failure of such tactics over the last century, coupled with the socio-economic changes brought by neoliberalism in the 1980s, revolutionary strategy has developed in more heterogeneous and non-representational directions. The aim of this book is thus to map an outline of these new directions by drawing on the theory and practice of two of its main inspirations: French political philosophers Gilles Deleuze and Félix Guattari and what many have called 'the first post-modern revolutionaries', the Zapatistas of Chiapas, Mexico (Burbach 1994, 1996; Carrigan 1995; Golden 1994, 2001).

There are two important reasons for undertaking a philosophical interrogation of this admittedly young revolutionary direction. First, political life does not have the leisure to wait until after the revolution for the hindsight of philosophical inquiry. If philosophy waited until a new political form of revolution had already come and gone, it would be useless in the formation of the revolutionary process itself. Thus, it is not in spite of, but rather precisely because of the fact that we are in the middle of this return to revolution that a philosophical interrogation and clarification of its practical meaning is needed. Second, since the turn of the century we have heard consistently from the Left (the alter-globalisation movement and the World Social Forum in particular) that 'another world is possible'. But what we have not heard is, more positively, what this alternative world to neoliberalism is. Beyond the political philosophy of possibility, what is needed is a more constructive theory and practice of this 'other world'. I believe we can locate the beginnings of this world in the work of Deleuze, Guattari and the Zapatistas.

The aim of this book is thus threefold: first, to provide a philosophical clarification and outline of the revolutionary strategies that both describe and advance the process of constructing real alternatives to state capitalism; second, to do so by focusing on three influential and emblematic figures of its history, mutually disclosive of one another as well as this larger revolutionary return: Deleuze, Guattari and the Zapatistas. Third, and more specifically, this work proposes four strategies[1] that characterise this return to revolution: (1) a multi-centred diagnostic of political power; (2) a prefigurative strategy of political transformation; (3) a participatory strategy of creating a body politic; and (4) a political strategy of belonging based on mutual global solidarity.

I. Methodology

Deleuze and Guattari

Thus, with the aim of developing these four strategies, I draw from Deleuze and Guattari's political philosophy by extracting from it the concepts that are most relevant and thematically productive to the problem at hand: revolution. More specifically, this work proceeds by way of four guiding questions that allow us to address the central issues underlying contemporary debates in revolutionary theory and practice: what is the relationship between history and revolution? What is revolutionary transformation? How is it possible to sustain and carry out the consequences of a revolutionary transformation? And how do revolutions connect with one another to produce a new form of worldwide solidarity? Deleuze and Guattari never wrote a book, or more than a couple of focused pages at a time, on the concept of political revolution.[2] In fact, the present volume is the first and only full-length work to centrally thematise this concept in their *oeuvre*. Because their usage of the concept of revolution was topical and problem-based, created to be put to use, so my own methodology will follow suit: I focus here exclusively on the problem of revolution. Additionally, this methodology allows for the most productive and focused use of their work, as it deals with one concept per chapter and provides a philosophical parallel to the political practices of the Zapatistas.

Deleuze and Guattari's political philosophy is not only conceptually advantageous to this effort, it is historically relevant as well. Deleuze and Guattari, unlike most of their philosophical contemporaries after the revolutionary events of May 1968, remained openly faithful to the concept of revolution throughout their work. In fact, it is in the aftermath of the failure of many of the political experiments that happened in the 1960s around the world that Deleuze and Guattari wrote their largest work of political philosophy, *Capitalisme et schizophrénie*, volumes one and two (1972, 1980). They were witnessing during these years the end of what Alain Badiou calls 'the last great emancipatory narrative: the revolutionary Party-State' (2010a: 101; 2010b: 67). Accordingly, in *Capitalism and Schizophrenia*, revolution is consistently valorised and juxtaposed against state-capitalism as well as state-socialism and the party/union bureaucracy, heavily criticised in France and around the world in the 1960s and 1970s. During the increasingly conservative and reactionary years of the 1970s and 1980s, Deleuze and Guattari worked tirelessly, in their single largest work, towards a political philosophy that would no longer be subordinated to state, party or vanguardism. If we want to look for some of the earliest philosophical origins of the contemporary revolutionary sequence, it is in these dark but fecund years (1970s and 1980s) that Deleuze and Guattari, perhaps more prolifically and more influentially than any other major philosophers at the time, created political concepts most consonant with the leaderless and networked horizontalism that characterises today's return to revolution practically demonstrated in Zapatismo, the alter-globalisation movement and the Occupy movement (Klein 2011).[3] Even Slavoj Žižek admits that 'Deleuze more and more serves as the theoretical foundation of today's anti-global Left' (2004: xi). But it was also during the 1980s that another revolution was emerging, not in France but in the mountains of the Mexican Southeast: a revolution that would more and more serve as the practical foundation for the 'alter-global Left'.

Yes, Deleuze and Guattari never wrote a book on political revolution, but this does not mean that they did not write about revolution extensively and consistently throughout their political philosophy. If the present book has adopted the method of creating concepts through the assembly of heterogeneous fragments from Deleuze and Guattari's philosophy of revolution, it is not only out of methodological affinity, but out of a practical necessity of doing so as well. And if the present book has chosen to extract these concepts from Deleuze and Guattari rather than from other political philosophers in this time period, it is because Deleuze and Guattari (in addition to their unique influence on the alter-global Left) never gave up on their belief that a worldwide revolution could emerge from the smallest of political experiments without the representation of the state, party, vanguard or proper class consciousness, as indeed it did with the Zapatistas.

Zapatismo

But if Deleuze and Guattari theorised this nascent revolutionary sequence so well, why the need to extract anything at all from the Zapatistas to outline these four strategies? Although not exactly the same, what I am calling the recent return to revolution[4] can be loosely associated with the popular emergence of what is often called the alter-globalisation movement (AGM). While the AGM and groups like Peoples' Global Action (PGA) and the World Social Forum are a significant part of the present revolutionary sequence, the sequence itself is not reducible to the features of these groups, in part because these meta-groups are composed of hundreds of sub-groups from around the world. In any case, the AGM did not start in Seattle in 1999. Most of the historical scholarship on the AGM dates it from 1994, that is, from the beginning of the Zapatista uprising (Notes from Nowhere 2003; Khasnabish 2008; Curran 2006; Engler 2007). Zapatismo and the Intercontinental *Encuentros* were the first and largest global anti-neoliberal gatherings of their kind and gave birth to several important groups like PGA (Khasnabish 2008: 238; Olesen 2005). And although they are obviously not the only source of inspiration, it is well documented that the Zapatistas' declarations against all forms of domination, their strategic refusal of capturing state or party power, their creation of directly democratic consensus-based communes, and their vision of a mutual global solidarity network were all highly visible and have had a lasting impact on revolutionary theory and practice today (Khasnabish 2008). Thus, understanding Zapatismo plays an important role in understanding the larger movement currently under way today.[5]

But my argument that we are witnessing a new revolutionary sequence is not merely an empirical one,[6] although many strong empirical arguments for the emergence of a new revolutionary sequence have been made (and in far more complete ways than I am capable of here).[7] I am thus truly indebted to those works; they are like the empirical companion to this philosophical work.[8] What I am arguing instead is that, in addition to this descriptive history of the past fifteen years of struggle, we can also define the emergence of this new revolutionary sequence by its creation of a set of novel and coherent strategies (that are both practical and theoretical). But since concretely locating these strategies in even the most active organisations of the last fifteen years is well beyond the scope of the present work, I want to focus on a deeper analysis of two of the earliest, most influential and most prolific sources of this often cited 'return to revolution': Deleuze and Guattari, and Zapatismo.

Accordingly, I try to give equal qualitative importance to extracting these strategies from both the political writings of Deleuze and Guattari and the actions of Zapatistas (although admittedly I spend more quantitative time with Deleuze and Guattari in this book). Politics, I hope to demonstrate in the case of Zapatismo, has its own thinking and does not need philosophy to think for it or represent its thought back to it (Lazarus 1996; Badiou 2005a; Foucault 1977). Rather, what the Zapatistas offer that other activists and philosophers do not is a particularly prolific and conceptually creative site at the beginning of this new and still-in-process revolutionary sequence. Many have gone as far as to call Zapatismo the first 'post-communist', 'post-modern' (Golden 1994) and 'post-representational' revolution (Tormey 2006; Proyect 2003). This book thus aims to contribute some novel philosophical clarifications, not for the Zapatistas themselves, but for others who wish to understand and continue the Zapatista struggle elsewhere. But as these practices appear only here and there in various writings and political actions over a fifteen-year period and never in a coherently self-described manifesto, the method of extraction and creative reassembly is one of necessity with the Zapatistas as well.

ASSEMBLY, RELAY AND CONTRIBUTION

But if Deleuze, Guattari and the Zapatistas share in common their being particularly early and influential sources of concepts for the philosophical development of what myself and others (Graeber 2002; Grubacic and Graeber 2004) are calling the present revolutionary sequence, what is their relationship to one another in a philosophical work, methodologically based on conceptual creation through extraction and reassembly? First, I certainly do not want to argue for a direct mutual influence between Deleuze and Guattari and the Zapatistas. Despite being more of a historical/empirical question than a philosophical one, it is also highly unlikely (and not worth trying to map their degrees of separation). Deleuze and Guattari, to my knowledge, were not aware of the early stages of the Zapatista uprising (before 1994), nor were the Zapatistas likely readers of Deleuze and Guattari's work leading up to 1994. Second, I do not want to argue that we should use Deleuze and Guattari's political philosophy to interpret, explain or understand the Zapatistas, as some scholars have done (Evans 2010)[9], any more than I want to argue that we should use the Zapatista uprising to legitimate, ground or justify Deleuze and Guattari's political philosophy. This approach not only presupposes a privileged foundationalism of theory over practice, or practice over theory, but also risks perpetuating a long legacy of Eurocentrism and theoretical imperialism (Spivak 2010). Third, the aim of this book is not to discover in either Deleuze and Guattari or the Zapatistas the philosophical foundations of all political life or 'the political', in part because this task is conceptually totalitarian, but also in part because this task is impossible and only reveals to us the ungrounded and anti-foundational character of political being as such (Lacoue-Labarthe and Nancy 1997). So rather than argue the point of political anti-foundationalism that has been argued elsewhere and much better, this book proposes a different project.

This book instead proposes to read Deleuze and Guattari and the Zapatistas side by side as parallel origins of the same strategies that have now become central to revolutionary and radical Left movements in the twenty-first century. To be clear, the four strategies common to Deleuze, Guattari and Zapatismo that I outline in this book are not models of all political action. Rather, they are only four (there are possibly others) of the transitional tools that have been and are likely to be deployed elsewhere in contemporary political theory and practice. My thesis is not to have discovered the four essential strategies that connect Deleuze, Guattari and the Zapatistas or the four foundations of revolutionary strategy as such. Rather, my thesis is that we can locate the origins of four of the most historically and theoretically influential revolutionary strategies of the late twentieth and early twenty-first century in the work of Deleuze, Guattari and the Zapatistas. They created these four common strategies at roughly the same time (1980s and 1990s) in two different regions of the world (France and Mexico) and in two different domains (politics and philosophy) without direct influence on one another.[10] Neither is founded or derived from the other, but understood together we gain a better sense of both. Additionally, these four common strategies can also be useful for understanding contemporary movements like the *indignados* in Spain or the global Occupy movement, to the degree that these draw heavily on these four strategies and the legacy of Zapatismo and the alter-globalisation movement.

By reading Deleuze, Guattari and the Zapatistas alongside each other we can see where a theoretical action is unclear, weak or too general, and where a practical action will clarify, strengthen or specify how to take theory in a new direction, and vice versa. Where one hits a wall, the other might break through, not as a substitute for the other but as a relay or assemblage of two heterogeneous actions: theory and practice (Foucault 1977: 207). This methodology of doing political philosophy by extracting and reassembling a system of useful practical-theoretical relays is one used by Deleuze, Guattari and Foucault, and one I follow in this book. Accordingly, philosophy, for Deleuze and Guattari, is political insofar as it is directed towards creating concepts that are 'adequate to what is happening around us. It must adopt as its own those revolutions going on elsewhere, in other domains, or those that are being prepared' (Deleuze 2004: 191/138; see also Deleuze and Guattari 1994: 96/100). This book thus adopts as its own the current revolution in preparation.

But this adoption and adequation is not a matter of representation or resemblance. Intellectuals do not simply stand at the front and off to the side of revolutionary struggles as its representatives (Foucault 1977: 208). Whether theory is supposed to inform practice or practice is supposed to inform theory, in each case their relationship has typically been a totalisation of one over the other (1977: 206). In contrast, the goal of developing a political philosophy of practical-theoretical relays is not to ground one in the other or to describe or interpret the world more accurately, but rather to *transform* the world itself using both theory and practice, side by side.

Theory does not cause praxis, nor does praxis cause theory: both are heterogeneous components constitutive *of* revolutionary strategy itself. The political analysis of revolutionary movements is thus never a question of representation, interpretation or 'speaking for others'. Rather, as Guattari says, 'It is a question of situating their trajectory to see whether they are in a position to serve as indicators of new universes of references that could acquire sufficient consistency to bring about a radical change in the situation' (2008: 328). But, as Guattari continues, because 'there are no universal scientific models with which to try to understand a situation . . . known in advance of the situation', one must continually develop new concepts that *help articulate* the situation, *not* represent it (2008: 343, 397). This is what I have aimed to do with the practical-theoretical relays (what I am calling 'strategies') I propose in this book: to extract four common strategies, which will help further articulate the current revolutionary conjuncture.

So, if there are no universal foundations or categories for all political life, as Guattari argues, then the goal of political philosophy changes significantly. If the role of leadership and critique are forever bound by the question of political foundations, then the alternative task of an engaged political philosopher is to intervene and contribute immanently to political struggles themselves just like anyone else. Or as Subcomandante Marcos says, 'We had to be honest and tell people that we had not come to lead anything of what might emerge. We came to release a demand, that could unleash others' (Marcos 2001c). Or perhaps, as Foucault says of his own philosophical interventions,

> So, since there has to be an imperative, I would like the one underpinning the theoretical analysis we are attempting to be quite simply a conditional imperative of the kind: if you want to struggle, here are some key points, here are some lines of force, here are some constrictions and blockages. In other words, I would like these imperatives to be no more than tactical pointers. Of course, it's up to me, and those who are working in the same direction, to know on what fields of real forces we need to get our bearings in order to make a tactically effective analysis. But this is, after all, the circle of struggle and truth, that is to say, precisely, of philosophical practice. (2007: 3)

In sum, the aim of the present volume, in addition to the aforementioned three aims, following Marcos, Marx and Foucault, is not to interpret the world, but to transform it by outlining some revolutionary strategies that might unleash something else. Thus the ultimate

8

criterion of success for this book is not that it has simply described the world, but that it will have been useful to those engaged in the present revolutionary task of changing the world.

II. Interventions

The question of general methodology having been addressed, what are the specific philosophical interventions being proposed in this book as regards the work of Deleuze and Guattari and the Zapatistas? That is, within what readings, contexts and assumptions do I propose to draw on these political thinkers? In this next section I propose two interventions, one into the scholarly literature on Deleuze and Guattari and one into the political commentary written on the Zapatista uprising. In both cases my conclusion is similar: to reject reading them as either theories of political representation or theories of political differentiation. I propose, rather, to read them as theories of political constructivism, that is, as contributions to the *creation* of a new collective political body. I deal firstly with Deleuze and Guattari.

DELEUZE, GUATTARI AND REPRESENTATION

Deleuze and Guattari's political philosophy, due in part to the increasing amount of anti-capitalist activity in the last fifteen years, has recently come to significant scholarly attention. With this attention, the concept of revolution has emerged as a central point of interest. Paul Patton has gone as far as to say that revolutionary deterritorialisation is the normative concept underlying their entire political philosophy (2000: 10).[11] And in his book *Deleuze and Guattari: An Introduction to the Politics of Desire*, Philip Goodchild locates their 'concern for the immanent transformation of society [revolutionary desire] as the sole purpose of their political philosophy' (1996: 5). But within this common interest one can see the formulation of at least two well-argued readings of this concept of revolution.

On the one side, Deleuze and Guattari's concept of revolution is read as a process by which marginalised or minor peoples come to be increasingly included and represented by the liberal democratic state. We can see this type of reading in the work of anglophone scholar Paul Patton (translator of *Différence et répétition*, 1968, and author of *Deleuze and the Political*, 2000), as well as that of francophone scholar Philippe Mengue (author of *Deleuze et la ques-*

tion de la démocratie, 2003). Revolution, as a real object of political aims, according to Mengue, should be considered as a process of becoming-mediated and becoming-represented under a democratic state. Non-mediated, non-representational politics, according to Mengue, are not only highly speculative but practically impossible and undesirable. Deleuze is thus, for Mengue, an ultimately anti-democratic thinker.

> What is the big difficulty of micropolitics? It is that it refuses all mediation and representation. It pretends to be capable of doing it, but – letting aside, for a moment, the problem of the theoretical or speculative validity of such a thesis – experience has shown that this refusal is absolutely impossible and not even desirable. Indeed, politics is linked to the function of mediation and representation – the *doxic* plane of immanence guarantees it . . . opinion is at the heart of politics. (2009: 172)

Paul Patton, however, highlights the concept of 'becoming-democratic' found in Deleuze and Guattari's later work and argues that, despite their lack of a normative political position, there are liberal democratic principles implicit in their political philosophy. Despite Deleuze and Guattari's frequent criticisms against modern state democracies, Patton argues that 'the appearance of "becoming-democratic" in *What Is Philosophy?* represents a new turn in Deleuze and Guattari's political thought' (2008: 178). Specifically, it takes a normative turn in favour of the institutions, rights and values of modern liberal democracy.

While this position may not be the dominant reading of Deleuze and Guattari's concept of revolution, the authors of this position have certainly contributed to a healthy debate over the concept. Despite agreeing with these authors in a host of other areas, I find a few problems with this position. Firstly, it seems a bit strange to say, as Mengue implies, that the historical practice of direct democracy (non-representational, non-mediated democracy) would be simply speculative. Countless volumes on the history of the Paris Commune, the Spanish Civil War, the Landless Peasants Movement in Brazil and others (not to mention those of many indigenous peoples like the Zapatistas) attest to the very non-speculative nature of direct versus representational democracy. There is a meaningful distinction between the two that remains unaddressed by both Patton and Mengue. Secondly, if these events have been experienced, as Mengue claims, they could not possibly be just speculative. The assertion that these experiments have been tried, and have failed, would seem already to indicate that some did find them desirable enough to start them and perhaps die for them. Thirdly, the determination of what is and is not possible and desirable is precisely what revolution aims to transform. I find the closure of this possibility politically suspicious. The brute fact that the liberal state has won a certain historical battle and is the presupposition of many political philosophers has nothing to do with the possible emergence of another more inclusive and desirable form of political organisation. In the end, given Deleuze and Guattari's clear and consistent critique of state representation and mediation, one has to disavow too much of their political work and explicit condemnations of state democracy in order to make them liberal democrats. Additionally, this move takes away one of Deleuze and Guattari's most original contributions to the history of political philosophy: a non-foundational theory of revolution (without state, party, vanguard or representation).

DELEUZE, GUATTARI AND DIFFERENCE

On the other side, Deleuze and Guattari's concept of revolution is more often read as the pure process of political becoming, uncaptured by all forms of political representation and mediation (territory, state and capital). We can see this type of reading in the work of American and Italian philosophers Michael Hardt and Antonio Negri (authors of *Empire*, 2000; *Multitude: War and Democracy in the Age of Empire*, 2004; and *Commonwealth*, 2010) as well as in the work of American scholar Eugene Holland (author of *Deleuze and Guattari's Anti-Oedipus: Introduction to Schizoanalysis*, 1999). Opposed to defining the aim of revolution by its inevitable incorporation into the liberal state apparatus, as Mengue and Patton do, Hardt and Negri draw from Deleuze and Guattari a theory of revolutionary potentiality or 'difference-in-itself' that they call the 'multitude'. Rather than basing revolutionary action on an analogy with, an opposition to, a resemblance with or a representation of the originally presupposed political bodies of territory, god, king, statesman or capital, Hardt and Negri propose a Deleuzian-inspired theory of political creativity located ontologically anterior to any constituted or mediating power, whether state, people or capital. Deleuze and Guattari's concept of revolution, according to Hardt and Negri, should not be read as a theory of possibility defined by what is dominantly understood to be 'possible' or 'feasible' (as Mengue argues), but rather as a pure potentiality 'to become other than one is'.

In Hardt and Negri's version of Spinozist-Deleuzian political ontology, the concept of the multitude stands, not as a new form of representation for global minority movements (that would speak for them), or as a negative movement 'against representation', but rather as an *expressive* potential that all such subjugated groups have 'to revolt', 'to create something new'. But since this potential is not a political object nor even a specific political event, but rather a pure 'becoming-revolutionary' that allows for the possibility of new conditions, elements and agencies in the political field as such, Hardt and Negri are able to avoid the restrictions of only thinking Deleuze and Guattari's theory of revolution as taking place within a representational political domain. Thus, 'the creative forces of the multitude that sustain Empire are also capable of autonomously constructing a counter-Empire, an alternative political organisation of global flows and exchanges,' as they claim in their book *Empire* (2000: 11–23). Examples of this potential for counter-empire, Hardt and Negri argue, are the alter-globalisation movement (2010: 368) and the nomadisms of refugees and immigrants who remain unrepresented in politics today. Their transformation-in-itself is the real sphere of 'the political', perpetually open to all those who potentially participate in its non-exclusive community.

Similarly, for Eugene Holland, 'it is not the entity but the process that has revolutionary potential' (2006: 100). Thus, 'Schizophrenia is the potential for revolution, not the revolution itself' (2006: 100). Opposed to any particular being or entity in the world, the revolutionary plane of immanence, according to Holland, is the 'principle of freedom in permanent revolution' (2006: 123).

Now, while I certainly think this reading is more faithful to the anti-representational dimension of Deleuze and Guattari's theory of revolution, I also want to steer clear of several dangers in this reading, as posed by recent critical scholarship. These dangers are worth recounting here at some length. Since 1997, three full-length books have been devoted to this critique: Alain Badiou's *Deleuze: The Clamor of Being* (1997, translated 2000); Slavoj Žižek's *Organs Without Bodies* (2004); and Peter Hallward's *Out of This World: Deleuze and the Philosophy of Creation* (2006). From these works, and several other critical essays, we can discern three distinct criticisms that, while perhaps not entirely fair to Deleuze (and Guattari), do outline several dangers posed by their philosophy: political ambivalence, virtual hierarchy and subjective paralysis.

(1) Political Ambivalence

'Affirming Difference in the state of permanent revolution,' as Deleuze says in *Difference and Repetition* (75/53), or affirming 'transformation as such' as a new revolutionary commitment that escapes the previous problems of vanguardism and the party-state poses the danger of becoming-ambivalent.[12] Such transformations *may* provide a new non-representational space of liberty, *or* it may provide a ruptured 'open' domain for a new discourse of rights and military occupation by the state, *or* it may merely reproduce a complicity with the processes of capitalist deterritorialisation necessary for new capitalist reterritorialisations. Slavoj Žižek, in particular, frequently attributes this capitalist ambivalence to Deleuze and Guattari's politics (2004: 184).[13] But to say that affirming the potentiality for transformation as such is to affirm a 'purely ideological radicality' that 'inevitably changes over into its opposite: once the mass festivals of democracy and discourse are over, things make place for the modernist restoration of order among workers and bosses', as Badiou and Balmès do, would be to overstate the problem (Badiou and Balmès 1976: 83).

Rather, it would be much more appropriate to say, with Paolo Virno, that 'the multitude is a form of being that can give birth to one thing but also to the other: ambivalence' (Virno 2003: 131). Accordingly, the affirmation of this ambivalence as a political commitment, and the 'politico-ontological optimism and unapologetic vitalism' it assumes in Hardt, Negri and Deleuze's work, according to Bruno Bosteels, remains radically insufficient (2004: 95). While the purely creative power of the multitude may be the condition for global liberation from empire, it is also the productive condition *for* empire as well. With no clear political consistency to organise or motivate any particular political transformation, such a 'vitalist optimism' can remain, at best, Bosteels argues, politically ambivalent, speculative and spontaneous. Showing the non-foundational or ungrounded nature of politics provides no more of a contribution for organised politics than does the creative potentiality of desire. 'A subject's intervention', Bosteels suggests, 'cannot consist merely in showing or recognizing the traumatic impossibility, void, or antagonism around which the situation as a whole is structured' (2004: 104), but rather, following Badiou, a 'political organization is necessary in order for the intervention, as wager, to make a process out of the trajectory that goes from an interruption to a fidelity. In this sense, organization is nothing but the consistency of politics' (Badiou

1985: 12). And insofar as Deleuze and Guattari, and those inspired by their work, do not offer developed concepts of political consistency and organisation that would bring differential multiplicities into specific political interventions and distributions, they remain, at most, ambivalent towards revolutionary politics.

(2) Virtual Hierarchy

In addition to the first danger, the problem of ambivalence, Deleuze's concept of revolution, according to Badiou and Hallward, risks a second danger, namely that of creating a political hierarchy of virtual potential. Badiou argues at length in *Deleuze: The Clamor of Being* that

> contrary to all egalitarian or 'communitarian' norms, Deleuze's conception of thought is profoundly aristocratic. Thought only exists in a hierarchized space. This is because, for individuals to attain the point where they are seized by their preindividual determination and, thus, by the power of the One-All – of which they are, at the start, only meager local configurations – they have to go beyond their limits and endure the transfixion and disintegration of their actuality by infinite virtuality, which is actuality's veritable being. And individuals are not equally capable of this. Admittedly, Being is itself neutral, equal, outside all evaluation ... But 'things reside unequally in this equal being' (Deleuze 1994: 60/37). And, as a result, it is essential to think according to 'a hierarchy which considers things and beings from the point of view of power' (Deleuze 1994: 60/37). (Badiou 1999: 12–13)

The political thrust of this argument is that if we understand revolutionary change as the virtual or potential for change as such, and not merely change for or against certain pre-existing powers, then, contrary to any kind of egalitarianism, there will instead be a hierarchy of actual political beings that more or less participate in this degree of pure potential transformation. The more actual political beings renounce their specific and local determinations and affirm their participation in the larger processes of difference-in-itself, the more powerful they become. Thus, if the point of examining any local political intervention is in every case to show to what degree it renounces its concrete determinations and might 'become other than it is' (as a virtuality or potentiality), there seems to be a risk of hierarchy in such a relationship of potential.

Similarly, Peter Hallward has argued that Deleuze's political philosophy is 'indifferent to the politics of this world' (2006: 162). Hallward claims that 'once a social field is defined less by its conflicts and contradictions than by the lines of flight running through it' (2006: 62 n16), any distinctive space for political action can only be subsumed within the more general dynamics of creation, life and potential transformation. And since these dynamics are 'themselves anti-dialectical if not anti-relational, there can be little room in Deleuze's philosophy for relations of conflict and solidarity' (2006: 162). If each concrete, localised, actual political being *is* only insofar as its actual being is subtracted from the situation into a virtual event, 'and every mortal event in a single Event' (Deleuze 1990: 178/152), the processional 'telos' of absolute political deterritori-alisation is completely indifferent to the actual politics of this world (2006: 97). By valorising this pure potentiality for transformation as such against all actual political determinations, Hallward argues, Deleuze is guilty of affirming an impossible utopianism. 'By posing the question of politics in the starkly dualistic terms of war machine or state – by posing it, in the end, in the apocalyptic terms of a new people and a new earth or else no people and no earth – the political aspect of Deleuze's philosophy amounts to little more than utopian distraction' (2006: 162).

(3) Subjective Paralysis

The differential reading of Deleuze and Guattari's concept of revolu-tion may be able to avoid the problem of representational subjectivity: that it can reject or affirm particular desires but never change the nature of the 'self that desires'. But it does so finally, only at the risk of diffusing the self into an endless multiplicity of impersonal drives: a self in perpetual transformation. This leads to the third danger, that of subjective paralysis. Firstly, to read Deleuze and Guattari's theory of revolutionary subjectivity as the 'simple fact of one's own existence as possibility or potentiality' (Agamben 1993: 43) or, as Paul Patton calls it, one's 'critical freedom' – the freedom to transgress the limits of what one is presently capable of being or doing, rather than just the freedom to be or do those things' (2000: 85) – suggests, as Bosteels' previous critique implies, an ambivalence. It is both the capacity for emancipation and the potentiality for enslavement.

Secondly, without a pre-given unity of subjectivity, how do agents qua multiplicities deliberate between and distinguish between differ-ent political decisions? Without the representational screen of reason, or the state-guaranteed grounds of political discourse, what might something like a dispute or agreement look like? If 'becoming other is not a capacity liberated individuals possess to constitute themselves as autonomous singularities' but 'what defines "autonomy" itself', as Simon Tormey argues (2006: 146), then the political danger, according to Hallward, is that the subject is simply replaced by the larger impersonal process of transformation as such: 'pure autonomy'. The radical affirmation of the ambivalent and unlocalisable processes of subjective potentiality (qua pure multiplicities) seems then to have nothing to contribute to an analysis of the basic function of participatory democracy and collective decision-making, which remains at the core of many of today's radical political struggles (see Starr, Martinez-Torres and Rosset 2011). Insofar as a theory of subjectivity is defined only by its potential for transformation, it is stuck in a kind of paralysis of endless potential change no less disempowering than subjective stasis. Or, as Hallward frames this criticism, Deleuze 'abandons the decisive subject in favour of our more immediate subjection to the imperative of creative life or thought' (2006: 163).

DELEUZE, GUATTARI AND CONSTRUCTIVISM

While this ongoing debate over the implications of Deleuze and Guattari's political philosophy, and in particular their concept of revolution, continues to be a productive one, I propose a third reading of Deleuze and Guattari's concept of revolution that does not fall prey to the dangers of the two previous ones. I term this a 'constructivist' reading, in a sense borrowed from Deleuze and Guattari's own writings. To explain this alternative reading, I proceed in three steps: first, I show how the concept of constructivism emerges in Deleuze and Guattari's work; second, I differentiate this approach from the previous two readings; and third, I demonstrate its significance for the thesis of this book.

Deleuze and Guattari's first major attempt at the creation of a concept of revolution came after the events of May 1968 in France. Their first book together, *Capitalisme et schizophrénie: L'Anti-Oedipe* (1972), set out as a critique of both psychoanalysis and Marxism in order to develop a new concept of revolutionary desire that was indexed neither to primitive, state or capitalist power (in all their familial and oedipal formulations), nor to class analysis or the vanguard party apparatus 'modelled after the state' in Marxism. Schizophrenia was their name for this new concept of revolution. These efforts were, however, subject to significant criticism. Critics immediately charged that Deleuze and Guattari had been too optimistic about the potentiality of art, 'minimalized the role of class struggle', 'militated in favour of an irrationalism of desire' and 'identified revolutionaries with schizophrenics' (Deleuze and Guattari 1983: 455/379). After its publication the authors expended no small effort clarifying and even modifying the concepts proposed in *Anti-Oedipus* (later, even criticising them). Revolutionaries are neither 'insane' nor self-marginalised, they insist:

> Some have said that we see the schizophrenic as the true revolutionary. We believe, rather, that schizophrenia is the descent of a molecular process into a black hole. Marginals have always inspired fear in us, and a slight horror. (Deleuze and Parnet 1987: 167/139)

Desire is neither irrational nor without determination in a particular political arrangement:

> We say quite the opposite: desire only exists when it is assembled or machined. You cannot grasp or conceive of a desire outside a determinate assemblage, on a plane which is not pre-existent but which must itself be constructed. (Deleuze and Parnet 1987: 115/96)

Revolutionary desire does not just blow apart the social into a pure flux:

> It is in concrete social fields, at specific moments, that the comparative movements of deterritorialization, the continuums of intensity, and the combinations of flux that they form must be studied. (Deleuze and Parnet 1987: 163/135)

Despite these qualifications, the concept of revolution in *Anti-Oedipus* remained admittedly underdeveloped. How were these lines of schizo-flight to provide a stable alternative to the history of representational politics (primitivism, statism, capitalism)? How were these 'desiring machines' to be assembled into a revolutionary movement? And what are some of its concrete characteristics? A crucial shift, though, took place in their political writings between *Anti-Oedipus* and *A Thousand Plateaus* (1980). The move from emphasising the unrestrained deterritorialisations of desire to the careful and more sober transformations of the concrete political arrangement (constructivism) became decisive.

Eugene Holland was perhaps the first to highlight this shift in Deleuze and Guattari's political philosophy:

> In as much as deterritorialization designated the motor of permanent revolution, while reterritorialization designated the power relations imposed by the private ownership of capital . . . deterritorialization looked 'good' and reterritorialization looked 'bad' . . . but in *A Thousand Plateaus*,

both de- and re-territorialization appear in a very different light. (Holland 1991: 58–9)

Aside from removing the last traces of humanism and anthropo-centrism from the 'psycho-social' machines of *Anti-Oedipus*, *A Thousand Plateaus*, Holland claims, introduces three kinds of deter-ritorialisation – relative, absolute negative and absolute positive (1991: 62). *A Thousand Plateaus* no longer valorises the uncritical excitement for absolute deterritorialisation or potential creativity found in *Anti-Oedipus* (and in Deleuze's previous works) but instead develops what they call the more sober task of a logics or construc-tivism of political assemblages. While Holland notes the 'less revolu-tionary and less romantic' character of *A Thousand Plateaus* (1991: 63), he also suggests that 'any lingering suspicion of an earlier exag-gerated or uncritical enthusiasm for "schizophrenia" should now be dispelled by the very cautious, nuanced treatment of deterritorializa-tion and the body-without-organs' (1991: 63).

A Thousand Plateaus also marks a shift away from Deleuze's earlier solo works, self-defined as the 'merger of philosophy and ontology' (1990: 201/179). While I disagree that Deleuze's previ-ous works can be characterised as entirely 'apolitical', as Badiou has argued (2009b), Deleuze had in fact developed very few political concepts, usually favouring more ontological or aesthetic ones. By contrast, *A Thousand Plateaus* clearly prioritises politics over ontol-ogy. Against accusations of 'ontological vitalism' and 'other-worldly politics' made by Peter Hallward, *A Thousand Plateaus* claims (1) to overthrow ontology: to replace the logic of the 'is' [*est*] with the logic of the 'and' [*et*]; and (2) that 'politics precedes being' [*avant l'être, il y a la politique*] (Deleuze and Guattari 1987: 37/25, 249/203). *A Thousand Plateaus* should therefore be read more primarily as a political text than an ontological one, thus distancing it significantly from Deleuze's earlier solo works as well as from much of Badiou, Hallward and Žižek's critical commentary that tends to focus almost exclusively on his pre-*A Thousand Plateaus* writings. While this by no means allows us to ignore the political dangers Badiou and others outline, it is important to recognise that the constructivist turn that occurs in Deleuze and Guattari's political philosophy has yet to be taken seriously (against the continuity thesis, for example, that is argued for explicitly by Hallward and implicitly by many others: that a single central thought guides all of Deleuze's work, such as imma-nence, the virtual, life and so on).

More recent scholarship on Deleuze and Guattari's political philosophy, though, has begun to shift more notably in the direction of the political constructivism begun in *A Thousand Plateaus*. Many scholars have noted the existence and importance of the constructivist (also called diagrammatic, pragmatic or cartographic) turn in Deleuze and Guattari's later work. The terrain, according to Alberto Toscano, 'seems to have shifted considerably with respect to the earlier [pre-*A Thousand Plateaus*] preoccupation that seemed to afford a certain continuity with naturalised or materialist accounts of ontogenesis' (2006: 176).[14] Eugene Holland speaks of the 'importance that *A Thousand Plateaus* ascribes to devising planes of consistency or composition where lines of flight can intersect and become productive instead of spinning off into the void' (1998: 69). Eduardo Pellejero emphasises that the 'creative articulation of the lines of flight in assemblages that allow them to mature is not just possible and desirable, but constitutes the constructivist vector of this new militant praxis' (Pellejero 2010: 108). Bonta and Protevi, too, have emphasised the centrality of having a 'working cartography ... to experiment with real intervention' (2004: 23). Not only do Deleuze and Guattari 'give us a theory of assemblages' (Patton 2006: 35) that 'would map out the complex terrain and conditions in which new modes of existence appear' (Smith 1998: 264), according to Paul Patton and Dan Smith, but even Bruno Bosteels has admitted the political importance of the 'basic scaffolding' of 'a formal and political theory of cartography' (1998: 150) developed by Guattari. We can even find the admission by Hardt and Negri, in the final chapter of *Empire*, that 'recognizing the potential autonomy of the mobile multitude, however, only points toward the real question. What we need to grasp is how the multitude is organized and redefined as a positive, political power' (2000: 394, 398). So the real question is not simply that of deterritorialisation over reterritorialisation or creative life versus the dead hand of capital, but rather the *constructive* ways revolutionary action takes on a consistency, a commitment and an organisation, and what forms of antagonism and relation it produces in a specific struggle.

Thus, while there may be politically dangerous tendencies in Deleuze and Guattari-inspired political philosophy, more or less emphasised in certain works, it is clearly inaccurate to say that Deleuze and Guattari and their readers after *A Thousand Plateaus* are not aware of the dangers of naively 'valorising the potentiality' of revolutionary deterritorialisation.[15] Revolution may, of course, move too quickly, too much, or end up in a black hole (marginality) with no consistency or connection at all. Contrary to the claim of *Anti-Oedipus* that 'We can never go too far in the direction of deterritorialization' [*Jamais on n'ira assez loin dans la déterritorialisation, le décodage des flux*] (458/382), *A Thousand Plateaus* warns us that we can in fact go too far and so must approach revolutionary struggles with sobriety, caution and construction.

But scholarly awareness, promising gestures and scaffolds hardly constitute a fully developed constructivist theory of revolution. Aside from the fact that no full-length work until now has been dedicated to developing Deleuze and Guattari's constructivist theory of revolution, there is a problem with such a project. Éric Alliez, in his essay 'Anti-Oedipus – Thirty Years On', has been the most emphatic about the political importance of Deleuze and Guattari's later constructivist text *What Is Philosophy?* (against the Badiouian charges of political spontaneity) (2006).[16] Yet the problem is that *What Is Philosophy?* does not even give politics its own proper register, like art (percepts), philosophy (concepts) or science (functives)! Accordingly, Alliez's book *The Signature of the World*, devoted to Deleuze and Guattari's constructivism, contains absolutely no discussion of politics.[17]

Even Manuel de Landa, who may have gone furthest in developing the details of such a social logic or what he calls a 'theory of assemblages' in *A New Philosophy of Society*, has expressed concern with such a project. 'The relatively few pages dedicated to assemblage theory in the work of Deleuze and Guattari hardly amount to a fully-fledged theory,' he says. And 'even in those cases where conceptual definitions are easy to locate, they are usually not given in a style that allows for a straightforward interpretation. This would seem to condemn a book on assemblage theory to spend most of its pages doing hermeneutics' (de Landa 2006: 3). But while de Landa's solution to this problem is, as Alberto Toscano says, to '"naturalise" the theory of multiplicities by recasting it as an ontology of models, much as if Deleuze were the heir of Husserl's metatheoretical project, now applied to the theory of complex systems' (2006: 86), the current work will not follow suit. The central concern of this book is neither social nor ontological, but political and constructivist, interested explicitly in the revolutionary transformation of existing society.[18] But this section has only framed the emergence of a constructivist turn in Deleuze and Guattari's work. The question now is how to define 'constructivism' as a meaningful interpretive category against the previous two, and to show how it contributes to a philosophical return to the concept of revolution.

Towards a Constructivist Theory of Revolution

By 'constructivism', I do not mean what is traditionally understood as 'social constructivism' in sociology and philosophy, namely, that revolutions are by-products or 'social constructs' produced by human minds, language, institutions, historical contexts, cultural values and so on. Such theories presuppose what needs to be explained in the first place: mind, society, culture and history themselves. Deleuze and Guattari rather define their philosophical method as constructivist in the sense that it is about the creative diagnosis and assembly of heterogeneous elements into a plane of consistency (see Deleuze and Guattari 1987: 93/73).[19] But given such a broad definition and the often scattered appearance of this method in their later work, one is almost forced to make, as de Landa correctly observes, some kind of interpretative or extractive move. I will thus make two: firstly, I limit my own methodological work with this concept to a strictly political interpretation, and in particular its revolutionary dimension; secondly, I break this constructivist method down into what I see as its four distinct yet coherent philosophical activities and try to reassemble them into four strategies paralleled by Zapatismo.

Asked succinctly, the question of this book is 'what would it mean to return to revolution today?' Answered succinctly, I argue that Deleuze and Guattari offer us several helpful concepts that respond to the four problematics of revolution mentioned previously. In response to the question of how to understand the dominant relations of power that revolution overcomes, they propose the concept of 'historical topology'. In response to the question of how to transform those relations of power, they propose the concept of 'deterritorialization'. In response to the question of what we can build instead of these power relations, they propose the concept of 'political consistency', and in response to the question of who belongs to the struggle, they propose the concept of 'nomadic solidarity'. Their constructivist theory of revolution is, thus, neither a utopian programme laid out in advance, the effect of 'social constructs', the capture of state power, an evolutionary development or the potentiality for revolutionary change as such, but rather the committed arrangement and distribution of heterogeneous elements or singularities without vanguard, party, state or capital: it is a politics based on autonomy and the self-management of political problems (see Deleuze 1994: 206/158; Deleuze and Guattari 1987: 588/471).

Much closer to what Badiou, Hallward, Toscano and Bosteels claim to be looking for in political concepts like 'consistency', 'intervention', 'commitment' and 'solidarity', the constructivist theory of revolution I am proposing is based on connecting the contingent and heterogeneous political practices that have broken free or been uprooted ('deterritorialised') through political crisis *to each other* to theorise the current revolutionary sequence (however nascent it may be) (see Žižek and Douzinas 2010). The current revolutionary sequence, and here I am in agreement with Toscano, has 'sketched out new regimes of organisation, new forms of subjectivity at a distance from the accepted forms of mediated representation. [Groups like] the Ejército Zapatista de Liberación Nacional in Mexico . . . [prompt us to] begin to think beyond the intra-State logic of representation' (2004: 224). Thus, the valorisation of 'lines of flight', 'rupture' and 'heterogeneity' as they break free from or within power, without a positive account of how such lines compose a new consistency of their own, are – and here I am in agreement with Badiou and others – 'the concrete definition of revolutionary failure', since revolutionary struggles cannot be sustained beyond the scope of isolated outbursts against or within power. Without a cohesive theory of how to diagnose, transform and create new political bodies connected through mutual global solidarity, I argue, we cannot hope to understand the philosophy of the present revolutionary sequence.

Thus, in my reading, the political project of *A Thousand Plateaus* is to develop such a positive account of how 'revolutionary consistencies' function and are sustained in the context of coexistent dangers. This positive account will address the following four questions: in what sense do the processes of representation pose dangers for revolutionary struggles? How do revolutions intervene politically in such situations? How are their conditions, elements and agencies arranged and distributed? How do they connect up to different struggles around the world? Drawing primarily from *A Thousand Plateaus* and *What Is Philosophy?*, I propose a constructivist theory of revolution that answers these questions without submitting revolution to an inevitable political representation or merely affirming a political potential to become-otherwise. But the philosophical elaboration of these concepts in Deleuze and Guattari's philosophy is not sufficient for developing the four revolutionary strategies I am outlining. What needs to be shown is their common but parallel development in the realm of political practice, specifically with Zapatismo.

Just as there are different ways to read the concept of revolution in Deleuze and Guattari's philosophy, so there are different ways to interpret the Zapatista uprising. Leaving aside all of those who reject the Zapatistas' struggle for dignity, land and democracy outright, readers of the Zapatistas fall more or less into two camps. On the one hand, there are those who see the uprising as an incomplete or failed struggle, insofar as it failed to mobilise the Mexican people to overthrow and capture the Mexican state (or even win significant representation for the indigenous of Mexico). This view can be found in the work of Argentine political theorist Atilio Boron (author of *State, Capitalism, and Democracy in Latin America,* 1995) and British Pakistani political analyst Tariq Ali in his 2004 essay 'Anti-neoliberalism in Latin America'. Boron argues that the postmodern celebration of diversity and local autonomy around Zapatismo is symptomatic of the Left's general retreat from class struggle. For Boron, popular movements, like Zapatismo, cannot afford the luxury of ignoring the struggle for state power and representation, especially in Latin America, where direct or indirect forms of US imperialism have so often undermined national sovereignty. To the degree that the Zapatistas have made no real gains for class struggle or state representation, they have failed (see Boron 2003: 143–82).

Similarly, Ali argues that the Zapatistas' slogan – 'we can change the world without taking power' – is a purely moral slogan with no real revolutionary teeth. As Ali says,

> I have to be very blunt here – [the Mexican State] [does not] feel threatened because there is an idealistic slogan within the social movements, which goes like this: 'We can change the world without taking power.' This slogan doesn't threaten anyone; it's a moral slogan. The Zapatistas – who I admire – when they marched from Chiapas to Mexico City, what did they think was going to happen? Nothing happened. It was a moral symbol, it was not even a moral victory because nothing happened. (Ali 2004)

There is certainly some truth to these claims: the Zapatistas (in their 1994 First Declaration from the Lacandón Jungle) did declare war on the Mexican state but failed to mobilise the Mexican people, and they were technically unable even to win the reformist San Andrés Accords with the Mexican government. Such criticisms are not wrong so much as they reduce the criteria of revolutionary success to the very narrow categories of state representation and class struggle. Firstly, if we are going to analyse what the Zapatistas have done, we must consider all the different dimensions on which their struggle has taken place (media, solidarity, local autonomy, democracy, gender, race and sexual orientation, as well as political economy and the state). The Zapatistas have won some things in some places but very little in others. Secondly, these narrow criticisms cover over one of the most original political contributions of the Zapatistas: not how they have been able to influence politicians and the state externally, but how they have created internally a new type of political consistency that has coherently organised a society of over 2,200 communities (over 200,000 people). These communities are federated into thirty-eight 'autonomous municipalities', each grouped into five local self-governments called the *Juntas de Buen Gobierno* (JBG) or Councils of Good Government (Ross 2006: 194). Thirdly, although perhaps one can judge the immediate effectiveness of a given slogan, it would be naive to think that slogans or symbols as such are not able to mobilise millions of people around the world, because they have, and they do so now more than ever. And as far as slogans go, 'change the world without taking power' has become a global one whose effects, I argue, have yet to be fully deployed. Regardless of its immediate effects, this slogan continues to express an emerging desire for a new politics without states. Perhaps the force of this slogan is best felt, for reasons that I will explain, in the future anterior.

Zapatismo and Difference

On the other hand, there are readers who argue that the Zapatistas' most important contribution is their strong suspicion of all forms of political representation (patriarchy, statism, capitalism and so on) and their affirmation of a political community and solidarity based on difference (across race, gender, class, sexual orientation, geography and so on). Although perhaps the majority of scholarship on the Zapatistas falls generally under this category (even though most disagree about how far the Zapatistas go in achieving this goal), I want to look at two of its more philosophical proponents: Simon Tormey and

John Holloway. Tormey's 2006 article '"Not in my Name": Deleuze, Zapatismo and the Critique of Representation' argues,

> The stance and philosophy of the Zapatistas is . . . remarkable in itself, but also symptomatic of a more general shift in the underpinnings of the political 'field', one that problematises and points beyond 'representation'. This is a shift that first announced itself in relation to philosophy, ethics and literature some decades ago, in turn spreading to black studies, feminism, queer and lesbian studies, and latterly to postcolonial and subaltern studies. It can now be felt and heard in what is sometimes termed 'the new activism'. (138)

But for Tormey, who draws theoretically on Deleuze's earlier work *Différence et répétition* (1968), the Zapatistas, 'as a group that insists that it is "exercising power" not on *behalf* of the people of Chiapas . . . but *with* the people of the Chiapas,' not only articulate a *demand* against all forms of political representation, but they, like Deleuze, also 'recognise and celebrate difference, not as negation . . . but as an affirmation, as something valued in itself' (2006: 142). Marcos, for example, does not represent the Zapatistas, but is himself a multiplicity; he 'is gay in San Francisco, a black in South Africa, Asian in Europe, a Chicano in San Isidro, an anarchist in Spain, a Palestinian in Israel . . . Marcos is every untolerated, oppressed, exploited minority that is resisting and saying "Enough!"' (Marcos 2001b: 101–6). Difference-in-itself, according to Tormey, is also realised in the internal organisation of the Zapatistas, whose form of direct democracy 'goes well beyond Marx's 'Paris Commune' model of immediate recall and rotation to embrace the demand that delegates listen to each and every "*compañero*" who turns up' (2006: 148).

Similarly, Holloway, in his 2002 book *Change the World Without Taking Power: The Meaning of Revolution Today*, argues that one of the most central contributions of the Zapatistas was to express a 'scream' of negation, dissonance and frustration with the present neoliberal system of political representation, which Holloway calls 'Fetishism' (2002: 1). The Zapatistas' struggle is one not only against the state and capital but against the entire system of political classification/representation as such. As Holloway puts it,

> We do not struggle as working class, we struggle against being working class, against being classified. Our struggle is not the struggle of labour: it is the struggle against labour. It is the unity of the process of classification (the unity of capital accumulation) that gives unity to our struggle, not our unity as members of a common class. Thus, for example, it is the

significance of the Zapatista struggle against capitalist classification that gives it importance for class struggle, not the question of whether the indigenous inhabitants of the Lacandón Jungle are or are not members of the working class. (2002: 88)

But Zapatismo is not just a rejection of representation; it is an affirmation of the potential to recover a new means of living, a 'power-to' or capacity for new action. As Holloway says,

> It is not enough to scream. Negativity, our refusal of capital, is the crucial starting point, theoretically and politically. But mere refusal is easily recaptured by capital, simply because it comes up against capital's control of the means of production, means of doing, means of living. For the scream to grow in strength, there must be a recuperation of doing, a development of power-to. That implies a re-taking of the means of doing. (2002: 127)

While I remain, for the most part, sympathetic to this kind of reading and to Tormey and Holloway's readings in particular, I think that their points of emphasis are not so much wrong as they are philosophically and politically incomplete or insufficient. It may be true that, with a few exceptions, the Zapatistas are critical of the dominant structure and categories of political representation (including narrow class analyses based on industrial development and factory labour) (see Kingsnorth 2004: 29).[20] And it is also true that the Zapatistas, to some degree, affirm and respect the multiplicity of differences that make up the global opposition to neoliberalism. However, the rejection of representation and the affirmation of difference or potential for 'power-to' tell us almost nothing about what positive philosophical and political alternatives the Zapatistas propose. Both Tormey and Holloway spend only a few short pages theorising the internal political organisation of the Zapatistas (direct democracy, consensus, rotational self-government, subjectivity, global solidarity and so on), and when they do, their conclusion is that these types of organisation (internal as well as global networks and so on) all simply express the Zapatistas' rejection of representation and affirmation of potential transformation (difference). But a pivotal question remains: how is this new type of post-representational politics constructed? How does it work? In what ways does it offer us a real political alternative to capitalist nation-states? What new types of political subjectivity does it create and how do they work? If the Zapatistas are not just practical examples of the philosophical insight that 'political representation has failed us, and we must become other than we are', then what do they offer us instead, philosophically and practically?

Perhaps many of the same criticisms addressed to 'differential readers' of Deleuze and Guattari's concept of revolution equally apply here: political ambivalence, virtual hierarchy and subjective paralysis. These are, in part, some of the Badiouian-inspired criticisms laid out by Mihalis Mentinis in his book *Zapatistas: The Chiapas Revolt and What It Means for Radical Politics* (2006). After moving through Gramsci, Laclou and Mouffe, Hardt and Negri, and Castoriadis, Mentinis argues for a Badiouian-inspired theory of militant subjectivity previously lacking in Zapatista scholarship. Despite providing an otherwise excellent survey of radical political theory and Zapatismo, Mentinis fails to reconcile his position with Badiou's explicit ambivalence towards Zapatismo as a truly universal event, and thus as having no real politically faithful subjects.[21] Some underemphasis on Zapatista constructivism in the scholarship may be simply historical, since it has taken the Zapatistas many years to develop a relatively distinct form of internal political organisation. But this does not explain more recent scholarship still committed to defining Zapatismo by its 'ontological priority of difference' (Evans 2010: 142). In any case, to sum up, difference-in-itself or the potential to develop our 'power-to' tell us very little about how to build a revolutionary strategy, or what concepts the Zapatistas offer for the reorganisation of political life.

ZAPATISMO AND CONSTRUCTIVISM

Subsequently, I propose, as I did in the case of Deleuze and Guattari's work, a constructivist reading of the Zapatistas that recognises not only their antagonism towards representation and their affirmation of political difference as the precondition for a radically inclusive global revolutionary movement, but, more importantly, what they have created in place of representation and how they have reassembled or built a maximum of political difference into their political practice. To be clear, this does not mean that I am proposing to use Deleuze and Guattari's philosophical method of constructivism to understand the Zapatista uprising, despite the strong similarities between the two methods of construction. What I am proposing instead is that the Zapatistas have invented their own political constructivism. While philosophy creates concepts, politics creates practices.

Between 8 and 10 August 2003, almost ten years after the 1994 uprising and almost twenty years after Marcos and company's first descent into the Lacandón Jungle, the Zapatistas announced a new direction in their struggle with the birth of the *Juntas de Buen Gobierno* (JBGs), or Councils of Good Government. Whereas their political energies and critiques had previously been focused on battling and negotiating with the Mexican government, paramilitary forces and corporations (rejecting the forces of political representation) and on affirming their autonomy and enlarging their global visibility through alternative media and global gatherings of heterogeneous struggles (affirming political difference), the birth of the JBGs marked a significant turn towards the *creation* of something new. While the Zapatistas certainly did not call this turn 'constructivist', I use this term to emphasise their turn towards creating new political practices, like building and sustaining their own autonomous municipalities of self-government, cooperative economics and environmental stewardship. It is in this turn, I argue, that we can learn the most from Zapatismo.

It is also during this time that one can see in the Zapatistas' communiqués, for the first time since the failure of the 1994 First Declaration to start a war against the Mexican government, a critique of themselves as they tried to build the world they wanted to see, in front of the world. It was announced that the Ejército Zapatista de Liberación Nacional (EZLN), the Zapatista Army of National Liberation, was overstepping its decision-making power in the municipalities and local governments, women were not being treated equally in terms of participation in the JBG and other areas, the environment was being harmed, drugs were being grown, human trafficking was taking place through Zapatista territory, and the five *caracoles* (regions of Zapatistas' territory, literally 'snail shells') were developing unevenly (Marcos 2006). Accordingly, the Zapatistas had to expand and multiply their analysis of power within their own territory: in terms of gender, the environment, local law, cooperative production and so on.

In undertaking this massive project of 'learning how to self-govern', the Zapatistas focused less on political reform with the state and more on creating a prefigurative politics: without overthrowing the state, they wanted to achieve a maximum of autonomy within it (and with others outside it). But one of the most difficult aspects of this was inventing a political body that would allow for the maximum inclusion of participation and autonomy with a minimum of exclusion and representation. This was created using a mixture of indigenous tradition, popular assemblies, consensus decision-making and rotational governance (positions changed every fifteen days to make sure everyone learned how to govern equally). In a word, they created a generalised direct democracy based on a maximum feedback loop of political participation. While certainly a work-in-progress, these were its practical horizons (see Marcos 2006).

But the Zapatistas have never been satisfied with local revolts, no matter how successful. While it may have appeared that during these years the Zapatistas became focused 'inward', one of the central purposes of this constructivist turn (not to be mistaken for an inward turn) was to be able to sustain a certain level of cooperative productive development based on common property (not private or public) and to share it with others, not just within the *caracoles* but with the world. Since 1994, the Zapatistas had been on the receiving end of international aid, but after 2003 one can see in their communiqués a sustained and novel effort to provide material and political support to struggles around the world against neoliberalism (textiles, dolls, maize, public endorsements, coffee and so on) (see Marcos 2006). Where previous concepts of solidarity had all been, for the most part, one way in direction (Soviet internationalism, Third World solidarity, international human rights and even material aid in the case of natural disasters and so on), the Zapatistas invented a whole new model of *mutual* global solidarity by sharing and encouraging others to mutually share support and aid, even in cases where they have very little (as the Zapatistas did). This kind of mutual support has resulted in a host of interesting solidarities, both political and economic (see Walker 2005).

These years leading up to *La Otra Campaña* (The Other Campaign), from 2003 to 2006 and beyond, have been misunderstood as 'years of silence' and under-theorised, in part due to a dearth of empirical research (compared to pre-2003 studies), but also perhaps in part because of a waning of interest in the 'newness' of Zapatismo. But it is from 2003 onwards, in my view, that the Zapatistas have the most to contribute to a philosophical investigation into how a revolutionary alternative to neoliberalism will have been built. I argue that the Zapatistas offer us several helpful concepts that respond to the four problematics of revolution mentioned previously. In response to the question of how to understand the dominant relations of power such that revolution is desirable, they propose the practice of what Marcos calls a *diagnóstico del sufrimiento* (a diagnostic of suffering) documented in *Beyond Resistance* (2010: 11). In response to the question of how to transform those relations of power, they propose the practice of building the autonomous *Juntas de Buen Gobierno*. In response to the question of what kinds of institutions we can put in their place, they propose the practice of *mandar obedeciendo* (leading by obeying), and in response to the question of who belongs to the struggle, they propose the practice of the global *Encuentro* (the encounter). In sum, their constructivist theory of revolution is quite similar to that of Deleuze and Guattari's: neither a utopian programme laid out in advance, the effect of 'social constructs', the capture of state power, an evolutionary development or the potentiality for revolutionary change as such, but rather the committed arrangement and distribution of heterogeneous elements or singularities without vanguard, party, state or capital. This politics, like that championed by Deleuze and Guattari, is based on autonomy and the participatory self-management of political problems.

III. Overview

Guided by the methodology of conceptual assemblage and the intervention of a constructivist reading, this book proposes to draw on the work of Deleuze, Guattari and the Zapatistas in order to extract a new political philosophy of revolution helpful for understanding and motivating the present, although perhaps young, revolutionary sequence. In particular, it proposes four specific revolutionary strategies or 'tactical pointers for the conditional imperative of political struggle': (1) a multi-centred diagnostics, (2) a prefigurative transformation, (3) a participatory process and (4) mutual global solidarity. Accordingly, the chapters of this book will propose and defend each of these strategies in turn. Additionally, each chapter is composed of three major subsections. The first section critically distinguishes the proposed strategy from two others: one based on political representation and the other based on political differentiation without construction. The second section then draws on at least one major idea from Deleuze and Guattari's philosophy to help assemble the strategy proposed in the chapter, before the third section draws on at least one major political practice from Zapatismo to help assemble the proposed strategy.

Chapter 1 argues that the return to revolution located in Deleuze, Guattari and the Zapatistas can be characterised by a diagnostic strategy of using history motivated by the relative rejection of all previous forms of historical representation (patriarchy, racism, statism, capitalism, vanguardism and so on) and a concern for their immanent diagnosis. Although this claim clearly rejects the representational readings of Deleuze, Guattari and Zapatismo, it is obviously quite similar to the philosophy of difference described earlier in this chapter. As such, it may seem relatively uncontroversial. But my argument includes three crucial and underemphasised dimensions of this rejection: firstly, that it is a *relative* rejection, meaning that political representation always plays a more or less active role in political life even if only in the mode of 'being warded off' by more participatory practices. That is, even in its relative absence, it still exerts force as an immanent historical potential of any political practice. Secondly, I argue that political representation is not a homogeneous philosophical category, since there are several distinctly different types of representation. These differences are found not only in terms of content, such as race, class, gender, economics and so on, but also in formal structure, such as coding, overcoding and axiomatisation. Thirdly, I argue that these types of relative representation always intersect and coexist with each other to different degrees in every political situation. Against the *necessary* historical emergence of these different types of political representation, but also against their *merely contingent and coexistent* emergence, I argue instead, drawing on Deleuze and Guattari's historical topology and what the Zapatistas call their diagnostic of suffering, that their return to revolution is characterised by their use of these types of representation as a way to understand the political dangers and opportunities presented in the situation to be transformed. But how then can one escape this matrix of political power and representation?

In Chapter 2, I argue that this return to revolution found in the work of Deleuze, Guattari and the Zapatistas is also characterised by a prefigurative strategy of political transformation aimed at constructing a new present within and alongside the old. Opposed to achieving revolutionary transformation by an evolutionary process of transition, progress and reform in representation, or achieving it simply through a spontaneous rupture with the present, prefigurative political transformations emerge as what will have been under way alongside the dominant political reality. Drawing on Deleuze and Guattari's theory of deterritorialisation and the Zapatistas' practice of the *Juntas de Buen Gobierno*, I argue that prefigurative revolutions are thus those types of transformation that are able to sustain the creation of a new present and connect it up to other struggles happening elsewhere. This type of political revolution is thus neither tied entirely to the determinations of its past (with its pre-given possibilities) nor to the potentialities of its future always yet-to-come. Rather, it is constructive of a new present that transforms both the past and the future. But how then can these revolutionary transformations be sustained beyond their relative autonomy and prefiguration?

In Chapter 3, I thus argue that we can locate in Deleuze, Guattari and the Zapatistas a participatory strategy for creating a revolutionary body politic that is able to sustain these prefigurative transformations. A participatory body politic does not simply establish new conditions for political life based on a 'more just' sphere of political action whose foundational principles are still controlled by political representatives. Nor does a participatory body politic merely aim to establish anti-institutions, whose sole purpose is to undermine all forms of representation and await the possibility that something new, and hopefully better, may emerge. Rather, a participatory and revolutionary body politic is built and sustained through an expressive process whose founding conditions are constantly undergoing a high degree of direct and immanent transformation by the various practices and people who are also transformed, to varying degrees, by its deployment. In particular, I argue in this chapter that this participatory 'feedback loop' can be located in Deleuze and Guattari's concept of consistency, found in *A Thousand Plateaus* and *What Is Philosophy?*, and in the Zapatistas' political practice of 'leading by obeying' (*mandar obedeciendo*). I argue that, in order to understand the structure and function of this consistency and of leading by obeying in this new body politic, we need to understand how their conditions, elements and agencies work differently than in representational and anti-representational institutions. I argue this by drawing on three concepts in Deleuze and Guattari's philosophy that correspond to the conditions, elements and agencies of consistent revolutionary institutions: the abstract machine, the concrete assemblage and the persona.[22] Just as these three concepts immanently transform one another in a relationship of 'order without hierarchy',[23] according to Deleuze and Guattari, so does leading by obeying provide the egalitarian framework for the revolutionary institutions of the Zapatistas (Deleuze and Guattari 1994: 87/90). But the participatory nature of a revolutionary body politic still leaves the question, 'how will these new political bodies be able to connect up with each other across their radical differences?'

Thus, Chapter 4 draws on all the previous chapters in order to argue that we can locate in Deleuze, Guattari and the Zapatistas a strategy of revolutionary political affinity based on the mutual global solidarity of such participatory political bodies. Revolutionary political affinity, I argue, is not simply a matter of integrating marginalised demands back into the dominant territorial-nation-state apparatus based on modifying specific criteria for citizenship or aiding those who need help. Nor is it a matter of recognising the universal singularity of all beings to become other than they are. Rather, revolutionary political affinity is a matter of solidarity: when revolutionary political bodies, namely those who remain unrepresented or excluded from dominant forms of political affinity, find in each other, one by one, the transuniversality and mutual aid of each other's singular struggles. Singular-universal solidarity is thus not a matter of recognition, charity or even radical difference, but rather a mutually federated difference or 'contingent holism' of heterogeneous singular-universal events in worldwide struggle. The task of this chapter is thus to avoid the dangers of exclusion and universal singularity and to propose a theory of political solidarity instead, drawn from Deleuze and Guattari's concept of nomadism and the Zapatistas' global practice of *Encuentros Intercontinentales*. In particular, I argue first against the concepts of 'citizenship' and 'difference' as desirable models of political belonging insofar as the former is structurally exclusionary and the latter is unable to theorise any concrete relations between multiple coexistent conditions. Secondly, I argue that, opposed to these two dangers, revolutionary solidarity should be defined instead by the federated connection between multiple singular-universal conditions without totality.

Finally, I conclude with a reconstruction and reflection upon the relative accomplishments of the chapters and the argument of the book as a whole. In particular, the conclusion addresses the problem remaining at the end of the book: how can mutual global solidarity take on a decision-making power such that the world's organised struggles against neoliberalism can form an acting counter-power without private property, necessary political exclusion, economic exploitation or a centralisation of this counter-power itself? While Deleuze, Guattari and the Zapatistas provide excellent resources for constructing a new political philosophy of revolution, they are only able to lay the groundwork to deal with this problem that has also yet to be resolved in the present revolutionary sequence at the level of the World Social Forum. This is a significant barrier to a real transition away from global capitalism and requires a further philosophical investigation into the currently emerging forms of political and philosophical experimentation that contribute to this problem's resolution.

Notes

1. By 'strategy' I mean something composed of both philosophical concepts and political practices.
2. It is important to mention here that Guattari has written several books, which more directly address the concept of revolution. However, Guattari's writings on politics and revolution are best understood, I believe, within the larger philosophical framework developed in Guattari's work with Deleuze. Nonetheless, Guattari's books *Molecular Revolution: Psychiatry and Politics* (1984), *Molecular Revolution in Brazil* (2008) and his short book with Antonio Negri, *New Spaces of Liberty, New Lines of Alliance* (1990), all offer invaluable contributions to the philosophy of revolution that I develop in this book.
3. The Occupy movement and the alter-globalisation movement have both been characterised as leaderless and horizontal movements (Hardt and Negri 2011). For an explicit strategic connection between these three movements see Klein 2011; Rodríguez 2011.
4. The return to revolution here should be understood as a differential return, a return that takes up again the charge of creating a new world but does so with entirely different strategies.
5. There are, however, a lot more influences on today's radical Left than the Zapatistas.
6. To be clear, I will not be drawing on my own empirical research (ethnographies, interviews and so on) of the Zapatistas. Rather, I will draw on the vast empirical research already produced by those more qualified in ethnography than myself.
7. In addition to all of the literature on the alter-globalisation movement cited in this book, I am indebted to the following articles that argue that a new revolutionary sequence has already begun: Harvey 2010; Graeber 2002; Grubacic and Graeber 2004.
8. The World Social Forum's *Charter of Principles* also supports several of the strategies I propose in this book (World Social Forum 2001).
9. Evans claims to offer 'a Deleuzian reading of the Zapatista experience'. He also claims that 'Deleuze provide[s] us with a meaningful basis for political action' (Evans 2010: 142).
10. This is what Deleuze and Guattari, following Rémy Chauvin, would perhaps call 'the *aparallel evolution*' of theory and practice (1987: 18/10).
11. 'In all cases, [Deleuze] presents a world understood as a complex of

interconnected assemblages (earth, territory, forms of deterritorialization and reterritorialization), where the overriding norm is that of
deterritorialization.'

12. 'Overturning all orders and representations in order to affirm Difference
in the state of permanent revolution which characterizes the eternal
return' (Deleuze 1994: 75/53). 'To make the simulacra rise and affirm
their rights' (Deleuze 1990: 303/262).

13. 'There are, effectively, features that justify calling Deleuze the ideolo-
gist of late capitalism' (Žižek 2004: 184).

14. Being is no longer naturally emergent, as in early works, according to
Toscano. In *A Thousand Plateaus* Deleuze and Guattari now claim
that political strategy precedes Being and that multiplicity must be
constructed.

15. Except Nick Land, who affirms deterritorialisation as absolute escape
without consistency; see Land 1993.

16. 'Desire is always assembled and fabricated on a plane of immanence or
composition which must itself be constructed at the same time as desire
assembles and fabricates' (Deleuze and Parnet 1987: 125/103). 'A tool
remains marginal, or little used, until there exists a social machine or
collective assemblage which is capable of taking it into its "phylum"'
(1987: 85/70; see also 115/96).

17. *The Signature of the World* deals with ethics, not politics.

18. In this way my approach is similarly distinct from Hanjo Beressem's
approach in 'Structural Couplings: Radical Constructivism and a
Deleuzian Ecologics' in *Deleuze/Guattari and Ecology* (2009). While
Beressem does gesture to a radical constructivism of some kind, he does
not understand it in the truly political and overtly revolutionary way
that Deleuze and Guattari do. 'When I use the term "radical ecology"
or "radical philosophy" these do not immediately concern what is
generally considered a "radical ecology" or "radical philosophy" or
a "radical politics"' (Beressem 2009: 58). A radical constructivism
that does not immediately concern what is generally and actually
considered radical politics is counter to the aims of the current book
and to the aims of Deleuze and Guattari's revolutionary strategy more
generally.

19. Constructivism is the concept Deleuze and Guattari mobilise against
accusations of political spontaneity. 'In retrospect every assemblage
expresses and creates a desire by constructing the plane which makes it
possible and, by making it possible, brings it about . . . It is in itself an
immanent revolutionary process. It is constructivist, not at all sponta-
neist' (Deleuze and Parnet 1987: 115–16/96).

20. 'We are not a proletariat, our land is not your means of production and
we don't want to work in a tractor factory. All we want is to be listened
to, and for you big-city smart-arses to stop telling us how to live. As for

your dialectic – you can keep it. You never know when it might come in handy' (Kingsnorth 2004: 29).

21. 'The examples of popular organization we know today are, therefore, either extremely experimental and localized (like the Zapatista movement) or theologico-political (like Hezbollah)' (Badiou 2008a: 656). 'Through a combination of constructions of thought, which are always global or universal, and political experiments, which are local or singular but can be transmitted universally, we can assure the new existence of the communist hypothesis, both in consciousness and in concrete situations' (Badiou 2008b: 117).

22. There are many types of abstract machines according to Deleuze and Guattari. In Chapter 1 I elaborate three kinds of abstract machines (territorial, statist, capitalist) but in Chapter 3 the concept of the abstract machine, concrete assemblage and machinic persona should be understood as referring only to the 'consistent' type of machines.

23. 'Pas hiérarchique, mais vicinal' (Deleuze and Guattari 1994: 87/90).

1

Political History and the Diagnostic of Revolutionary Praxis

Neither Marx nor Engels ever came close to developing a theory of history, in the sense of an unpredictable historical event, unique and aleatory, nor indeed to developing a theory of political practice. I refer here to the politico-ideologico-social practice of political activism, of mass movements and of their eventual organizations, for which we possess no concepts and even less a coherent theory, in order for it to be apprehended in thought. Lenin, Gramsci, and Mao were only able to partially think such a practice. The only theorist to think the political history of political practice in the present was Machiavelli. There is here another huge deficit to overcome, the importance of which is decisive, and which, once again, sends us back to philosophy.

(Althusser 1994: 48)

Introduction

In light of its apparent exhaustion, how is it possible to return to revolution? This is the central question of this book. Given the scope of such a question, I proposed in the introduction to focus my philosophical interrogation of this question on three figures in the history of the present revolutionary sequence who have been particularly influential to its development: Deleuze, Guattari and the Zapatistas. Thus, in order to shed some light on the larger revolutionary sequence that began to take place at the end of the twentieth century, I also proposed four distinct revolutionary strategies that help us clarify and develop this new political philosophy of revolution. These four strategies respond to four important questions concerning revolution and correspond with each chapter of this book. What is the relationship between history and revolution? What is revolutionary transformation? How is it possible to sustain and carry out the consequences of a revolutionary transformation? And how do revolutions connect with one another to produce a new form of worldwide solidarity?

The introduction not only laid out the larger task of the book as a whole but proposed a method for assembling the four proposed strategies and an interpretive intervention for locating them in Deleuze, Guattari and the Zapatistas. Along with this method I also proposed to make a contributing intervention into the literature on Deleuze, Guattari and the Zapatistas by reading them not as political theories and practices aimed at merely reforming the process of political representation or aimed at simply affirming the ontologically differential conditions of their potential for transformation, but reading them instead as political constructivists engaged in the creation of positive alternatives to state, party and vanguard politics.[1]

Given the above philosophical framework I have put forward, this chapter responds to the first of the four questions above: what is the relationship between history and revolution today? In reply, this chapter argues that the return to revolution influenced by Deleuze, Guattari and the Zapatistas can be characterised by a 'diagnostic' strategy of political history motivated by the relative rejection of all previous forms of political representation (statism, capitalism, vanguardism and so on) and a concern for their immanent diagnosis in revolutionary praxis. My argument is a *relative* rejection not only of the content of representation (race, class, gender, economics and so on) but of its forms, which always intersect and coexist in varying degrees in any political situation.

In order to defend these claims, this chapter is divided into three sections. The first begins by rejecting two notions of universal history: the notion of the *necessary* and sequential emergence of different types of political power, and the notion of the *merely contingent and coexistent* emergence of different types of political power. Both of these notions, I argue, are unable to conceive of a sustained alternative to representational politics. The next two sections then propose an alternative strategy of using history based on its specifically diagnostic ability to help discern the immanent political dangers and opportunities for revolutionary praxis. Section two argues that Deleuze and Guattari's theory of historical topology functions as such a multi-centred political diagnostic, and section three argues that the Zapatistas' practice of 'diagnosing suffering' used in *La Otra Campaña* also functions as such a multi-centred political diagnostic (Marcos 2004b: 314).

I. *Revolution and Universal History*

In this first section, I distinguish the concept of a multi-centred political diagnostic from two competing notions of universal history both unable to conceive of a sustained alternative to representational politics.

<small>THE UNIVERSAL HISTORY OF SUCCESSION</small>

According to the first concept, universal history is the succession of inevitable moments of crisis moving towards increasingly superior forms of political organisation. Revolution is thus a progressive, evolutionary and teleological force. The notion that political history functions through the sequential passing of distinct instants or epochs relies on the idea of a unity, ground or identity beneath these epochs such that they can be distinguished both from each other and from the ground upon which they pass. Each epoch is distinct but connected causally to the previous one under the condition of an underlying arrow of history itself. But whether this universal political succession is teleological, evolutionary or progressive, it still defines revolution as the transformation of one state into another, guided by the knowledge of an underlying historical continuity between them. Revolutionary movements, according to this theory, proceed by a successive and increasingly accurate transformative repetition of states towards their predefined goal: the perfect state-form itself, state-liberalism, state-communism, state-capitalism and so on.

The problem that this theory of universal historical succession poses, however, is that because it assumes a pre-given synthesis of identity to account for the passing of causally different instants, it ends up reproducing only repetitions of the same historico-political presupposition without the possibility of external change or contingency. It is ultimately a universal history of states and their capture of non-state forces. It defines history as the tendency of the development of 'x', where x is the perfection of the present dominant political ideology: the state form. In other words, the concept of succession presupposes a given present moment and then understands the past and future as repetitions of this present moment: as effects of its primary cause. This closes off the possibility that a contingent and revolutionary event might undermine this unity; that it might change the very presuppositions of history (and not simply repeat its underlying laws of relation: resemblance, representation, acquisition of state power and so on). Historical succession can thus allow for change, but only within pre-given parameters themselves unchanged by new political events. There may be non-state power, but only as a developmental stage moving towards the perfection of state power.

What this theory of revolutionary history has failed to think, however, is a concept of non-state historical novelty. The question of a revolution's positive composition as a real form of power apart from the telos of state seizure has not yet been taken seriously. Revolutionary Marxism, although Marx's theoretical aims were ultimately anti-state, has only succeeded in replacing the bourgeois state-body with the communist party-state, but what has yet to be thought and practised today is a new kind of non-state body that would replace both party and state.[2]

THE UNIVERSAL HISTORY OF CONTINGENCY

According to the second concept, universal history is the coexistent potentiality of multiple and contingent forces. Revolution in this case is the potentiality of transformation as such. The universal history of contingency rejects the concept of historical progress, teleology, the state and an underlying historical unity. Unfortunately, the mere contingency and coexistence of historical political forms is insufficient for understanding how it is that revolutions actually emerge. One way of reading Deleuze and Guattari's concept of political history is to read it as the universal history of contingency and coexistence.

In *Deleuze and Guattari's Philosophy of History*, Jay Lampert argues precisely this. The universal history of succession 'assumes', Lampert argues, 'that events have their primary causal impact on just those events which they resemble; it treats events as if they were entirely determined by prior causes unaffected either by chance or by subsequent events, and it reads events teleologically' (2006: 7). Opposed to succession, Lampert argues instead that

> we might think of time as the folding and unfolding of a topological field. When folded over on to itself, the field is present one small square at a time, with its other parts moved to the back – present but backgrounded. When unfolded again, the presents get reorganised, and new foregroundings take place. Instants are always being reformulated on the shifting topology; as the smallest possible points of view, they are in a sense real. In sum, the smallest points, and their order of presentation, are dependent on the foldings and unfoldings of the general field that envelops them. (2006: 16)

If we consider 'universal history [as] the history of contingencies, and not the history of necessity', and historical events as folded
intersections of all 'previous, present, and future' events (some more
foregrounded, others more backgrounded), then there can be no
necessary or pre-given teleology, evolution or progress in history,
only different arrangements of temporally heterogeneous moments
continually open to recomposition (Deleuze and Guattari 1983:
163/140). According to Deleuze and Guattari,

> It is thus right to understand retrospectively all of history in the light of
> capitalism, on condition that we follow exactly the rules formulated by
> Marx: first, universal history is one of contingencies, and not of necessity;
> of breaks and limits, and not of continuity. For it required great chances
> [*grands hasards*], astonishing encounters, which could have been pro-
> duced elsewhere, previously, or might never have been produced, in order
> that fluxes escape coding, and, escaping, would constitute no less a new
> machine determinable as a capitalist *socius* . . . In short, universal history
> is not only retrospective, it is contingent, singular, ironic, and critical.
> (1983: 163–4/140)

Deleuze and Guattari's concept of universal history is thus ironic in
the sense that it begins from the perspective of the 'end' of history
(capitalism), but that this 'end' is not its final end. It is critical in the
sense that it is continually pushing beyond the limits of capitalism
towards the ever new elements that continue to break free from it,
and it is singular in the sense that historical events are based on contingent encounters that do not express the same unified condition.

History is universal, for Deleuze and Guattari, not because a
pre-given social identity is able to see itself in all its predecessors,
but because capitalism has detached beings from their 'natural' or
'proper' space-times to be exchanged on a world market. These deterritorialised historical events are then able to bear directly upon the
constitution of the present. According to Lampert, the way around
the neoliberal cul-de-sac of political history is thus the 'revolutionary
potential of co-existential history' (2006: 140). 'In short,' Lampert
argues, following Deleuze and Guattari's claim that 'the undecidable
is *par excellence* the germ and the place of revolutionary decisions'
(Deleuze and Guattari 1987: 590–1/473), '[revolutionary] events are
contingent not because they do something new, but because they do
something undecidable' (Lampert 2006: 169). If history is universally
contingent and some or any of its revolutionary events of the past,
present or future may be contingently revived at any moment (the
French revolution, May 1968, events to come and so on) then the

41

concept of revolution can never be exhausted and 'the Deleuzian historian' becomes 'the revolutionary who reorganizes bodies into war machines' and affirms the undecidable coexistence of all events as the potential for a new revolution (2006: 111).

While I believe Lampert's account is well written and not inaccurate, I also believe that its contribution to a political philosophy of revolution is, as it is for Deleuze and Guattari in *Anti-Oedipus*, radically insufficient. While it is true that a universal history of contingency and coexistence can be located in Deleuze and Guattari's philosophy and is able to avoid the problems of succession, the undecidable affirmation of revolutionary coexistential potentiality, however, remains ultimately ambivalent. On this point I am in agreement with Badiou's criticisms of *Anti-Oedipus* in 'Flux and the Party' (2004a). Simply valorising or affirming the historical potentiality of the political situation to 'become other than it is' through the aleatory re-emergence of revolutionary historical events may be emancipatory just as much as it may mean the return of more archaically violent forms of repression or a new market opportunity for capitalism. While the universal history of contingency certainly admits the possibility of revolution, it does not directly contribute to its clarification or actual development.

In some places, however, Lampert's reading of Deleuze and Guattari's philosophy of history does seem to offer us some clues to continue developing a theory of revolution based on this contingent coexistence of political events. 'For a historical event', Lampert insists, 'to be actualized at a particular moment in time means nothing other than for it to exhibit all four kinds of temporal relations [territorial, statist, capitalist and nomadic] at once, all of which are real, and all of which are diagrammed together concretely' (2006: 17). Lampert may not have used this method to understand the actualisation of revolutionary praxis, but it is the aim of this chapter to do so.

II. Deleuze and Guattari's Historical Topology

WHAT IS POLITICAL HISTORY?

How then are we to understand political history such that non-representational revolutionary praxis is not only possible but actually constructed? So far I have argued that it cannot be by necessity, progress and state-seizure, nor can it be by mere contingency and coexistence. Neither of these offers us a way to understand a sustained political alternative to the history of representational politics. Taking Lampert's lead seriously, however, I argue in this next section that we can use Deleuze and Guattari's theory of historical topology as a multi-centred diagnostic of revolutionary praxis. Doing so, we can extract a truly revolutionary use of political history untethered to representation and the affirmation of undecidable contingency. Although first begun in *Anti-Oedipus*, I believe the best resources for reading Deleuze and Guattari's theory of history as a revolutionary diagnostic are to be found in *A Thousand Plateaus*. While Deleuze and Guattari do not directly describe their theory of historical topology as a 'multi-centred political diagnostic', nor do they use it for the sole purpose of assessing the positive power of revolutionary struggle, I argue that doing so will resolve our dilemma and help us assess the dangers of building a revolutionary praxis: by diagramming all its four kinds of temporal relations together, concretely (see Deleuze and Guattari 1987: 542/435).[3]

To this end, and following the above quotation from *A Thousand Plateaus*, in this section I outline three of the historical political processes described by Deleuze and Guattari in *Capitalism and Schizophrenia* and argue that these processes are useful for diagnosing the dangers and opportunities for revolutionary transformation, even though Deleuze and Guattari did not completely do so themselves. To what degree does a revolutionary situation operate by territorial coding, statist overcoding or capitalist axiomatics? What dangers do these pose to revolutionary praxis?

But the argument that Deleuze and Guattari's theory of history should be used as a political diagnostic is not an original argument on my part and has, to some degree, been made by others, whose work I draw on in my own reading (Bell and Colebrook 2009). What is original in my reading, however, is that I focus this diagnostic specifically on the question of the actualisation of revolution and the dangers it faces as a positive (not merely potential or undecidable) form of power.

At this point, however, the reader might be wondering from where Deleuze and Guattari have derived these three political processes and why we should draw on them to understand the contemporary return to revolution. Firstly, the political processes of territorial coding, statist overcoding and capitalist axiomatisation did not fall from the sky. Deleuze and Guattari spend the vast majority of *Anti-Oedipus* and a good part of *A Thousand Plateaus* extracting

the general characteristics of these processes from the concrete practices and events of political history by drawing on a variety of well-
known sociologists, anthropologists, archaeologists and historians.
For Deleuze and Guattari, these political processes are not universal
categories imposed upon history and political life from the outside.
But neither are they merely reducible to the concrete empirical phenomena that they are meant to characterise. Statist overcoding, for
example, is not an empirical state, nor is it a universal category given
in advance and by necessity; it is, as Foucault says, a 'process of statification' (2008: 77). For Deleuze and Guattari, these three processes
of political power have no fixed essence or universality independent from the contingent and concrete effects that compose them. In
fact, they are themselves nothing but effects, the mobile shape of a
perpetual process in the sense that they are incessant transactions
which modify, move or change. But within these changes there are
still general characteristics of each process that remain 'transcenden-
tally empirical' (see Sauvagnargues 2010). That is, they are transcendental in the sense that they describe the conditions under which a
wide variety of phenomena occur, but they are also empirical in the
sense that they are real, singular, mutable and historically contingent
themselves. Being contingent, however, also means that they may
reappear and disappear at different moments in history and in different combinations.[4]

Secondly, and accordingly, we should use Deleuze and Guattari's
theory of historical topology to understand the relationship between
history and revolution because, unlike the political history of succession, which Lampert rightly critiques, historical topology is able to
theorise the possibility of the novel and non-representational process
that characterises the contemporary return to revolution. Opposed to
assuming a prior historical unity based on states, and here I am in full
agreement with Lampert, Deleuze and Guattari develop a political
history of contingency based on revolutionary potential. If we want
to be able to think a return to revolution that is not based on the teleological political development of state, party or vanguard representation, then we need to be able to think of history as both contingent
and topological. Exactly how Deleuze and Guattari succeed at this
task is the subject of several scholarly works (see Burchill 2007).
However, the argument I put forward in this section moves beyond
the scholarship on this topic that has for the most part read Deleuze
and Guattari as proposing a merely potential and topological theory
of history. I argue instead that Deleuze and Guattari's philosophy

of political history is not merely topological, but that it should be used as a diagnostic of political power in order to construct a positive revolutionary praxis. We should use Deleuze and Guattari's historical topology as more than the mere accurate description of the world and its potential for transformation; we should use it to build another world within it that actively replaces representational politics.

Before describing the general characteristics of each of these processes and arguing for their use as a multi-centred political diagnostic of revolutionary praxis, I want to highlight the four central characteristics of Deleuze and Guattari's topological theory of political history that guide my argument. Political history, according to Deleuze and Guattari, is (1) topological, (2) applied immanently 'in the course of events' [*qu'ils s'exercent au fur et à mesure, sur le moment*] (1987: 307/251), (3) a mix of political processes, and (4) able to help us to avoid the dangers of political representation.

(1) Political History is Topological

> It was a decisive event when the mathematician Riemann uprooted the multiple from its predicate state and made it a noun, 'multiplicity'. It marked the end of dialectics and the beginning of a typology and topology of multiplicities. (Deleuze and Guattari 1987: 602/482–3)

Taken from mathematics, the concept of a topological field is a single surface composed of multiple heterogeneous points that are connected together by foldings or morphisms in their surface (like a piece of origami). Independent of linear contiguity, succession or dialectics, topological shapes move and change by folding themselves into new networks of relations. Sierpiński's sponge, von Koch's curve without tangent and Mandelbrot's fractals are examples of iterated topological fields in geometry.[5]

The concept of a specifically topological theory of political history thus provides a way to consider political events as having several overlapping and contingent tendencies at once, each to a greater or lesser degree. For example, perhaps a political event has a strong anti-capitalist tendency but also has a strong territorial or religious tendency towards patriarchal norms that weakly manifests as a non-national solidarity across borders. This heterogeneity is not a matter of contradiction or exclusion. Topologically speaking, there is no central axis or 'essential political ideology' operating here. There is only a relative mix of political tendencies folded on top of each other without a fixed centre or necessary relationship. All of these political tendencies, according to Deleuze and Guattari, act as the 'loci of a topology [*lieux d'une topologie*] that defines primitive societies here, States there, and elsewhere war machines' (1987: 537/430). Thus, topologically speaking, these political tendencies or types are really distinct insofar as they occupy different locations, and yet they can also be contingently connected insofar as the coexistent space itself folds them together. If political events are like successive points on a line, then there is no way for one point to directly affect another except through a mediated chain of causal unity. However, if political events are heterogeneous points on a one-dimensional folded surface, then any event can be directly connected to any other in any combination by spatial proximity: without mediation or causal unity.[6]

The consequence of this political coexistence, according to Deleuze and Guattari, is that 'these directions are equally present in all social fields, in all periods. It even happens that they partially merge' (1987: 446/360). All political types merge and coexist simultaneously in all social fields at once in the sense that they actively ward each other off and prevent what is to come while also providing the conditions for their replacement. Kinship relations in primitive societies, for example, Deleuze and Guattari argue, actively anticipate the state capture of their surplus storage and the decoded flows of capital, but also actively ward them off through specific practices of potlatch and alliance (marriages, dowries) with other tribes. In this sense there is a 'presentiment' or action of the inexistent future upon the present already in action, even if the 'future' form does not empirically exist yet.

> Primitive societies cannot ward off the formation of an empire or State without anticipating it, and they cannot anticipate it without its already being there, forming part of their horizon. And States cannot effect a capture unless what is captured coexists, resists in primitive societies, or escapes under new forms, as towns or war machines. (Deleuze and Guattari 1987: 542/435)

Thus, 'To ward off is also to anticipate' [*Conjurer, c'est aussi anticiper*], they say (Deleuze and Guattari 1987: 537/431). Even contemporary physics and biology have developed similar notions of 'reverse causalities' that are without finality but testify to the action of the future on the present, or of the present on the past (Prigogine and Stengers 1997).

(2) Political History is Applied in the Course of Events

But Deleuze and Guattari's historical topology or 'speculative cartography ... is not there to provide an inventory of modes of existence' (Stivale 1998), or to provide an exhaustive taxonomy of beings. Such an inventory would presuppose a higher unity or totality of being from which to derive its universality. Only when a political history, Deleuze and Guattari say, 'ceases to express a hidden unity, becoming itself a dimension of the multiplicity under consideration', does it cease to represent a political situation and become constitutive of it (1987: 33/22). That is, the revolutionary situation does not pre-exist its topological construction, it 'must be made' [*Le multiple, il faut le faire*] (Deleuze and Guattari 1987: 13/6) or expressed through the diagnostic labour itself, such 'that one cannot distinguish it from the existential territory' (Stivale 1998: 219). There is thus, as Deleuze and Guattari say, 'no difference between the map and the territory. That means that there is no transposition, that there is no translatability, and therefore no possible taxonomy. The modelization here is a producer of existence' (Stivale 1998: 219).

For example, when Deleuze and Guattari describe the kinship relations of credit and debt in primitive societies or the desert wanderings of Moses' nomads, these are not anthropological or historical claims meant to represent or factually reference some past 'state of affairs', accurately or inaccurately, as some critics have misunderstood (Miller 1993). Representational anthropology and history presuppose a prior unity of humanity and time such that one point may stand in for another through succession and identity. Rather, Deleuze and Guattari draw on anthropology and history to isolate certain political concepts, concepts which are proper to politics but which can only be formed philosophically (see Deleuze 1989: 365/280). Such political concepts do not bear any resemblance to the situation but are a dimension of it, constitutive and expressive of it.

Thus, historical topology does not ask if characteristics accurately represent the truth of the state of affairs or what they mean, signify, symbolise or stand for. Instead it composes a practical dimension of how they work and what they do. Topology is thus a creative practice: a constructivism itself transformed by what it transforms.

(3) Political History Exists as a Mix of Political Processes

But if political history is not the continuous evolution of a single telos, or the pure potentiality of coexistence as such, but rather the contingent, multiple and folded mix of 'aggregates of consistency' or 'consolidations of very heterogeneous elements' in coexisting historical events, then how can we explain time: the quasi-historical phenomena of limited political sequences, retroactive interpretations, dates, causes and breakdowns (Deleuze and Guattari 1987: 414/335)? If every event in history is coexistent then how are we to distinguish different topologically mixed 'blocks of becoming' from one another?

Every situation, or 'block of becoming', as Deleuze and Guattari call it, has its own particular admixture of political types that are more or less anticipated or prevented. For instance, different political processes may create blockages to transformation in a situation through different modes of historico-political succession: territorial successions of genealogy and filiation, state successions-in-coexistence of pre-given laws and despots, and capitalist coexistences of successions through axiomatic exchange on the world market.[7] Succession exists, then, not with a presupposed unity of time, but as a secondary effect of a more primary network of folds in a political topology.

These 'mixed regimes', Deleuze and Guattari say, 'presuppose these transformations from one regime to another, past, present, or potential (*as a function of the creation of new regimes*)' (my italics) (1987: 181/145). That is, because all political events are potentially or virtually active in any given event (and must be warded off or precipitated), they do not constitute a necessary succession but can produce the effect of one. A political topology based on thresholds and neighbourhoods (statism here, territorial formations there and so on) accounts for distinct 'sequences' through transhistorical folding. Completely heterogeneous space-times are held together through a particular 'sequence' of resurrected and prefiguring components given a historical name and date to mark their configuration. Sequence is then constructed from topological heterogeneity. Dates and names thus do not refer to or represent past or future political events but are simply markers indicating the creation of a 'sequence'.

'Contrary to the Marxist view,' according to Paul Patton, 'no single logic of development governs the direction of history understood in these terms. All events are the effects of the interplay of forces, as things are transformed or reinterpreted to serve new ends' (2000: 56). Instead of asking how a political event further articulates the becoming of a pre-given 'end of history', we should ask instead, what are the relative blockages, anticipations and mixed political processes at work in a given event, how do future events transform

those of the past and present, and how do those of the past transform those of the future? That is, what is the relative mixture of the
event's political anticipations and repressions and how can we avoid
the dangers of representation while creating a constructive alternative? In this way we can use Deleuze and Guattari's political topology
as a diagnostic to avoid the blockage of an identity-based universal
history (that understands difference only as a difference from the
same) and the ambivalence of a universal history that merely affirms
the potentiality of revolutionary coexistence.

(4) Political History Helps Us Avoid the Dangers of Political Representation

The goal of political history as a strategy is to aid in determining
the dangers that confront a revolutionary praxis. As Deleuze and
Guattari pose the issue after writing *Anti-Oedipus*,

> The problem one always comes up against is how to ensure that the
> movements of decoding, the movements of deterritorialization, are revo-
> lutionarily positive, but at the same time that they do not recreate artifi-
> cial forms like perversion or the family, that is, that they do not create in
> their own way types of codes and territorialities. (Deleuze 1972)[8]

In order to effectively avoid 'social orders of representation'
[*genres de représentation*], as Deleuze and Guattari call them, a political and topological history must be able to distinguish between types
and deselect the ones that isolate, self-destruct or try and capture all
other modes of valorisation (1983: 312/262). The monomania of
movements demanding recognition of their single-issue causes, the
subjection of citizens by legal and representational statism, global
enslavement by techno-capitalist market production, and no less the
lines of escape from these dangers that fail to create new alternatives, potentially falling instead into the black holes of revolutionary
purity, drugs or cynicism, are all coexisting potential dangers.

But as Deleuze and Guattari say, 'politics is by no means an apo-
dictic science. It proceeds by experimentation, groping in the dark,
injection, withdrawal, advances, retreats. The factors of decision and
prediction are limited' (1987: 575/461). Since the very practice of
historical topology is, as they define it, constitutive of the situation,
any 'identification' of 'what types are functioning here' is both effec-
tive and effected by acts of determination. Hence historical topology
is by no means axiomatic or formally unaffected by the determinations it makes. Rather, it is at each point reciprocally transformed

in an experimental feedback loop always in danger and requiring caution. Revolution is thus not an unrestrained unleashing of desire, freedom or lines of flight, nor is it a matter of having 'the right plan'. Rather, it is a risky experimentation requiring caution and commitment to lay out a practical diagnostic of action: adding one more dimension or fold to the last.

Revolution is neither about a progressive strategic assault on state power, nor an absolute potential to contingently allow things to become other than they are. Rather, a revolutionary situation is a specifically held tension of heterogeneous historical/political forces of anticipation and prevention. It is the diagnostic creation of new space-times or consistent events simultaneous and coexistent to the forces and dangers of political representation. It is not a radically external force, but rather an exterior force folded into the interior of the situation: it is, or can be, as Guattari says, an 'anti-capitalist force within capitalism' (1996: 89).[9] How then should we use Deleuze and Guattari's concept of historical topology as a creative diagnostic of the positive (not merely potential) power of revolutionary praxis?

HISTORICAL TOPOLOGY AS DIAGNOSTIC OF REVOLUTIONARY PRAXIS

I have thus far argued two points: firstly, that the emergence of a non-representational revolution is blocked by two theories of universal history. If history is the unity of successive moments culminating in political representation, then non-representational revolutionary novelty is impossible. If history is a virtual coexistence of contingent moments, then revolutionary novelty is possible but ambivalent. Secondly, I argued that Deleuze and Guattari's concept of political history provides an alternative to both these theories insofar as it is (1) topological, (2) applied immanently 'in the course of events', (3) a mix of political processes, and (4) able to help us to avoid the dangers of political representation (although the exact details of these dangers will be addressed in the following section). I will argue in this next section that this historical topology should be understood as indicative of a new revolutionary strategy based on its use as a diagnostic of revolutionary praxis.

In order to do this I examine each one of the political processes described by Deleuze and Guattari (territorial coding, statist over-coding and capitalist axiomatisation) in detail and show how each diagnoses a type of representational process that poses a danger for revolutionary praxis: (1) territorial representation poses the dangers of monomania and microfascism; (2) state representation poses the dangers of fear, machinic enslavement and subjectification; and (3) capitalist representation poses the dangers of total war, and a new form of machinic enslavement.

(1) Territorial Representation

Territorial political representation, a concept Deleuze and Guattari extract[10] from the practices of 'primitive societies', is characterised by what they call coding, supple segmentation and itinerancy. But, they ask, 'why return to the primitives, when it is a question of our own life?' (Deleuze and Guattari 1987: 254/209). One of the more politically significant (and yet under-attended) moves Deleuze and Guattari make away from *Anti-Oedipus* is to extend their political typology, previously restricted to libidinal and economic domains, into a broader 'general logic of assemblages' [*une logique générale*] in *A Thousand Plateaus* (Deleuze 2006: 163/177). According to Deleuze, the features that previously characterised the historical, libidinal and economic sequences of primitivism, statism and capitalism in *Anti-Oedipus* become, in *A Thousand Plateaus*, the general political and topological features of all kinds of assemblages. Following this, the present approach extracts only the most basic and transferable aspects of these three logics without suturing their origins to the narrowly historical context in which they emerge in *Anti-Oedipus*. Topologically, as I have shown, the basic characteristics of all historical political processes can be just as operative in the past as they can be in the present or future.[11]

(1.1) Coding, Supple Segmentation and Itinerancy

Territorial representation, according to Deleuze and Guattari, is thus characterised by the use of polyvocal codes, supple kinds of segmentation and itinerant territories. These are the basic processes, according to Jason Read, by which social 'traditions, prescriptions, and rules bearing on the production and distribution of goods, prestige, and desire' are represented in a political situation (2008: 142). They are the 'natural' norms of social life. Territorial processes express the pre-given, essential and proper limits and usage of persons and objects in a given situation by repressing decoded flows (the unexplainable) and (re)presenting others as coded (meaningful) ones. Codes are thus naturalised as 'related to the past, to an inscription of memory, "this is how things are done, how they have always been done"' (2008: 142). According to *Anti-Oedipus*, these 'qualitatively different chains of mobile and limited code' (1983: 294/247) are formed by three basic actions: (1) 'a selection cut' allowing something to pass through and circulate; (2) 'a detachment cut' that blocks part of that circulation; and (3) a 'redistribution of the remainder' to begin a new chain of code.

The process of coding, Deleuze and Guattari say, begins not on the basis of a primary code but from a territorial repression of 'uncoded or decoded flows': a kind of primordial chaos inherent to the earth itself. Before there are any social norms or traditions there is a more primary 'scission' (1983: 177/152) where the 'whole process of production is inscribed, on which the forces and means of labor are recorded, and the agents and the products distributed' (1983: 164–5/ 141). Confronted with the 'terrifying nightmare' (1983: 164/140) of this essentially chaotic and fragmented world, territorial peoples repress these uncoded flows and inscribe upon this chaos their own territorial representations (1983: 164/140).

The first synthesis of territorial coding (the synthesis of connection) attempts to ward off this chaos by making a 'selection cut' from these uncoded flows, allowing some of them to pass through while others are blocked. This primary repression of non-codable flows accomplishes two things: it wards off an absolutely chaotic world by deselecting some of its flows, and it puts into circulation and connection the others to be coded. By marking a separation of some of these non-coded flows the connective synthesis is able to serialise and qualitatively organise them into an identity, 'coded stock', or what Deleuze and Guattari call an 'inscription on a full body' or 'socius'. The 'entry pole' of selection here initiates a filiative line following a genealogical or hereditary descent of hierarchically coded stock: codes of kinship, codes of worship, codes of communication, codes of exchange, codes of location (places of worship, places for eating, places for rubbish). Everything has its proper code: the proper time for revolution, the proper people to undertake it.

The second synthesis of territorial coding (the disjunctive synthesis or 'detachment cut') also accomplishes two tasks: it blocks some of these connections from attaching themselves to the political body (by code prohibitions, limits and so on) so that a finite stock of code may circulate within a qualitatively distinct territory, and it detaches a remainder or 'residual energy' in order to begin a new chain of code further along. These are the borders to towns, prohibitions on kinship, and boundaries to racial, ethnic and gender identities. The revolutionary vanguard similarly detaches itself from the proletariat mass and forges ahead of them. These are the limits produced by the disjunctive synthesis.

The third synthesis of territorial coding (the conjunctive synthesis or the 'redistribution of the remainder') wards off the fusion of all codes into a single qualitative stock by producing a residuum, but also begins a new line of code by redistributing this surplus through an alliance with different lines of code. There are many different mechanisms for warding off the fusion of codes and redistributing surplus code through alliances with other lines of code: practices of potlatch (giving away wealth in order to gain prestige), practices of struggle (itinerant raids and theft eliminating accumulation), practices of dowry (giving away wealth and establishing alliances with other kinship lines), gifts and counter-gifts, and so on.

These codes, lineages and territories 'form a fabric [*tissu*] of relatively supple segmentarity' (Deleuze and Guattari 1987: 255/208). Codes and territorial representations segment us from all around and in every direction, Deleuze and Guattari say in *A Thousand Plateaus* (1987: 254/208). 'The house is segmented according to its rooms' assigned purposes; streets, according to the order of the city; the factory, according to the nature of the work and operations performed in it' (1987: 254/208). There are, according to Deleuze and Guattari,

> multiple *binary* segments following the great major dualist oppositions: social classes, but also men-women, adults-children, and so on, *circular* segments, in ever larger circles, ever wider disks or coronas, like Joyce's 'letter': my affairs, my neighborhood's affairs, my city's, my country's, the world's, and *linear* segments, along a straight line or a number of straight lines, of which each segment represents an episode or 'proceeding': as soon as we finish one proceeding we begin another, forever proceduring or procedured, in the family, in school, in the army, on the job. School tells us, 'You're not at home anymore'; the army tells us, 'You're not in school anymore.' (1987: 254/208)

Sometimes the segments belong to individuals or groups, and sometimes the individuals or groups belong to many segments at once and change according to the perspective. Territorial segments frequently have a leeway between the two poles of chaotic scission and static fusion. They have considerable communicability between heterogeneous elements such that one segment may fit with another in many ways without the prior determination of a base domain (economic, political, juridical, artistic and so on). They have situated properties and relations independent of any structure and have a continuous activity such that segmentarity is always segmentarity-in-progress, operating by outgrowths, detachments and mergings.

Finally, 'by switching territories at the conclusion of each operation period (itinerancy, itineration)', and within each operation period repeating a temporal series that tends towards its marginal or limit object, primitive political distributions create a 'disequilibrium of excess and deficiency' (see Deleuze and Guattari 1987: 548–50/440). That is, every time a territory is delimited, an outside or surplus is produced through this process of delimitation or 'detachment'. This surplus or credit is then redistributed to another line (through an alliance) where it will again produce a surplus and so on in a perpetual disequilibrium: making its very dysfunction an essential element of its ability to function ('c'est pour *fonctionner qu'une machine sociale doit* ne pas fonctionner bien') (1983: 177/151). But what would it mean to use this as a diagnostic of a positive revolutionary praxis?

(1.2) Errors and Dangers of Territorial Representation for Revolutionary Praxis

As a diagnostic tool, and not as a mere historical contingency, territorial representation reveals two errors and two dangers within revolutionary praxis. 'The first [error]', Deleuze and Guattari say, 'is axiological and consists in believing that a little suppleness is enough to make things "better"' (1987: 262/215).

Supple reforms based on the representation of an essential group identity only appear to be transformative when in fact they leave deeper structural problems intact. That is, if revolutionary movements produce their own coded (and thus restricted) values, essential meanings and segmented territories, they may appear to have made important reforms by legitimating their own identities/values. But by representing their culture as a coded identity, they are only that much easier to incorporate into the larger processes of state overcoding or a profitable and tolerant multiculturalism.

'The second [error]', Deleuze and Guattari say, 'is psychological, as if the molecular [territorial] were in the realm of the imagination and applied only to the individual and interindividual. But there is just as much social-Real on one line as on the other' (1987: 262/215). That is, territorial social struggles may not be state politics but that does not mean that they are 'social-imaginaries', reducible to psychological or phenomenological cases of subjects-who-imagine.

Segmentary distributions are real political representations even if they are not represented by the state.[12]

The first danger of supple segmentarity, Deleuze and Guattari say, is the clarity of 'monomania'. That is,

> Interactions without resonance. Instead of the great paranoid fear [of the state], we are trapped in a thousand little monomanias, self-evident truths, and clarities that gush from every black hole and no longer form a system, but are only rumble and buzz, blinding lights giving any and everybody the mission of self-appointed judge, dispenser of justice, policeman, neighborhood SS man. (1987: 279/228)

Monomania is the danger that revolutionary movements can become what Deleuze and Guattari call 'neoterritorialities': gangs, bands, minorities, margins and 'tribalisms' that 'continue to affirm the rights of segmentary societies' but tend to persist within the interiority of the state. These neoterritorialities remain relatively independent from each other by presuming a coded clarity of their own issue, campaign or identity. However, the clarity afforded by independent single-issue struggles is ultimately unable to form a cohesive alternative to state-capitalism.

> These modern archaisms are extremely complex and varied. Some are mainly folkloric, but they nonetheless represent social and potentially political forces (from domino players to home brewers via the Veterans of Foreign Wars). Others are enclaves whose archaism is just as capable of nourishing a modern fascism as of freeing a revolutionary charge (the ethnic minorities, the Basque problem, the Irish Catholics, the Indian reservations) . . . (neighborhood territorialities, territorialities of the large aggregates, 'gangs'). Others are organized or promoted by the State, even though they might turn against the State and cause it serious problems (regionalism, nationalism). (1983: 306–7/257–8)

The revolutionary potential of these groups should not be dismissed. But political isolation and single-issue reform campaigns without the larger horizon of revolution are in danger of being exceptions that only prove the rule of state-capitalism (see Žižek 1997).

The second danger of supple segmentarity for revolutionary praxis is what Deleuze and Guattari call 'microfascism'. Coded revolutionary movements, bands, gangs, sects, families, towns and neighbourhoods can recreate, on their own territorial scale, the hierarchical, authoritarian organisation present at the state bureaucratic level. Within revolutionary struggles, patriarchal, racist, classist and so on codes and segments can all reappear. These microfascisms spare no one. 'Leftist organizations will not be the last to secrete microfascisms,' Deleuze and Guattari warn us. 'It's too easy to be antifascist on the molar level, and not even see the fascist inside you, the fascist you yourself sustain and nourish and cherish with molecules both personal and collective' (1987: 262/215). Supple segmentarity may undermine the rigid state segments, 'but everything that it dismantles it reassembles on its own level: micro-Oedipuses, microformations of power, microfascisms' (1987: 251/205).

But what dangers are posed for revolutionary praxis when these segmentary processes begin to resonate together in a process of state overcoding?

(2) State Representation

The second type of historical political process that Deleuze and Guattari describe in *Capitalism and Schizophrenia*, and that I argue can be used as a diagnostic of revolutionary praxis, is state representation. Just as territorial representation operates between the two poles of fusion and scission, state representation operates between two poles: the despotic and the juridical. While the first pole of the state brings coded territories into a resonance of concentric circles through the process of what Deleuze and Guattari call 'overcoding', the more developed juridical pole of the state disciplines the territories through law and 'social subjection'. While the first creates public stocks of land, work and money in order to extract rent, profit and tax, the second creates private property and legal contracts in order to circulate land, work and money horizontally among symmetrically related citizens. The despotic pole of the state is characterised by overcoding and rigid segmentation and poses two dangers for revolutionary movements, fear and machinic enslavement, while the juridical pole of the state poses the danger of social subjection. I examine each pole of the state and its dangers for revolutionary praxis in turn.

(2.1) The Despotic State Pole

Despotic state representation is characterised by its overcoding of territorial codes and its rigid segmentation of territorially supple segments. Instead of the surplus code generated through territorial representation that would normally form an alliance with other blocks of code, this surplus of code may instead begin to form an unchecked accumulation (agricultural, social, political and so on) requiring the maintenance of a specialised body. This special body of accumulation then reacts back upon the territories and brings them into resonance around a centralised point of transcendence: the despot. The extended filiations of old communities and groups are then replaced by the direct filiation of the despot to his deity, while the lateral alliances are replaced by a new alliance of the despot with his people. Overcoding, according to Deleuze and Guattari, thus

> makes points resonate together, points that are not necessarily already town-poles but very diverse points of order, geographic, ethnic, linguistic, moral, economic, technological particularities. It makes the town resonate with the countryside. It operates by stratification; in other words, it forms a vertical, hierarchized aggregate that spans the horizontal lines in a dimension of depth. In retaining given elements, it necessarily cuts off their relations with other elements, which become exterior, it inhibits, slows down, or controls those relations; if the State has a circuit of its own, it is an internal circuit dependent primarily upon resonance, it is a zone of recurrence that isolates itself from the remainder of the network, even if in order to do so it must exert even stricter controls over its relations with that remainder. (1987: 539–40/433)

State overcoding is thus characterised by centralised accumulation, forced resonance of diverse points of order, 'laying out [*en étendant*] a divisible homogeneous space striated in all directions' (Deleuze and Guattari 1987: 272/223), and by its vertical and redundant centre (on top), scanning all the radii. The figure of the despot or emperor, as he is called in *A Thousand Plateaus*, is the 'sole and transcendent public-property owner, the master of the surplus or the stock and the source of public functions and bureaucracy' (1987: 533/427–8). The state is the bond or knot that deterritorialises the polyvocal political segments and forces them into a new regime of overcoding.

Just as there are three kinds of supple segmentation, Deleuze and Guattari also describe three kinds of rigid segmentation proper to the process of statification: binary, circular and linear. Whereas binary supple segmentations are defined by multiple binaries that are always determined by a third (an alliance between the two), binary rigid segmentations are self-sufficient and assure the prevalence of one segment over the other (hierarchy). Whereas circular supple segments do not imply the same centre but a multiplicity of centres (round but not quite circular), circular rigid segments form a resonance of concentric circles around an axis of rotation, converging on a single point of accumulation. Whereas linear supple segmentation functions by 'segments-in-progress', alignments but no straight line, and supple morphological formations, linear rigid segments function by homogenised segments geometrically organised around a dominant segment through which they pass: a space or *spatio* rather than a place or territory.

But there remains no opposition between the central and the territorial. The state is a global whole, unified and unifying, but it is so only because it implies a constellation of juxtaposed, imbricated, ordered subsystems: a whole micropolitical fabric (pedagogical, juridical, economic, familial, sexual). As Foucault similarly observes, the most general character of the statification consists in organising these micropolitical arts of governmentality around a sovereign agency (Foucault 2007: 11–12). Hierarchy is, thus, not simply pyramidal, it is differential because territorial and state distributions are 'inseparable, overlapping and entangled . . . forming a supple fabric without which their rigid segments would not hold' (Deleuze and Guattari 1987: 259–60/213).

(2.2) The Dangers of State Representation for Revolutionary Praxis
Despotic state representation, I argue, poses at least two significant dangers for revolutionary praxis: fear and 'machinic enslavement'. Despotic regimes create a generalised terror and paranoia of scission resolvable only by a transcendent unity: 'National security is at risk! Let the executive decide.' 'The more rigid the segmentarity, the more reassuring it is for us,' Deleuze and Guattari say (1987: 277/227). States often declare a 'state of emergency' in order to suspend normal law and stop riots, demonstrations or potential revolutions. The more violent the state's response to popular revolt, the 'safer' the population is under the state's protection. Revolutions themselves also risk creating a party-state apparatus that makes everyone a piece in a single megamachine. 'There is enslavement', Deleuze and Guattari say, 'when human beings themselves are constituent pieces of a machine that they compose among themselves and with other things (animals, tools), under the control and direction of a higher unity' (1987: 570/456–7). Socialist states in Russia and China are examples of revolutions turned state megamachines.

(2.3) The Juridical State Pole
At the other pole of the state overcoding process is the juridical pole of the city-state defined by its topical conjugations and its danger of social subjection. According to Deleuze and Guattari, while despotic states certainly included towns, depending on how complete the state's monopoly over foreign trade is, town distributions tend to 'break free when the State's overcoding itself provoke[s] decoded

flows' (1987: 541/434). Eastern empires, they say, had created large stockpiles that trading towns (like ancient Athens) took advantage of without having to constitute a stock of their own (1987: 539/432). Juridical town distributions thus formed topical conjunctions that were achieved through this autonomy, or else through corporative and commercial networks freed from the despotic state-form of Asiatic production.

As despotic rigid segmentations unleash flows of decoded functionaries necessary for collecting taxes, rent and profit, keeping laws, and policing, so legal conjunctions harness and engender these flows into towns but keep them from streaming together. Topical conjunctions are magisterial or legal structures immanent to towns that 'stand as so many knots or recodings' (Deleuze and Guattari 1987: 564/452) and act as distinct focal points in resonance with the state. Yet they also form their own network of camps, fortifications and 'boundary lines' in place of the previous territorial segments-in-progress. Imperial law thus undergoes a mutation, becoming subjective, disciplinary and conjunctive. 'And unlike the relatively uniform imperial pole, this second pole presents the most diverse of forms. But as varied as relations of personal dependence are, they always mark qualified and topical conjunctions' (Deleuze and Guattari 1987: 563/451).

(2.4) The Danger of Juridical Representation for Revolutionary Praxis

> There is subjection when the higher unity constitutes the human subject linked to a now exterior object, which can be an animal, tool, or even a machine. The human being is no longer a component of the machine but a worker, a user. He or she is subjected *to* the machine and no longer enslaved *by* the machine. (Deleuze and Guattari 1987: 570/457)

Opposed to being a cog in a megamachine, the processes of juridical subjectification constitute human beings as subjects of an external machine. Revolutionary praxis risks either subordinating itself to juridical representation as a form of resistance against the despotic state (law suits, human rights, legal representation and so on), or it risks recreating juridical representation in its own autonomous territories (popular justice, Maoist people's courts and so on). Laws, contracts and conventions discipline and create private citizens. These laws are then enforced by local revolutionary officials. Private individuals are users of contracts and workers of animals, tools and machines, no longer just one more part in a megamachine. They are users of machines held together by the transconsistency of being subjects of the law. But the egalitarian pretensions and human face of such subjection should not conceal the local centralisation of power, hierarchy and disciplinary apparatuses of juridical representation set in motion to force the coordination of subjects.[13]

(3) Capitalist Representation

The third type of historical political process that Deleuze and Guattari describe in *Capitalism and Schizophrenia*, and that I argue can be used as a diagnostic of revolutionary praxis, is capitalist representation. Where Deleuze and Guattari defined territorial representation by its codes and microfascisms, despotic representation by its overcoding and machinic enslavements, and juridical representation by its topical conjugations and social subjections, they define capitalist representation by its axiomatisation and its new form of machinic enslavement.

(3.1) Axiomatics

Deleuze and Guattari define capitalist representation by its processes of axiomatisation. An axiom, they say, is an independent or disengaged point that forces unqualified elements into homologous quantitative relations (1994: 130/137–8). Axioms are not theoretical propositions, they say, but 'operative statements that enter as component parts into the assemblages of production, circulation, and consumption' (1987: 575/461). That is, Deleuze and Guattari do not mean the word 'axiomatic' as a scientific 'metaphor'; *social* axiomatics are not derived from scientific, mathematical or logical axiomatics,[14] but the reverse: the true axiomatic is that of the social machine itself, which takes the place of the old codings and organises all the decoded flows, including the flows of scientific and technical code, for the benefit of the capitalist system and in the service of its ends (see Deleuze and Guattari 1983: 299/251).

So whereas codes determine the qualities of flows (types of places, types of goods, types of activity) and establish indirect relations (of alliance) between these incommensurable, qualified, mobile, limited codes, and overcodes (as well as topical conjunctions) capture and recode these flows through extra-economic forces (political or juridical), capitalist axioms establish a strictly economic general equivalence between purely unqualified (decoded) flows.

The axiomatic, however, is not the invention of capitalism,

Deleuze and Guattari say, since it is identical with capitalism itself. Rather, capitalism is the offspring or result, which merely ensures the regulation of the axiomatic; 'it watches over or directs progress toward a saturation of the axiomatic and the corresponding widening of the limits' (1983: 300/252–3). Capitalist axiomatics create denumerable finite representations of social processes divested of their qualities. Each independent from the others, they are added, subtracted and multiplied to form more or less saturated markets for the generation of wealth.

Just like the other political types, two poles also form capitalist distributions. What capitalism continually decodes at one pole, it axiomatises at the other (1983: 293–4/246). Deleuze and Guattari give several examples of the 'decoded flows' constituting capitalist axiomatisation. For the free worker, decoding means: (1) the deterritorialisation of the soil through privatisation, (2) the loss of the means of consumption through the dissolution of the family, and the decoding of the worker in favour of the work itself or of the machine (industrial production). For capital it means: (1) the deterritorialisation of wealth through monetary abstraction, (2) the decoding of the flows of production through merchant capital, (3) the decoding of states through financial capital and public debts, and (4) the decoding of the means of production through the formation of industrial capital (1983: 266–7/225).

While territorial representation 'implies' that qualified pieces of labour correspond to a particular quantum of abstract labour (activity required to create a given artefact), and state exchange introduces the general equivalent of currency formally uniting 'partial objects' (goods and services) whose overcoded value is determined by non-capitalist (imperial or juridical) decisions, neither decode or dequalify exchange to the degree that capitalism does.

In Rome, for example, Deleuze and Guattari say, there may have been a privatisation of property, a decoding of money through the formations of great fortunes, the decoding of producers through expropriation and proletarianisation. But despite all these decoded conditions, it did not produce a capitalist economy, but rather reinforced feudal offices and relations in a regime based on slavery (1983: 264/223). Capitalism goes further. At one pole it decodes qualitative relationships through the privatisation of all aspects of social life, free trade, advertising, freeing of labour and capital, imperialism; and, at the other pole, it axiomatises them as 'productions for the market'.

Here, however, it is crucial not to make the error Slavoj Žižek and others have made by concluding from this that all 'decoded flows' are necessarily contributions to capitalism (Žižek 2004: 184). Neither, I argue, should we conclude the opposite: that decoded flows are necessarily revolutionary. The struggle over the assembly of decoded flows is a revolutionary struggle and far from decidable in advance. Revolutionary praxis struggles to unite a consistency of decoded flows, and capitalism struggles to have them 'bound into a world axiomatic that always opposes the revolutionary potential of decoded flows with new interior limits' (Deleuze and Guattari 1983: 292–3/246). The details of this struggle are developed at length in Chapter 3.

Capitalism is thus constituted by two decoded flows: on the one hand the flow of naked labour, freed from serfdom and able to sell its labour capacity, and on the other hand the pure flow of capital, independent from landed wealth, that is capable of buying labour. The first 'has its roots in simple circulation where money develops as means of payment (bills of exchange falling due on a fixed date, which constitute a monetary form of finite debt)' (1983: 272/229) and is distributed as 'income' to wage earners for the purchase of products and services. The second, however, is the money inscribed on the balance sheet of the firm and is based on the circulation of drafts rather than money. This second money constitutes what Deleuze and Guattari call the capitalist form of infinite debt.

> Rather than using preexisting currency as a means of payment, finance capital is an instantaneous creative flow that banks create spontaneously as a debt owing to themselves, a creation *ex nihilo* that hollows out at one extreme of the full body a negative money (a debt entered as a liability of the banks), and projects at the other extreme a positive money (a credit granted the productive economy by the banks), 'a flow possessing a power of mutation' [*flux à pouvoir mutant*] *that does not enter into income and is not assigned to purchases*, a pure availability, non-possession and non-wealth. (1983: 282/237)

This so-called stateless, monetary mass that circulates through foreign exchange and across borders forms a supranational ecumenical organisation in many ways untouched by governmental decisions. For example, ninety-six per cent of money circulated in the United States alone is financial capital. This money does not exist as concrete payment or exchange money but rather as credit or investment money loaned out by banks (to other banks, or other investors) at specific interest rates. How much this investment capital is 'worth' at any given moment depends on an incredibly complex host of speculations, desires, predictions, interest rates, stock prices and so on that no one can predict with total accuracy. At any given time, US banks are required to have no less than three per cent of their total money as payment money to distribute for bank withdrawals.[15]

This dualism between types of money – 'the formation of means of payment and the structure of financing, between the management of money and the financing of capitalist accumulation, between exchange money and credit money' (Deleuze and Guattari 1983: 271/229) – is fundamental to the capitalist system: but how are such unqualified monetary flows then quantified by an axiomatic?

It would be a simplistic reading of Deleuze and Guattari's analysis to say that capitalist axiomatics were defined solely by the 'abstract quantification of decoded flows'. In part, this is the case because the quantification of the creative flow of financial capital poses a real difficulty: 'no one knows exactly where to draw the line' on this speculative, non-existent monetary mass. But what makes the capitalist social field unique is that its quantifications are based on 'differential conjunctions' between flows of unqualified labour and flows of unqualified capital. That is, simple 'quantity' as a variable relation between independent terms (goods and services) has taken upon itself the independence. Denumerable quantification no longer depends on the independent qualities of the terms being exchanged, but is determined independently of these concrete terms. Just as axioms remain 'independent' and 'disengaged' from their social or mathematical demonstrations, so the capitalist market also determines the quantitative value of commodities independently of their qualification; that is, it determines them 'axiomatically'.

The capitalist machine thus begins when capital ceases to be a capital of alliance (a variable relation between two qualified terms) to become filiative capital (an independent determination of abstract quantities) where 'money begets money, or value a surplus value' (1983: 269/227). Capitalism's 'differential conjunctions', as Deleuze and Guattari describe them, are precisely the axiomatisation of this 'differential relationship', 'where Dy derives from labor power and constitutes the fluctuation of variable capital, and where Dx derives from capital itself and constitutes the fluctuation of constant capital ("the definition of constant capital by no means excludes the possibility of a change in the value of its constituent parts")' (1983: 269–70/227–8). The relation is differential (dy/dx) because both terms are decoded and unqualified. But by measuring (quantifying) these two orders of magnitude, non-existent (unqualified) finance capital and variable (unqualified) labour, in terms of the same analytical unit, Deleuze and Guattari claim that capitalist axiomatics are 'a pure fiction, a cosmic swindle, as if one were to measure intergalactic or intra-atomic distances in metres and centimeters' (1983: 273/230).

These 'cosmic fictions' are the basis of an endless accumulation of profit. Unlike a surplus value of code, defined by the difference between labour capacity and the value created by labour capacity, capitalist 'surplus values of flux' are defined by the incommensurability between two flows that are immanent to each other (free capital and free labour). The difference between what labour can do and what it can be sold for is its profit. But by completely decoding labour and capital and axiomatising their incommensurable relation, capitalism is able to generate 'surplus flux' or profit without the limitations created by certain kinds of codes (or qualities). 'Anything whatever' can be axiomatised and circulated on the world market. Under the capitalist axiomatic, according to Deleuze and Guattari, profit accumulation has been unleashed from any external limitations.

(3.2) The Dangers of the Axiomatic for Revolutionary Praxis
The first danger of axiomatisation is that it harnesses a worldwide war machine that sets out to reorganise the entire world based on the exploitation of planetary resources. 'War', as Deleuze and Guattari say, 'clearly follows the same movement as capitalism' (1987: 582/466). The growing importance of finance capital in the axiomatic means that the depreciation of existing capital and the formation of new capital take on the speed of a war machine incarnated in the state as models of realisation that 'actively contribute to the redistributions of the world necessary for the exploitation of maritime and planetary resources . . . The power of war always supersaturates the system's saturations, as its necessary condition' [*La puissance de guerre venait toujours sursaturer la saturation du système, et la conditionnait*] (Deleuze and Guattari 1987: 582/466). States no longer appropriate the war machine but constitute a war machine of which they themselves are only the parts: the worldwide capitalist war machine. As states increase military, techno-scientific spending to absorb or compensate for the massive surplus values of corporations, they find their new object in the absolute 'peace' of terror or deterrence, Deleuze and Guattari say. State-organised capitalism operates

against an 'unspecified enemy' as an organised insecurity. The danger for revolutionary praxis is that this war machine, unlike the state, has no centre that can be 'overthrown'. Capitalist resistance then must take a very different form than the mere capture of the state.

Another danger of capitalism is the disappearance of enjoyment as an end, and its replacement with the sole end of abstract wealth and its realisation in forms other than consumption. Where the despotic state had emperors of anti-production to consume surplus, the bourgeois field of immanence has no such external limit and has integrated anti-production inside production itself. It has instituted an unrivalled slavery, an unprecedented subjugation. No longer are there any masters but only slaves commanding other slaves, slaves of the social machine. 'The bourgeois sets the example,' Deleuze and Guattari argue:

> He absorbs surplus value for ends that, taken as a whole, have nothing to do with his own enjoyment: more utterly enslaved than the lowest slaves, he is the first servant of the ravenous machine, the beast of the reproduction of capital, internalization of the infinite debt. 'I too am a slave' – these are the new words spoken by the master. (1983: 302/254)

The social subjection of juridical statism combined with the machinic enslavement of states by the market create a new form of machinic enslavement in which states and capitalists alike are merely parts of a larger social machine that no one is in control of: the capitalist world market. The excessive surpluses are so large they cannot be enjoyed but merely absorbed through other mechanisms. The danger for revolutionary praxis is to be enslaved by this process.

In response to the question 'what is the relationship between history and revolution?', I have argued in the above section that what I am calling the 'return to revolution', influenced by the political philosophy of Deleuze and Guattari, can be characterised less by the theory of necessary historical succession (whether chronological or dialectical) or by the theory of a purely contingent historical rupture, but rather by a historico-political diagnostic of multiple coexisting political dangers to be replaced by revolutionary praxis. Deleuze and Guattari were the first to lay the philosophical groundwork for this theory of diagnostic analysis based on the topological mixture of past, present and future political forms. Today, the field of political struggle is not dominated by a single or central figure, like the state, proletariat, capital and so on, that can orient all revolutionary analysis. Rather, it is much more like 'a motley painting of everything that has ever been believed' (1983: 42/34). The challenge, then, is to understand and avoid all these motley processes of political representation and create something new. But this chapter has so far only been a theoretical interrogation. In the next and final section, I argue that we can locate in Zapatismo the parallel practical invention of a multi-centred political diagnostic.

III. The Zapatistas' Diagnostic of Suffering

Zapatismo is one of the first and most sustained non-representational revolutionary efforts to diagnose political power from the perspective that 'there is no single front of struggle'. The Zapatistas' return to revolution can thus be characterised by a practical analysis of power based on a multi-centred diagnostic of political history. This analysis is motivated by the relative rejection of all previous forms of historical representation both in form (coding, overcoding and axiomatisation) and in content (patriarchy, racism, statism, capitalism, vanguardism and so on), as well as a concern for their immanent diagnosis. The Zapatistas' rejection and diagnostic of these processes is demonstrated through the practice of what Marcos calls a 'diagnostic of suffering' used in *La Otra Campaña*. During this campaign the Zapatistas travelled across Mexico listening and taking note of people's problems and sufferings. The Zapatistas, contrary to centrist or vanguard analyses that revolve around a privileged method/science, site or dimension of struggle, offer instead an inclusive intersectional analysis that does not necessarily privilege any single method, front or site of struggle. Revolution, according to Marcos,

> is about a process which incorporates different methods, different fronts, different and various levels of commitment and participation. This means that all methods have their place, that all the fronts of struggle are necessary, and that all levels of participation are important. This is about an inclusive process, which is anti-vanguard and collective. The problem with the revolution (pay attention to the small letters) is then no longer a problem of THE organization, THE method, THE *caudillo* [dictator, political boss]. It becomes rather a problem which concerns all those who see that revolution is necessary and possible, and whose achievement is important for everyone. (Marcos 2004b: 164)

Even the Zapatistas' own uprising forms a 'motley historical assemblage'. Consider the way in which they have selected some moments from Mexican history (Emiliano Zapata's peasant uprising of

1910–1917), some components from Marxist history (red stars, the use of the word 'comrade' and so on), some components from their own indigenous history (consensus decision-making, autonomous village networks and so on) as well as some components of the future (the promise of a non-neoliberal future) to compose the historical hodgepodge of their own political event. In what follows, I argue that the Zapatistas use a practical diagnostic to understand and defend against the three coexisting political dangers found in the parallel historical topology of Deleuze and Guattari: territorial coding, statist overcoding and capitalist axiomatisation.

ZAPATISMO AND TERRITORIAL REPRESENTATION

By 2004, the Zapatistas had lost many battles but still held strong in their commitment to dignity and autonomy. It is around this time that the Zapatistas also turned their critical diagnostic to their own forms of organisation. They began to look at the various different ways that their movement was creating forms of political represen- tation: not at the traditional level of the state or capital, but at the territorial level. That is, they began a multi-centred or intersectional diagnostic of their own revolutionary praxis. 'There are two mis- takes', Subcomandante Marcos says in a 2004 communiqué, 'which seem to have persisted in our political work (and which flagrantly contradict our principles): the place of women, on the one hand, and, on the other, the relationship between the political-military structure and the autonomous governments' (Marcos 2004a). These are two mistakes/dangers that have been historically neglected by revolution- ary movements, in part because they are more supple non-state kinds of social power ignored by dialectical and insurrectionist theories of history. Rejecting the premise that the only revolutionary praxis that matters is that of the historical progress of the state, the proletariat and so on, the Zapatistas have attempted to diagnose and ward off the processes of territorial coding. But the problem of patriarchy in the Zapatista revolution existed in the indigenous communities well before the EZLN arrived in Chiapas in 1983.

> Before Zapatismo the conditions women lived in were dreadful: sexual abuse was rife through rape or early forced marriage, domestic violence was high, giving birth to large families ruined a woman's body and gave them a heavy responsibility for social reproduction through household chores. Moreover they were expected to reduce their food intake so that the husband and children could eat sufficiently, though even this was

unable to staunch the high rates of infant mortality. In short they were virtual slaves in their own villages. (Yakubu 2000)

This type of patriarchy uses a process of territorial coding. Certain patriarchal and filial lines of hierarchically coded male stock are selected (genealogically) from the decoded flows of the earth and detached at certain places through violence (domestic and otherwise) to create the essential ethnic, gender and spatial boundaries/identities between men and women, adults and children, and different lineages of indigenous peoples. Without forming a complete fusion of all these codes, however, the remaining surplus code (an unmarried woman) is then used to form itinerant alliances between male filiations through arranged marriages. As Deleuze and Guattari say, 'Through women, men establish their own connections; through the man woman disjunction, which is always the outcome of filiation, alliance places in connection men from different filiations' (1983: 194/165). The pre-given linear codes of male power and violence are then repeated and represented through each new alliance.

But by allowing women '*insurgentas*' and '*comandantas*' the EZLN political-military structure (by no means entirely egalitarian) creates a relative decoding of this patriarchal filiation and alliance by permitting 'young indigenous women [to] go to the mountains and develop their capacities more, [creating] consequences in the communities' (Ramírez 2008: 312) and giving them 'the right to choose their partner and not [be] obliged to enter into marriage', to 'occupy positions of leadership in the organization and hold military ranks in the revolutionary armed forces', as well as other rights detailed in the EZLN's 'Women's Revolutionary Law' (EZLN 1994). These laws are being increasingly implemented in the autonomous townships through new women's alliances (craft cooperatives, women's councils and so on). However, the decoding of certain patriarchal traditions comes at the risk of creating a new set of vanguard military codes, hence the second territorial mistake or danger.

> These groups operate through detachment, election, and residual selection: they detach a supposedly expert avant-garde; they elect a disciplined, organized, hierarchized proletariat; they select a residual sub-proletariat to be excluded or reeducated. (Deleuze 2004: 278/198)

As Deleuze warns (and the EZLN is well aware), the detachment of EZLN commanders living in the mountains (particularly from 1983 to 1993) that elects/recruits *campesin@s* from the villages to be disciplined, organised, hierarchised into the EZLN, and then creates a residual selection of *campesin@s* to be excluded/re-educated in ever widening circular segmentations, risks creating new military codes that undermine the autonomy and self-management of the Zapatistas. As Marcos says,

> The idea we had originally was that the EZLN should accompany and support the peoples in the building of their autonomy. However, accompaniment has sometimes turned into management, advice into orders and support into a hindrance. I've already spoken previously about the fact that the hierarchical, pyramid structure is not characteristic of the indigenous communities. The fact that the EZLN is a political-military and clandestine organization still corrupts processes that should and must be democratic. (Marcos 2004a)

Patriarchy and militarism in Zapatismo are two examples of what Deleuze and Guattari call microfascism. Microfascism is a significant threat to be diagnosed in revolutionary praxis: 'everything that [supple segmentation and coding] dismantles [at the level of the state] it reassembles on its own level: micro-Oedipuses, microformations of power, microfascisms' (Deleuze and Guattari 1987: 251/205). Zapatismo, as a revolutionary movement, also risks falling prey to what Deleuze and Guattari call 'monomania' by becoming a strictly ethnic struggle for indigenous rights. Segmentary societies, indigenous peoples, gangs and ethnic minorities without a 'shared acceleration' or solidarity beyond the narrow 'self-evident clarities' of their individual causes (for indigenous rights and so on) risk, at worst, extermination by the state or, at best, becoming a 'rumble or buzz' under its heel. As a revolutionary movement with an intersectional diagnostic, the Zapatistas have rejected this monomania by universalising their struggle and making it a global one against neoliberalism, inclusive of everyone engaged in this struggle: 'We are all Zapatistas!'[16] But what dangers does the process of statification pose to the Zapatista uprising?

ZAPATISMO AND DESPOTIC STATE REPRESENTATION

In addition to their diagnosis of territorial coding, the Zapatistas also deployed a significant and vocal diagnostic analysis of the danger of state overcoding. What external and internal dangers does it pose to the flourishing of their revolutionary praxis? Despotic state representation (overcoding) in the executive branch of the Mexican government aims to force indigenous 'activity' into work, to extract taxes from its communities, to create a concentric political resonance of its territories (states, cities, neighbourhoods and autonomous territories) into exchangeable and rentable land through forced relocation and redistribution to large land owners (*latifundistas*), and to establish a stockpile of exchange into currency (the peso) mostly withheld from the *campesin@s*. While the modern Mexican state certainly has more than just despotic components, its despotic components, more or less socialist or capitalist, threaten to enslave every aspect of life into the work-model. State representation thus creates by force the conditions of land, taxes, work and exchange that will be necessary for the emergence of a specifically capitalist axiomatic of privatisation and global circulation distinct from the work-model of the state.

Any and all states, according to the Zapatistas, pose similar dangers and threats of capture for revolutionary struggles insofar as collective action becomes the mere representation or resemblance of this central executive authority. In the case of Mexico, the agricultural surpluses of indigenous labour (controlled by the *latifundistas*, through sugar, coffee and rubber production) create an unchecked accumulation requiring the maintenance of a specialised (political-military) body for its management that replaces the multi-lineal filiations of the older coded communities with the direct filiation of a despot or president. The Mexican executive system thus makes a very diverse group of points (geographic, ethnic, linguistic, moral, economic and technological) resonate together under a single hierarchised and transcendent unity.

The Mexican state captures the territories not by the opposition of overcoding to diverse territorial codes, but by unifying the constellation of imbricated, micropolitical systems. Each territory is given a place as a piece of a single megamachine of public-works. The state's hierarchy is thus not pyramidal but vertically held together by innumerable coded territories. On the one hand, Zapatismo confronts this danger as an external one because state overcoding, despite its juridical pretensions to negotiation (the betrayal of the San Andrés Accords),[17] is unable to accept decoded flows or coded ones that do not resonate around its central unity. The state thus aims to exterminate them or bring them into resonance as subordinate parts of its central machine.[18]

> More than 6,000 displaced by the war are the result of the attacks of paramilitary bands and state police, both directed by the state government, with the blessing of the federal government. (Ramírez 2008: 162)

Assassinations, intimidations, dozens of arrested, tortured and jailed, military and paramilitary harassment, thousands displaced, and the burning of autonomous townships were the norm during these seven months of the year 1998. (Ramírez 2008: 175)

However, Zapatismo also confronts the danger of statist overcoding as an internal one. In both its early (1983) vanguard strategy to militarily overthrow the Mexican government and seize power in a popular revolutionary style familiar to Mexico and Latin America, and in its later (1994–2007) strategy to intervene in electoral politics without becoming partisan or a political party, Zapatismo risked overcoding. While the likelihood of the Zapatistas actually seizing state power is slim, the dangers of reproducing the processes of overcoding are real. As Marcos says, 'The worst that could happen to [the EZLN] . . . would be to come to power and install itself there as a revolutionary army' (Marcos 2001a).

> Every vanguard imagines itself to be representative of the majority. We not only think that is false in our case, but that even in the best of cases it is little more than wishful thinking, and in the worst cases an outright usurpation. The moment social forces come into play, it becomes clear that the vanguard is not such a vanguard and that those it represents do not recognize themselves in it. (Marcos 2001c)

Mexican state representation and rigid segmentation, according to Marcos, deploy the paranoiac fear that national security will crumble if the indigenous are given autonomy. War, the state threatens, will only continue if the rigid state segments do not prevail. This fear, the state claims, can only be resolved if everyone submits to being part of a machinic enslavement orchestrated by the state. But this is only half the story of the danger of the state. Zapatismo also confronts the danger of being subjected to the juridical power of the state.

ZAPATISMO AND JURIDICAL STATE REPRESENTATION

Despite their early interest in establishing legal rights and representation for indigenous people across Mexico, the Zapatistas have remained diagnostically aware of the danger of becoming merely incorporated into the judicial norms of the state by having their demands satisfied and/or redefined. Marcos describes the juridical state as 'the aspect which incorporates popular struggles and their demands, and regulates, through judicial norms, the satisfaction of such demands and/or their redefinition' (Marcos 2004b: 311). Once revolutionary demands are met, the revolution is over, overcoded and conjuncted as one more subject of law.

Additionally, what Mexican despotic/federal overcodes are not entirely able to capture (autonomous peasant movements, local laws, personal contracts, state functionaries, tax collectors and local ranchers), other channels of unofficial power in Chiapas, like paramilitary groups and the *caciques* (local self-appointed bosses and landowners), are able to recode through legal structures immanent to the region. Much more flexible, diverse and personal, these recoding focal points for the state are all the processes that endlessly negotiate with the peasants and indigenous movements without ever granting them autonomy, create local laws like not allowing *campesin@s* to walk in the street in San Cristóbal de las Casas, harass and abuse Zapatista communities in the name of 'tax collection', legally sanction paramilitary groups like the ones responsible for the Acteal massacre (while federal troops 200 metres away did nothing) (Ramírez 2008: 164), and fund local *caciques* who

> deliver some of the basic demands of the campesino and mediate his needs. They are usually older men who are involved in local commercial activities and have a reputation as fixers, usually with some access to local state funds. Many are PRIistas, most are corrupt and violent and all believe they 'serve the people'. In fact they serve to demobilize and suppress rural struggle and are invaluable to the landowners. (Yakubu 2000)

But such legal mediations and democratic pretensions found in city halls, private property owners and local law enforcement should not disguise the real disciplinary apparatuses of juridical representation set in motion to force the coordination (recoding) of revolutionary subjects like the Zapatistas.

Zapatismo and Capitalist Representation

The Zapatistas' political diagnosis of capitalism is no more central or foundational than any of their other analyses of power. The territorial coding of patriarchy and militarism within Zapatista communities, the statist overcoding of fear, war and centralisation, and the juridical recoding of legalisation and local management are all equally important dangers that need to be diagnosed and avoided within their revolutionary praxis. As they say, 'all fronts are important', not just the front against state power or capitalism. That said, they do have a diagnosis of capitalist representation.

In Chiapas, the previous (1876) forms of non-innovatory local capital (private cattle ranchers and cotton, sugar and coffee *latifundistas*) that had turned many small landholders and *ejidos* (communal production units) into either poorly paid day-labourers (that is, seasonally employed) or debt-peons (little more than slaves) gave way to new patterns of accumulation in the 1970s: free/unqualified labour and mobile decoded capital. As capital increasingly freed itself from national boundaries, transforming itself into highly mobile finance capital, investment flooded away from the industrial heartlands of both North America and Mexico to the Pacific Rim economies (Yakubu 2000).

> The local farmers and ranchers that previously needed very small amounts of quasi-slave labor and large areas of land in Chiapas are now selling their land to make way for the region's new importance as a resource for hydroelectric power, oil, eco-tourism, patented genetic technology, and uranium for national and international accumulation. (Yakubu 2000)[19]

And while it may make up a small part of this accumulation, Zapatismo itself has been turned into a market in several ways that it is well aware of: as a revolutionary tourist destination, as a cultural commodity, as the content of revolutionary kitsch sold around the world (even by those who do not sympathise with the EZLN) like Zapatista dolls, posters, T-shirts and condoms ('for those who rise up') (Kersten 1997). In other words, what the processes of capitalism decode with one hand (land, family, work, wealth, states and production),[20] they continually axiomatise with the other. By privatising previously coded and overcoded relations in Chiapas and placing them all for sale or investment on a world market, their 'qualities' or 'unique specificities' have become completely relative to the speculative investment patterns of a transnational ecumenical organisation (themselves relative to the abstract 'forces of the market') (Yakubu 2000).

Capitalist representation, as the differential relation (dy/dx) between these decoded flows of unqualified *campesin@* labour, Lacandón Jungle, rivers, culture (participatory democracy, Zapatismo resistance and so on) on the one hand, and the decoded flows of financial capital (world stock speculation, bank finance, international investment and so on) on the other, fixes both into an abstract 'differential' quantification or axiomatic equivalence for the sole purposes of profit.

The 'war in Chiapas' is an instance of how the Mexican state has become a 'model [or axiom] for the realization of international capital' by 'actively contribut[ing] to the redistributions of [Chiapas] necessary for the exploitation of maritime and planetary resources' (Deleuze and Guattari 1987: 582/466). In the case of Chiapas, state and capital are, at the current historical conjuncture of neoliberalism, highly intertwined. As Marcos says, 'the indigenous peoples at a global level (who number more than 300 million) are located in zones that possess 60% of the natural resources of the planet. The reconquest of these territories is one of the principal objectives of the capitalist war' (Fuentes 2007). The Mexican state is now less an appropriation of its own war machine (a standing army), but rather forms a mere part in the larger worldwide capitalist war machine aimed at securing the axiomatisation of the unqualified flows of oil, water, biogenetic code and Zapatista resistance culture for their exchange on the global market.[21] 'Neoliberalism', as Marcos puts it, 'is the catastrophic political management of catastrophe' (Marcos 1995). This new form of capitalist machinic enslavement, as Deleuze and Guattari call it, however, takes little enjoyment in the massacres, humanitarian crises and ecological devastations that result from its 'structural readjustments' in Chiapas. Rather, capitalist axiomatisation has dequalified all other coded values of enjoyment except for one pre-given condition for representation to which everyone is enslaved (to a certain degree): the abstract accumulation of wealth. Zapatismo faces an external capitalist war of resource extraction against Chiapas, but also faces an internal appropriation of its resistance by the culture industry.

But here the reader may wonder if this analysis of Zapatismo might be significantly undermined if the Zapatistas were to do something that suddenly rejected their previous use of a multi-centred diagnostic (if they became class-struggle Marxists, for instance). Since I am not arguing that the Zapatistas themselves are a model for revolution but rather that the practices that they have created may be useful, then I still think we can mobilise such practices elsewhere without deferring to the 'authority' of their struggle. A multi-centred political diagnostic, whether the Zapatistas keep using it or not, remains a practice that was at one time useful and that could be adapted for further use by others.

Conclusion

What is the relationship between history and revolution in the contemporary return to revolution? In short, I have argued that political history is used strategically as a multi-centred political diagnostic to develop a non-representational revolutionary praxis. In order to defend this response I drew on two early and influential figures of its practical and theoretical use: Deleuze and Guattari, and the Zapatistas. Deleuze and Guattari were some of the first to develop the philosophical basis for an analysis of interlocking forms of oppression based on a topology of multiple, heterogeneous axes of political power, in content (class, race, gender and so on) and in form (coding, overcoding, axiomatisation). Contrary to the universal history of succession and necessity based on the political body of the state and its representation, political topology understands history as a single folded and refolded surface. Events are not tied by chronological or dialectical causality but by contingency and proximity to one another in space-time. Without unity or identity, political history is thus capable of producing non-representational revolutionary political forms. However, beyond the mere affirmation of revolutionary historical potential, my argument was that this historical topology should be used instead as a diagnostic by which we can assess the dangers confronting revolutionary praxis itself.

Practically, Zapatismo is one of the first and most sustained non-representational revolutionary efforts to diagnose political power from the perspective that 'there is no single front of struggle'. No one single type of power threatens their autonomy and self-determination 'in the last instance', but rather a mix of several different processes from history coexist in recombined forms both external and internal to their struggle. With no single front or axis on which power turns, there is also no single type of marginalised subject, nor is there a single axis or pivot by which to discern the proper direction, critique or teleology of history. There are simply different types of multiplicities in need of diagnosis and redirection. My argument was that without the predicative power of Marxist science, or a determinate universal history, the Zapatistas' revolution has become contingent, non-representational and flexible like a folded topological shape. Zapata's peasant rebellion can emerge from the past, direct democracy can emerge from the future, and both can bear directly on the transformation of the present. Zapatismo, in this sense, is a creation of the past and a nostalgia for the future at the same time.

These arguments were accomplished in three sections. The first outlined and problematised two theories of universal history (succession and contingency) and showed how each failed to conceive of a sustained alternative to representational politics. The second laid out, in turn, four basic characteristics of an alternative concept of revolutionary history drawn from Deleuze and Guattari's historical topology. I then expanded this theory and argued that it should be used as a political diagnostic based on three contingent, coexisting and recombinable political processes: territorial coding, state overcoding and capitalist axiomatisation. Each of these types was developed in turn to show how they inform revolutionary praxis. The third and final section showed how the Zapatistas also practise a multi-centred political diagnostic based on their 'diagnostic of suffering'. What remains to be addressed, however, is how such a folded intersection of representational processes is transformed through the process of concrete revolutionary intervention. This will be the subject of the following chapter.

Notes

1. While Deleuze and Guattari's critics do well to pinpoint certain shortcomings, risks or tendencies, particularly in Deleuze and Guattari's pre-*A Thousand Plateaus* writings (political ambivalence, virtual hierarchy and subjective paralysis), I also argued in the introduction that there is a third approach to retheorising the concept of revolution in their philosophy that has been left out of this debate, namely one that does not simply affirm deterritorialisation or difference-in-itself as a sufficient political concept, nor that merely relies on a critical analysis of power, but rather picks up where Deleuze and Guattari left off: with the creation of political concepts proper to concrete revolutionary situations. By drawing on Deleuze and Guattari's work after their 'constructivist turn' in *A Thousand Plateaus*, I maintain that a specifically constructivist theory of revolution provides a viable third reading of their political work that is better equipped to overcome the dangers hindering a new return of revolution today. This is similarly the case with the Zapatistas, whose post-2003 constructivist turn is so often misunderstood as an 'inward' and 'silent' one.
2. A 'collective' or 'participatory-body': a political horizontalism.
3. I deal with the fourth kind of temporal relation in Chapters 3 and 4.
4. Beyond their usefulness as diagnostic tools, these processes have no universally descriptive power.

5. See Deleuze and Guattari 1987: 608/487 for diagrams of these images.
6. This point is similarly argued in Lampert 2006: 16.
7. I use here Jay Lampert's historico-political distinction between these three regimes of representation.
8. Deleuze, seminar of 7 March 1972:

> Le problème auquel on se heurte toujours, c'est comment faire pour que les mouvements de décodage, les mouvements de déterritorialisation soit à la fois révolutionnairement positifs et qu'à la fois ils ne recréent pas des formes comme perverses ou des formes artificielles de famille, c'est à dire qu'ils ne recréent pas à leur manière des espèces de codes et de territorialités. (Deleuze 1972)

9.
> I am in favor of market economy but not geared only at profit and its valorization of status, hierarchy and power. I am in favor of an institutional market economy, one founded on another mode of valorization. Instead of being more capitalistic, we want to make anti-capitalism within capitalism. (Guattari 1996: 89)

10. Deleuze and Guattari do not claim to be representing actual primitive peoples' lives or doing anthropology (even though they cite anthropologists). Their goal is to create concepts that are heterogeneous to these practices but that can still connect to them and coexist alongside them.
11. Nick Thoburn offers an excellent account of this topology in action on the subject of political militancy (see Thoburn 2009).
12. There are two other dangers. 'Third, the two forms [state and primitive] are not simply distinguished by size' but by type of distribution. Fourth, finally, the qualitative distinction between the two (state overcoding and territorial coding) does not preclude the two cutting into each other or boosting each other in inverse proportion (1987: 262/215).
13. See 'On popular justice: a discussion with Maoists' in Foucault 1980: 1–37.
14. Badiou claims that mathematics (specifically axiomatic set theory) alone is the thinking of being qua being. Social and political being, for Badiou, are thus derived from the more primary ontological axioms of set theory that are independent from phenomenological or political transformations and their affections. So when Badiou claims that Deleuze has no political philosophy but only an ethics, this cannot be the case since axiomatics, according to Deleuze and Guattari, are primarily social and political mechanisms: they are not purely mathematical, but rather social.
15. According to the Monetary Control Act of 1980.
16. This slogan is one of several practices that creates the universality of Zapatismo. Others are discussed in Chapter 4.
17. The Mexican government negotiated and agreed to the San Andrés Accords but never followed through with them. While they negotiated

they also escalated military relocation, murder and harassment of the indigenous.

> In the [San Andrés] agreements the government promised to recognize the right to autonomy of Indian peoples in the constitution, to broaden their political representation, to guarantee full access to the justice system, and to build a new legal framework that guaranteed political rights, legal rights and cultural rights. The government promised also to recognize indigenous people as subjects of public rights. (Ramírez 2008: 138)

18.
> There was the scene when on Dec. 22, 1997, one of the most atrocious and sadly predictable massacres in the history of the nation occurred. In the community of Acteal, located in the township of Chenalho in Los Altos of Chiapas, forty-five indigenous people, most children and women belonging to the civilian group 'Las Abejas,' were massacred with firearms and machetes by sixty armed men from a paramilitary band made up of indigenous from the PRI and the Cardenist Front (PFCRN). The shooting lasted over six hours, while dozens of Public Security police remained 200 meters away from where the killings took place, listening to the shots and screams without lifting a finger. (Ramírez 2008: 164)

19.
> New dams were built in this period to provide electricity for petrochemical plants in Tabasco and Veracruz: Chiapas is Mexico's largest producer of hydroelectricity, though half of its homes have no power. Dam construction has provided sporadic employment for some parts of the indigenous population, while others have had to abandon their villages to rising flood waters. Further dam construction is planned, much of it targeted at the Zapatista stronghold of Las Cañadas (the Canyons), a region of Los Altos ... The importance of hydroelectricity pales in comparison with the discovery of oil, however. The deposits in the north-east of the state are part of the Gulf of Mexico field that produces 81% of Mexico's crude export. But new deposits have also been found in the east, just north of the Guatemalan border (the so-called Ocosingo field), bang in the middle of Zapatista territory. Most of this new oil is not yet being pumped, but exploratory wells have been drilled both by PEMEX, the national oil company, and international oil interests. (Yakubu 2000)

20. Deterritorialisation is not only a capitalist process. Deleuze and Guattari describe four different types of deterritorialisation that I will describe in detail in Chapter 2 as they are relevant to the situation in Chiapas. For further discussion of these types in *A Thousand Plateaus* see pages 274–5/225. What distinguishes capitalist deterritorialisation from territorial, statist and nomadic (or revolutionary) deterritorialisation is what happens afterward. This process is what Deleuze and Guattari call a 'relative deterritorialisation': a process that changes but only in order to expand and further reproduce itself and block other processes of transformation. What is unique about capitalism is that it axiomatises or transforms deterritorialised elements into commodities whose original value or meaning is stripped away but then becomes

entirely relative to the fluctuations of the global market in particular. Everything is rendered meaningless, but only in order to give it a single meaning: as capital. In Chapter 2, I examine how each of these types of deterritorialisation both close off and open up the possibility of a revolution in Chiapas.

21. As a part in the global war machine of capitalism the Mexican government has aimed to secure international capital in a variety of ways: (1) the creation of highways into Zapatista territory for the construction of dams, extraction of oil and uranium, and militarisation of eco-logical preserves (for the purposes of bioprospecting); (2) the forced relocation of indigenous peoples from their land that was sold by the Mexican government to private companies; and (3) the harassment of indigenous peoples living in these 'capital rich' areas by tanks, aeroplanes and government-funded para-military attacks (see Ramírez 2008).

2

Intervention and the Future Anterior

Unlike history, becoming cannot be conceptualized in terms of past and future. Becoming revolutionary remains indifferent to questions of a future and a past of the revolution; it passes between the two. Every becoming is a block of coexistence.

(Deleuze and Guattari 1987: 358/292)

Introduction

In Chapter 1, I argued that political history should be used as a multi-centred political diagnostic to construct a revolutionary praxis. But how do revolutionary events emerge from this polyvalent intersection of representational processes (coding, overcoding, axiomatisation) and sustain something new? How are these processes 'warded off by other means'? This is an important question left unanswered both by Deleuze and Guattari's concept of historical topology and by my proposed concept of a multi-centred diagnostic. While Deleuze and Guattari's theory of political topology may be able to provide us with the tools to diagnose the three processes of political representation, it is unable to account for how such processes are replaced by revolutionary interventions. That is, if a political arrangement is composed of multiple, coexistent processes (present to varying degrees), as discerned by an immanent diagnostic of the event, how can the situation then be transformed? How can we assess the risks of such an intervention? Who and what is intervening, and upon what do they intervene?

This chapter is thus organised into three sections. In the first section I argue that the contemporary return to revolution is defined neither by a mere reaction to pre-existing political ills (processes of representation), nor by an absolute insurrectionary break with the dominant situation. In the second section I argue that the contemporary return to revolution is instead characterised by a transformation that emerges through a careful labour of evental prefiguration, connection and condensation that brings together what seemed to be

80

inexistent and invisible elements within the arrangement into a new existence and visibility. This process of revolutionary intervention brings into existence a new world of the present, not as a consequence of the past, or as the potential for a new future 'to come', but through the construction of a new present in a future anterior that 'will have been'. My argument here is that this strategy of prefiguration is able to provide an alternative to the transformative methods posed by opposition and insurrection. To help develop this strategy of prefiguration I draw on two concepts from Deleuze and Guattari: Aiôn (the time of the future anterior) and deterritorialisation (their theory of change). In the third section I further develop this argument, drawing on its practical deployment in the Zapatistas' creation and maintenance of the *Juntas de Buen Gobierno* (Councils of Good Government).

I. Revolution and Political Intervention

OPPOSITION/NEGATION

Political interventions can create transformations by opposing or negating the dominant arrangement of political power. Given the specific mixture of codes, overcodes and axioms that define the field of political subjects and objects, reactionary forces can intervene but only by first accepting the pre-given parameters of the political problem at hand to be changed: they must accept *a priori* the identity and unity of what they are in opposition to. Revolutionary interventions and transformations, in this way, aim at a modification of this unity. They intervene in the internal development and transformation of legitimate political processes (territorial, legal, economic and so on) by accepting the terms in which the political problems and questions are posed and then modifying their relations.

In more traditional revolutionary struggles, oppositional interventions can be seen in the teleological imperative to seize the state apparatus and reappropriate its bureaucratic, legal and military mechanisms towards other ends. What remains the same in these struggles, however, is the identity of their initial parameters for collective social organisation: hierarchy, militarism and state bureaucracy. In the case of more social democratic struggles, this internal reform of legal and economic processes opposes the present mechanisms of representation, not from a different non-representational perspective, but with the aim of correcting political mis-representation. Its transformative intervention aims for an increasingly accurate representation of the differences not yet represented. While this strategy may function as one front or dimension of a larger revolutionary movement, on its own it merely accepts the given conditions of political life and representation.

This kind of oppositional intervention, however, is always an *internal* difference: an oppositional difference subsumed into the unity of a state apparatus, an economic market or a new identity. Revolutionary opposition can thus create political change, but only insofar as such a change is a change *within the regime of representation*: a new election, a new more environmentally friendly capitalist market, or a new, more democratic state apparatus. We can thus define such an interventional tendency as the modification of an existing domain of objects and identities without a change in the fundamental conditions and coordinates of the political problem itself.

INSURRECTION AND THE REVOLUTIONARY CONDITIONS FOR THE PRODUCTION OF THE NEW

In 'Events, Becoming and History' Paul Patton argues that Deleuze and Guattari propose a compelling alternative to revolutionary opposition. 'Far from being the actualisations of a particular pre-existing event,' Patton argues, '[revolutions] are eruptions of "eventality", pure eventness or becoming: absolute deterritorialisation' (Patton 2009: 43). Rather than define revolutionary events as simply expressing oppositions or internal reforms to the pre-existing domain of political givens (identities, subjects, rights, private property and so on) that would condition in advance what new forms of collective action were possible in a situation, Patton argues that Deleuze and Guattari provide a theory of revolution based on difference or deterritorialisation-in-itself.

> Deleuze defines the pure event as that part of every event that escapes its own actualisation. Pure eventness in this sense is the highest object of historical thought. It is what must be thought from [a] historical point of view, but at the same time that which can never, or never exhaustively, be thought since it is only given to us through what actually happens. (2009: 47)

Revolution, according to Patton, is a groundless, unconditioned, unthinkable (in-itself) difference 'that is the condition of there being events at all' (2009: 42). Insofar as actual political struggles exhibit this 'hermeneutical sublime in the highest degree . . . they realise the potential break with existing frameworks of understanding' (2009: 43). They constitute a 'pure exteriority and metamorphosis' (2000: 114) (absolute deterritorialisation) from the state of affairs and its processes of representation. Rather than presuppose existing political conditions, revolution, or the pure eventness of transformation, change and becoming itself, Patton argues, must be considered as 'the source or condition of the emergence of the new' (2009: 50).

Similarly, as Dan Smith argues in 'Deleuze and the Production of the New', 'if identity (A is A) were the primary principle, that is, if identities were already pregiven, then there would in principle be no production of the new (no new differences)' (2008: 151). Thus, Smith continues, 'for Deleuze, the conditions of the new can be found only in a principle of difference' (2008: 151), 'no less capable of dissolving and destroying individuals than of constituting them temporarily' (Deleuze 1994: 56/38). While Patton and Smith accurately develop the important concept of 'difference-in-itself' drawn from Deleuze's earlier works, I believe that this concept not only remains unable to account for a theory of revolutionary intervention and political change but even risks blocking it by affirming the unconditioned ambivalence and non-relational 'exteriority' of political action. By valorising revolution as the unconditioned (real) potentiality for 'change as such' (liberatory change as well as non-liberatory change) or what Patton calls 'critical freedom' (2000: 83), radical politics remains optimistically tied to an ultimately indifferent and ambivalent principle of difference for its own sake: the aleatory temporal constitution no less than the destruction of individuals; or spontaneous insurrection.

However, the contemporary return to revolution, I argue, is more than an affirmation that 'another world is possible'. And insofar as revolution affirms pure eventness 'as that part of every event that escapes its own actualisation' exterior to history, it remains ultimately (in its pure form) abstracted from all actual and concrete political relations as well as different political events in their specificity. To be clear, this is not the same criticism well refuted by John Protevi in his review of Peter Hallward's *Out of This World* (Protevi 2006). It is not the case that the virtual simply remains abstractly above the actual as a spiritual realm. Insofar as revolution is the 'general transformative movement *between* actualization and counter-actualization', it remains non-related to any determinate quasi-causal political event and its singular concrete consequences. It remains unable to conceptualise the multiple intermediate stages of any local political intervention. I disagree that concrete revolutionary struggles are radical only insofar as they abandon their actual relations and affirm 'only' their capacity to become-other-as-such in a pure becoming-actual-becoming-virtual.

II. A Time for Revolution

THE FUTURE ANTERIOR

How then are we to understand political transformation such that a non-representational revolutionary praxis is not merely possible but actually constructed? Distinct from the notion that revolutionary intervention is based on opposition and from the notion that it is a form of pure 'eventness' that conditions all events as such, in this next section I argue for a third position. In order to understand the contemporary return to revolution we need to analyse four intermediate and concrete stages that take place *between* the processes of representation (developed in Chapter 1) on the one hand, and the so-called pure exteriority of 'eventness' or 'absolute deterritorialisation' on the other. Between the pre-given facts, subjects and objects of the situation and their history (the past) and the radically unconditioned potentiality for their transformation 'to come' (the future), I argue, there are four intermediate stages of political transformation distributed by a revolutionary event.

Within these four intermediate stages of political transformation, the fourth stage, in particular, describes the type of revolutionary transformation that defines the contemporary return to revolution. This fourth type of revolutionary transformation is prefigurative and takes place in the time of the future anterior. But the purpose of the future anterior is not to create a 'pure becoming' of the past and future as such, or to privilege one against the other (the pre-evental over the post-evental or vice versa). Rather, what I propose instead in this section is a strategy of revolutionary intervention that accounts for both the concepts of revolutionary precipitation and its post-evental consequences.

My aim here is also to understand prefiguration as a revolutionary strategy composed of both conceptual and practical components. Thus, in order to help develop this strategy I draw on Deleuze and Guattari's theory of deterritorialisation that describes four modes of change. The first type of change is what they call 'relative negative deterritorialization'. This is a change that is able to break free from the processes of political representation (coding, overcoding and axiomatisation) but only momentarily and in such a way that obstructs further transformations. The second type of change is what they call a 'relative positive deterritorialization'. This type of change succeeds in creating an undecidable point of tension within the processes of political representation that might lead to revolution, but may also lead to a mere reform of power. The third type of change is what Deleuze and Guattari call an 'absolute negative deterritorialization'. This type of change creates a radical rupture within the processes of representation but fails to connect to any others and enters a line of isolated self-destruction. The fourth type of change is what they call an 'absolute positive deterritorialization'. This type of change is not only able to break free from power but is also able to connect up to other such ruptures and create a collective alternative to representational politics in the future anterior.

These different modes of change, their mixtures, temporalities and relations are the conceptual tools Deleuze and Guattari have to offer for understanding the process of revolutionary transformation. This chapter aims to demonstrate their usefulness first conceptually, against the concepts of opposition and insurrection, and then practically, as they are paralleled in the Zapatistas' prefigurative *Juntas de Buen Gobierno*. However, before I continue with this demonstration, two problems pertaining to the usage of the temporality of the future anterior need be clarified and avoided up front. In the next three subsections I thus argue that the future anterior should (1) not be understood as a complete synthesis of the past and future (an 'event of becoming'), (2) nor should it be understood as merely privileging pre- or post-eventual actions; it should rather (3) be understood as the creation of a new present.

(1) The Future Anterior is Not an Event of Becoming

The process of revolutionary prefiguration, I am arguing, takes place in the time of the future anterior, that is, as an event which will have been. But the conjunction of past, present and future that creates the future anterior should not at all be understood as a global synthesis of these three times as such. If we define revolutionary transformation as the synthesis – even the differential one Deleuze describes in *Difference and Repetition* (96–168/70–128) – of the past, present and future, then the revolutionary future anterior would be the absolute conditions for all change as such. That is, the revolutionary future anterior would be the principle of difference-in-itself. As such, revolution would have no actual, concrete existence or political force by which to offer an alternative to the competing processes of political representation.[1] Revolution would be the mere potentiality of change, not any actual, positive political power. Put simply, if revolution is the 'event of pure becoming' between all pasts, presents and futures, then there is only one ambivalent event that conditions all types of political power.

Truly different revolutionary events with their own conditions for action, agency and organisation could therefore not exist but would instead only be derived as effects from a single eternal event: genesis, the *'event of being'*.[2] Following many others who also hold that *The Logic of Sense* 'is Deleuze's most noteworthy effort to clarify his concept of the event' (Badiou 2009a: 382), Alain Badiou locates what I believe to be a significant danger for a Deleuzian theory of revolutionary intervention: if the condition for all transformation itself is an event, then there can be no real change, only the endless modification of a single event. In *Logics of Worlds*, Badiou argues that if, as Deleuze says in *The Logic of Sense*, there is only 'one single event for all events; one and the same *aliquid* for that which happens and that which is said; and one and the same being for the impossible, the possible, and the real' (Deleuze 1990: 211/180), then such an ontological condition becomes both the condition and the conditioned, leaving no room for real disjunction, rupture and change (Badiou 2009a: 385).

If, as Badiou says, 'the event is always a synthesis of past and future ... The expression of the One within becomings' or 'what lies between a past and a future, between the end of one world and the beginning of another', it expresses the eternal and continual being of time itself, and not the separation or disjunction necessary for thinking a determinate political change in the world (2009a: 382–3). Ultimately, Deleuze's theory of the event is caught between two poles, neither of which is able to account for the emergence of a new revolutionary present: either the present is split entirely into the future and past and thus does not exist, or the present is the eternal synthesis of all futures and pasts and is thus everything.

However, while it may be the case that Deleuze's earlier works, *Difference and Repetition* and *The Logic of Sense*, develop the concepts of 'event' and 'becoming' at length, I maintain, following Alberto Toscano, that in *A Thousand Plateaus*

> The terrain seems to have shifted considerably with respect to [Deleuze's] earlier preoccupation with conditions of realization – a preoccupation

that seemed to afford a certain continuity with naturalised or materialist accounts of ontogenesis. The individuations that Deleuze and Guattari foreground in *A Thousand Plateaus* are not of the sort that engender individuals; rather, they traverse already constituted individuals, drawing them towards impersonal becomings, compositions of one multiplicity with another. (2006: 176)

In *A Thousand Plateaus* (a work from which Badiou and other critics rarely draw), Deleuze and Guattari no longer privilege the so-called 'ontological conditions for the production of events as such' but proceed from the principle that 'politics precedes being' (1987: 249/203), replacing earlier theories of 'structure and genesis' (1987: 326/266) with a theory of strategy, political relation and a logic of assemblages (Deleuze 2006: 163/177). That is, rather than aiming to show that 'difference-in-itself' or 'pure becoming' is the ontological condition and singular 'event of being', Deleuze and Guattari's later work instead develops a complex political logic (or constructivism) of the various types of assemblages that compose the immanent relations of and among political events and their degrees of transformation. Lacking the political typology and the more nuanced theory of change (deterritorialisation) found only in *A Thousand Plateaus*, *The Logic of Sense* and *Difference and Repetition* remain, I believe, not unhelpful or 'pre-political' but wholly inadequate for retrieving a concept of revolutionary intervention based on the future anterior.[3]

(2) The Future Anterior is Neither Pre- Nor Post-Evental

Just as the revolutionary future anterior cannot be understood in terms of an absolute synthesis of the future and the past (the 'event of becoming'), neither can it be understood as a pre- or post-evental intervention. In his essay 'What Is a Political Event?' Iain Mackenzie distinguishes between two approaches to understanding the emergence of political events: a pre-evental approach developed by Deleuze and a post-evental approach developed by Badiou. Ultimately, Mackenzie concludes that 'Deleuze's "pre-occurrence" approach is more persuasive than Badiou's "post-occurrence" theorisation' because it does not require a subject to miraculously nominate the event (Mackenzie 2008: 2). True or not, what I find interesting about this account is the way that Mackenzie and others have framed the problem of political transformation.

From a Deleuzean perspective, and in stark contrast to Badiou's emphasis upon the revolutionary event, events usually occur when we are least aware of them. Yet, it is as an effect of these apparently insignificant moments that significance is produced; the possibility of meaning enters the world, we might say, behind our backs. (Mackenzie 2008: 15)

For Deleuze, Mackenzie argues, it is only when we are least aware, or at our most impersonal, that a whole host of seemingly insignificant elements that we do not control can come out of nowhere and create an evental disjunction with the (actual) state of affairs. Rather than requiring any active precipitation, construction or evental surveillance, the Deleuzian pre-occurrence of potential forces will suddenly rise up from behind our backs and disjoint us from the actual pre-determinations of the past and towards the revolutionary future 'to come'. Far from being reducible to identifiable, epochal shifts, Deleuzian pre-evental singularities are, according to Paul Patton, 'molecular', 'indiscernible' and 'happening all the time' (2000: 108).

This is in contrast to the post-evental philosophy of Alain Badiou which is concerned primarily with the consequences, fidelities or 'truth procedures' that happen only after an event has occurred and vanished. 'Self-belonging', or the evental site, as Badiou says, 'annuls itself as soon as it appears. A site is a vanishing term: it appears only as disappearing. The problem consists in registering the consequences of the appearing' (2009a: 392). Badiou's clear privileging of evental 'retroaction' and 'post-evental commitment' has led critics (Hallward 2003; Bensaïd 2004; Marchart 2005) to argue that such a clear denial of pre-evental conditions leads Badiou into a kind of quasi-religious mysticism of evental miracles. That is, if there are no 'pre-evental subjects' and one is unable to pre-eventally precipitate events or even locate their precursors, then how and why events happen seems entirely miraculous. All that remains coherent are the militantly faithful subjects to events past. While this dilemma has led others like Adrian Johnston and Nick Srnicek to try and supplement this pre-evental shortcoming in Badiou's work (Johnston 2007; Srnicek 2008), I would like to proceed in a different direction.

The apparent split between Deleuze's 'pre' and Badiou's 'post' theory of the event, as Badiou himself observes, 'exposes the original ambiguity in the notion' of the event (2009a: 382). Adopting either position (the future-looking pre-evental or the backward-looking post-evental), it seems, we end up affirming a kind of mysticism of the political event. Either we simply sit around, do nothing and wait for the invisible, pre-evental and spontaneous potentialities to mystically bring about real revolutionary transformation behind our backs, or the mystical event has 'always-already' occurred (insofar as we are subjects of it) and we just need to 'get out there' and be militantly faithful to its consequences. This characterisation may seem like a straw man or polarisation of the problematic, and perhaps I have over-emphasised to demonstrate a debate in the literature on this topic. But even Deleuze and Badiou's most generous readers have acknowledged a real difference in emphasis between these two temporalities (Johnston 2007; Srnicek 2008).

Thus, it must also be admitted that the issue is a bit more subtle than this. Traces of the pre-evental exist in Badiou (in both *Being and Event* and *Logics of Worlds*), just as traces of the post-evental exist in Deleuze and Guattari (*The Logic of Sense* and *A Thousand Plateaus*). But even this observation still misses the point. 'Traces' hardly constitute a full resolution to this problem. The temporality of political intervention in Deleuze, Guattari and Badiou is poorly understood in terms of pre- and post-eventality. What I am arguing instead is that Deleuze, Guattari and Badiou all share a theory of political intervention based in the future anterior that has yet to be sufficiently examined (Badiou 2005b: 201–11; Badiou 2009a: 357–80; Deleuze 1990: 74–83/58–65; Deleuze and Guattari 1987: 284–380/232–309). So while Deleuze, Guattari and Badiou have all, at one point or another, clearly stated that revolutionary events do not emerge miraculously *ex nihilo*,[4] what remains to be developed in detail is a theory of such a revolutionary intervention that is demonstrably consistent with such a position. This is the aim of the present chapter.

(3) The Future Anterior is a New Present

With the aim of proposing a theory and practice of revolutionary prefiguration I have first distinguished two perilous sides of the future anterior to be avoided: on the one hand, a past and future fused together in the 'eventness' of a 'pure becoming' where the revolutionary present has disappeared, and on the other hand a past and future divided into pre- and post-evental worlds where the present has been infinitely divided into an empty or absent time. The first fails by equating revolutionary events with the absolute condition for all events as such. The second fails by positing a miraculous origin at the heart of any given event. What I am proposing instead is a concept of the future anterior that functions as a new present moment within and alongside the other processes of political and temporal representation. This new present moment is not an infinitely split time but a productive one that both projects a new future and retrojects a new past.[5] It is, as Deleuze says, the creation of a whole new space-time (Deleuze 1995: 239/176).

In the last few lines of series twenty-three (of Aiôn) in *The Logic of Sense*, Deleuze distinguishes between three kinds of present: (1) a subverted present (empty and infinitely split), (2) an actualised present (diffused into everything), and (3) a third present that acts as the 'quasi-cause' of a distinctly new past and future: a present-past and present-future (1990: 196/168). 'It would seem, no doubt,' Deleuze says, 'that the Aiôn cannot have any present at all, since in it the instance is always dividing into future and past. But this is only appearance' (1990: 196/168). In reality, the third present (of the future anterior) is a real 'quasi-causal' condition for a new past and future transformed immanently within the old. But how exactly is this new present precipitated? How are its consequences concretely distributed without becoming representational? What are its dangers? How are we to understand the more intermediate degrees of such a transformation? And what is its relationship to the political situation and its typology of different representational processes? These questions are not fully answered in *The Logic of Sense*.

In fact, Deleuze and Guattari are not able to fully answer them until 1980, when they co-write *A Thousand Plateaus*: their first constructivist effort.[6] What is important to distinguish, however, in this concept of the third present of the future anterior, introduced in *The Logic of Sense*,[7] is that such a present is capable of becoming the 'quasi-causal' or real condition for a new world neither diffused nor split. Once this 'moment' emerges it reconditions not only the political situation of the new present but also that of a new past and future. Revolution is thus not an opposition nor an *ex nihilo* insurrection, it is a prefiguration in the sense that it creates a new world parallel to the old one. This prefiguration takes place in the future anterior in the sense that it does not assume a pre-given past which it opposes or a merely possible future which it hopes to attain. Revolutionary prefiguration is instead future anterior insofar as it creates, as Deleuze says, an entirely new space-time of its own (1995: 239/176). It creates the past and future it wants to see in the present. According to Deleuze and Guattari, this is the positive meaning of presentiment: not the inert hope that 'another world is possible', but the direct action of that particular world within the present.

> In order to give a positive meaning to the idea of a 'presentiment' of what does not yet exist, it is necessary to demonstrate that what does not yet

exist is already in action, in a different form than that of its existence. (Deleuze and Guattari 1987: 537/431)

This real action of the constructed past and future within the present is what Deleuze and Guattari call, following the British historian Arnold Toynbee, 'neo-archaism' and 'ex-futurism' (1983: 309/257). If space-time is a topological plane of various contingent and heterogeneous processes connected together through folding and morphism, as was argued in Chapter 1, then a revolutionary intervention does not emerge dialectically or developmentally, or *ex nihilo*; it emerges by creating a new fold or connection between various points in space-time: a new arrangement of past, present and future. Thus revolution today does not seize the state, it creates something better from below.

I will return to this concept of revolutionary prefiguration and the future anterior in my development of Deleuze and Guattari's concept of absolute positive deterritorialisation. But with the concept of the future anterior distinguished from a synthesis of the past and future and from a complete split between past and future, the problem now is how to understand the role this revolutionary prefiguration plays and what dangers it faces in the larger process of political transformation. In order to do so, in the next four subsections I draw on Deleuze and Guattari's theory of transformation, or what they call 'deterritorialisation'.

Four Concepts of Change or 'Deterritorialisation'

The concept of change is arguably one of the most central concepts throughout Deleuze and Guattari's work, and while it has undergone many different names and terminological shifts over time, it remains safe to say that there are two concepts in their work that are the most important for understanding the concept of transformation: 'becoming' and 'deterritorialisation'. It is of no coincidence, then, that the chapter most centrally devoted to these two concepts not only composes the largest of all the chapters in *A Thousand Plateaus* (99/77 pages) but is also the only place in the book where the concept of the future anterior (Aiôn) is deployed: *1730: Becoming-Intense, Becoming-Animal, Becoming-Imperceptible . . .*

Given the clear centrality of these two concepts in Deleuze and Guattari's work, I propose to draw from them a theory of revolutionary transformation that provides an alternative to strategic opposition and revolutionary 'eventness', as well as to the synthetic and divided concepts of the future anterior. Additionally, my argument is that a theory of revolutionary intervention in the future anterior, or what I am calling strategic prefiguration, cannot be understood without also understanding the four concepts of change in the theory of deter-ritorialisation. In the next four subsections I thus develop the four concepts of change briefly outlined at the beginning of this section (relative negative, relative positive, absolute negative and absolute positive deterritorialisation). Afterwards, in the third and final major section of this chapter, I argue that the Zapatistas deploy a practice of revolutionary prefiguration in the *Juntas*.

(1) Relative Negative Deterritorialisation

The first type of change is what Deleuze and Guattari call 'rela-tive negative deterritorialisation'. This is a change that is able to break free from the processes of political representation (coding, overcoding and axiomatisation) but only momentarily and in such a way that the change obstructs further transformations. A relative negative deterritorialisation is a normalised transformation inter-nal to the functioning of a representational process that secures its further expansion. It is a mistake to think that power is ever total or homogeneous. Rather, the opposite is true. Representational power, according to Deleuze and Guattari, functions only through its inter-nal breakdowns: relative negative deterritorialisations.

In the processes of territorial coding, for example, there are certain prohibitions and boundaries that define the limits proper to a society: how things are to be used, how desire is to be directed, where activi-ties are to take place and so on. A coded territory is thus what it is only by virtue of where it draws the disjunctive limits of its code. On the one side it connects qualitative codes, while on the other side it disjuncts a remainder or surplus yet to be coded. But since territorial coding is based on the primary repression of 'uncoded or decoded flows' (absolute deterritorialisation), something is always escaping outside the limits of a given block of code. As each coded territory approaches its marginal limits, after which it will cease to be what it is, it undergoes an internal transformation by conjuncting and redistributing the surplus to another line of code (through alliance). 'By switching territories at the conclusion of each operation period' territorial coding becomes itinerant (Deleuze and Guattari 1987: 549/440): creating multiple binary segments-in-progress. That is to say, its power to represent the natural codes of social life functions only through a perpetual disequilibrium of excess and deficiency (1983: 175–6/150). Relative negative deterritorialisation (stabilised dysfunction) is thus an essential element of its very ability to function. Elements are structurally excluded, only to be reintegrated under a new hierarchy later on.

Statist overcoding also functions through internal breakdown and transformation, but in a different way. Opposed to the territorial coding of primarily unstable flows of absolute deterritorialisation, statism is itself a deterritorialised and uncoded remainder from the territorial stock that becomes a centralised point of accumulation (of land, work, currency and so on). This point of accumulation in turn performs a relative negative deterritorialisation back upon the qualitative territorial codes by removing their heterogeneous qualities and stratifying them into a single vertical and hierarchical line of machinic enslavement within a central overcoding apparatus (Deleuze and Guattari 1987: 533/427–8). But in retaining given coded elements, the state necessarily cuts off relations with other elements, which become exterior to it. Opposed to territorial itinerancy that merely begins a new line of code with the remainder, the state's form of relative negative deterritorialisation aims either to destroy all remainders or to capture them 'once and for all'. But since neither of these are possible (due to the inexhaustible contingencies of political history discussed in Chapter 1), the state is continually entering into increasingly violent states of security, emergency and internal change: relative negative deterritorialisation. The state is thus paranoiac and ultimately impotent. But 'it is precisely its impotence [*impuissance*] that makes power [*pouvoir*] so dangerous', as Deleuze and Guattari say (1987: 279/229). The more power and security a state deploys, the more its impotence grows; the more its impotence grows, the more power is required to secure it, and so on.

> This is both the principle of their power and the basis of their impotence. Far from being opposites, power and impotence complement and reinforce each other in a kind of fascinating satisfaction that is found above all in the most mediocre Statesmen, and defines their 'glory.' For they extract glory from their shortsightedness, and power from their impotence. (Deleuze and Guattari 1987: 275/225)

Above all, capitalist axiomatisation is the representational process most adapted to the rapid and fluid process of internal transformation, that is, relative negative deterritorialisation. Opposed to the paranoiac and totalitarian drive towards total capture or destruction that requires so many 'states of emergency' and paranoiac suspensions of law, capitalist axiomatisation takes non-totality and incompleteness to be its point of departure. Opposed to codes that qualify, and overcodes that bring codes into a single resonance, axioms function by directly conjugating unqualified and decoded flows themselves. Thus capitalism goes furthest in its relative negative deterritorialisation. At one pole it deploys an aggressive decoding of qualitative relationships through the privatisation of all aspects of social life, free trade, advertising, freeing of labour and capital, imperialism and so on, and at the other pole it conjugates them as abstract quantities for exchange on the world market (Deleuze and Guattari 1983: 293/246).[8] Where the despotic states had emperors of anti-production to consume and capture surplus, the bourgeois field of immanence has no such external limit; it has integrated anti-production inside production itself. Since axiomatisation takes contingency, change and deterritorialisation to be its presupposition, it also makes the internal and inevitable destruction or saturation of markets themselves the condition for its ever widening limits (1983: 292–3/253).

(2) Relative Positive Deterritorialisation
The second type of political change described by Deleuze and Guattari is defined as a real transformation of political representation that prevails over secondary reterritorialisations (codes, overcodes and axioms) but fails to connect with other positively deterritorialised elements or create a new arrangement. Relative positive deterritorialisation on its own is thus only the mere affirmation that something has escaped the dominant regimes of political representation at the borderlines. This kind of change is ultimately insufficient to sustain a revolutionary struggle. It is thus a mistake to think that just because something has escaped political representation, it is inherently revolutionary. Again, the opposite is true. Political transformations, according to Deleuze and Guattari, are experimental and require sustained and committed connections with others to become revolutionary.

> It is because no one, not even God, can say in advance whether two borderlines [bordures] will string together or form a fiber, whether a given multiplicity will or will not cross over into another given multiplicity, or even if given heterogeneous elements will enter symbiosis, will form a consistent, or cofunctioning, multiplicity susceptible to transformation. No one can say where the line of flight will pass: Will it let itself

get bogged down . . . Or will it succumb to another danger, for example, turning into a line of abolition, annihilation, self-destruction [*d'auto-destruction*], Ahab, Ahab . . . ? We are all too familiar with the dangers of the line of flight, and with its ambiguities. The risks are ever-present, but it is always possible to have the good fortune of avoiding them. Case by case, we can tell whether the line is consistent, in other words, whether the heterogeneities effectively function in a multiplicity of symbiosis, whether the multiplicities are effectively transformed through the becomings of passage. (Deleuze and Guattari 1987: 306–7/250)

Relative positive deterritorialisation is thus a borderline phenomenon, a 'thing, which arrives and passes at the edge', that functions as the two-sided limit of political representation (Deleuze and Guattari 1987: 299/245). Because 'the politics of becomings', for Deleuze and Guattari, are so 'extremely ambiguous', this borderline is split in two: on the one side it exists as an 'anomalous' element unaccounted for within the state of affairs but still recognisable as an exception, and on the other side it exists as an 'exceptional individual' that holds together the increasing connections of a new world in formation (Deleuze and Guattari 1987: 302/247). Insofar as it ceases to be a definable aggregate in relation to the majority, it reveals both the possibility of further connection and the possibility of inevitable co-optation (1987: 356–7/291).

(3) Absolute Negative Deterritorialisation
The third type of political change described by Deleuze and Guattari is defined as a real transformation that moves absolutely beyond all the borderlines of territorial, state and capitalist representation.[9] But in doing so it not only fails to connect with other deterritorialised elements and create a new arrangement, it deterritorialises too fast, too much, and becomes self-destructive. Ultimately, it ends up strengthening the processes of political representation. Radical political transformation is thus not merely ambiguous. This would be putting things too lightly; it can be dangerous. 'Staying stratified – organized, signified, subjected – is not the worst that can happen,' Deleuze and Guattari warn. 'The worst that can happen is if you throw the strata into demented or suicidal collapse, which brings them back down on us heavier than ever' (1987: 199/161).

When a 'line of flight' or a degree of political transformation 'makes [change] an unlimited movement with no other aim than itself', this is what Deleuze and Guattari call fascism (1987: 525/421).[10] Provided that we do not strictly apply this concept to its narrow and literal reference in the traditional categories of political ideology, there can be all kinds of fascisms in the degree to which they exhibit a certain 'passion for self-destruction'. There is a molar fascism when a totalitarian state values war over its own self-preservation, as in the case of Nazi Germany in Hitler's final days. 'If the war is lost, may the nation perish,' Hitler declares in telegram 71. 'Here,' Deleuze and Guattari say, 'Hitler decides to join forces with his enemies in order to complete the destruction of his own people, by obliterating the last remaining resources of its life-support system, civil reserves of every kind (potable water, fuel, provisions, etc.)' (Deleuze and Guattari 1987: 282/231; Virilio 1993: 1–15; Arendt 1979: 326). There is a molecular fascism when groups or individuals collapse in on themselves in isolation: 'a rural fascism and city or neighborhood fascism, youth fascism and war veterans fascism, fascism of the left and of the right, fascism of the couple, family, school and office' (Deleuze and Guattari 1987: 261/214). It is a general thirst for every kind of destruction, 'whose only outcome is death' (1987: 201/162).

Therefore, it is because one is unable to 'reach the . . . plane of consistency, by wildly destratifying' (1987: 199/160) that Deleuze and Guattari, for the first time in their work together, advise not wisdom but 'injections of caution' into the process of political transformation (1987: 175–6/150).

(4) Absolute Positive Deterritorialisation

Absolute positive deterritorialisation is the fourth, final and most important type of political change described by Deleuze and Guattari. It is a kind of transformation that not only escapes the absolute limits and borders of political representation, but also connects up to an increasing number of other absolutely positive deterritorialised elements whose ultimate collective aim is the immanent transformation of the present intersection of political processes through the prefigurative construction of a new world (Deleuze and Guattari 1987: 179/142). But it would be a mistake to think that this radical transformation is a kind of *ex nihilo* miracle or absolute Other/Outside of political representation. Deleuze and Guattari are quite clear, and the previous types of change have shown, that absolute deterritorialisation is already presupposed as the absolute internal limit immanently confronted by all other forms of social organisation. Absolute positive deterritorialisation is thus in no way transcendent, oppositional or merely potential, but rather a kind of immanent and creative process from within the situation that harnesses all of its inevitable breakdowns and exclusions. It does so not in order to develop a new form of political representation, or to stabilise the old ones, but to create a new non-representational social body.

But is it really sufficient to say that absolute positive deterritorialisation is merely the connection of all such heterogeneous breakdowns and exclusions? Not at all. It is precisely this move that reads absolute positive deterritorialisation as a transcendental condition for all political change as such: difference-in-itself, potentiality or pure becoming. While Peter Hallward's book *Out of This World* is perhaps the most extreme formulation of this 'theophantic' conclusion, it should indicate to us the risks of such a position and the necessity of thinking of absolute positive deterritorialisation as a real, concrete revolutionary force. I thus present the following alternative reading.

Absolute positive deterritorialisation does not form a single transcendental or ontological condition for all revolutionary change. Deleuze and Guattari are extremely clear about this when they say that 'politics precedes being' and that 'the plane of consistency does not preexist the movements of deterritorialization that unravel it, the lines of flight that draw it and cause it to rise to the surface, the becomings that compose it' (1987: 330/270). Rather, case by case, very specific, singular elements become dislodged, marginalised and deterritorialised from the intersection of representational political processes (or what Deleuze and Guattari call 'the plane of organisation'). These singular elements then 'combine into blocks [of becoming]' (1987: 328/268) based on a topological zone of proximity that marks their belonging to each other in a given situation (1987: 335/273).

Far from forming a muddy and inconsistent multitude, each relational 'block of becoming' that is assembled from the immanent breakdowns and unrepresentable elements within the situation 'does not have the same forces or even speeds of deterritorialization as another; in each instance, the indices and coefficients must be calculated according to the block of becoming under consideration, and in relation to the mutations of an abstract machine' (Deleuze and Guattari 1987: 377/306–7). Far from affirming the vague and ambivalent potentiality of transformation as such, Deleuze and Guattari insist on the 'fragment by fragment' political calculation, comparison and assembly of powers of deterritorialisation (Deleuze and Parnet 1987: 175/146; see also Deleuze and Guattari 1987: 378/307). Thus, and this is crucial to the entire thesis of this book, 'it is in concrete social fields, at specific moments, that the comparative movements of deterritorialization, the continuums of intensity, and the combinations of flux that they form must be studied' (Deleuze and Parnet 1987: 163/135).

Absolute positive deterritorialisation is prefigurative in the sense that it follows out the consequences of a specific event immanent and parallel to the processes of representation. 'The question' of sustaining the event, as Guattari puts it, 'is how to ensure that the singular processes – which almost swerve into the incommunicable – are maintained by articulating them in a work, a text, a way of living with oneself or with others, or the invention of areas of life and freedom to create' (2008: 259). In other words, absolute positive deterritorialisation doesn't just lay preparatory groundwork for an event, it also 'captures the [unrepresentable] elements of the situation' and 'constructs its own types of practical and theoretical references, without remaining dependent in relation to global power, whether in terms of economy, knowledge, technology, or segregations, and prestige that are disseminated' (2008: 62).

To return to the central thesis of this chapter, contemporary revolutionary transformation, according to Deleuze, Guattari and the Zapatistas, occurs as the prefigurative emergence of a particular new present (within and alongside the old) that both 'rewrites and reinterprets the totality of potentials that already existed in stratified form' (Guattari 2008: 252) as well as creates 'an action of the future on the present' and 'the present on the past' (Deleuze and Guattari 1987: 537/431). This is what Deleuze and Guattari call 'reverse causalities'. More than a break or zigzag in history, they argue, what is to come already acts upon 'what is' before the future can appear, insofar as it acts as a limit or threshold continually being warded off by the past's attempt to preserve itself. But once a new present emerges it is seen to have been on its way the entire time (1987: 537/431). If, from the perspective of the plane of organisation, revolutionary novelty may seem to emerge 'out of nowhere', this is only because it was unable to see or represent the prefigurative labour of deterritorialisation before it had transformed the political conditions under which it could be seen and understood as such. However, from the perspective of the revolutionary struggle, the emerging event appears entirely consistent and intelligible as that which will have been. This prefigurative labour, according to Guattari, consists in detecting the outlines, indicators, and crystals of molecular productivity. If there is a micropolitics to be practiced, it consists in ensuring that these molecular levels do not always succumb to systems that coopt them, systems of neutralization, or processes of implosion or self-destruction. It consists in apprehending how other assemblages of the production of life, the production of art, or the production of whatever you want might find their full expansion, so that the problematics of power find a response. This certainly involves modes of response of a new kind. (2008: 339)

The new revolutionary present thus emerges from strategic sites of struggle that draw it 'in negative outline', Deleuze and Guattari say. 'But for it to be realized there must be a whole integral of decoded flows, a whole generalized conjunction that overspills and over-turns the preceding apparatuses' (1987: 564/452). That is, it must 'cause the other elements to cross a threshold enabling a conjunction of their respective deterritorializations, a shared acceleration. This is . . . absolute, positive deterritorialization' (1987: 179/142). The future anterior is not only an escape but the creation of 'new weapons' (Deleuze and Parnet 1987: 164/136): 'the creation of great machines of struggle' (Guattari 2008: 210). To be clear, this type of revolutionary struggle only appears to be parasitic from the perspective of the status quo. From the perspective of the revolution, it is political representation that is parasitic on the will of the people, whose will must first exist before it can be (mis)represented in the first place.

However, lest I risk arguing in favour of a purely subterranean and imperceptible form of revolutionary transformation, I should highlight – because some often forget to – that the purpose of absolute positive deterritorialisation is not simply to become-imperceptible in relation to the plane of organisation for the sake of doing so: this has too much fascist potential. The purpose of prefigurative revolutionary interventions are to render everything 'fragment by fragment' imperceptible from the plane of organisation in order to create 'the plane of consistency, which is nevertheless precisely where the imperceptible is seen and heard' (Deleuze and Guattari 1987: 308/252). The task is not to relish the theory of an impossible and invisible revolution, but rather to 'bring the imperceptible to perception' by changing the dominant conditions for visibility (1987: 326/267). It is neither by oppositional destruction nor by *ex nihilo* creation but 'by conjugating, by continuing with other lines, other pieces, that one makes a world that can overlay the first one, like a transparency' [*comme en transparence*] (Deleuze and Guattari 1987:

343/280). In the case of revolutions this new world becomes the popular and more powerful world.

III. The Prefigurative Politics of Zapatismo

It would be a mistake to think that the Zapatistas or any other revolutionary political struggle were ever confined to expressing only a single type of political transformation. Just as in the previous chapter we saw how the Zapatistas use an intersectional diagnostic to assess the external and internal dangers of their struggle on all fronts, so in this chapter we see to what degree they have chosen to intervene in each of the above four ways. Zapatismo thus takes place at a particular intersection of all four types of political change, although ultimately, I argue, their greatest degree of intervention is in the prefigurative future anterior.

Relative Negative Deterritorialisation: the EZLN, the Peace Accords and Biopiracy

Power is never total or homogeneous, and thus change, dysfunction and breakdown are inevitable aspects of any intersection of social orders. To the degree that the Zapatistas intervene in their political situation, they always risk having any transformations they contribute not only neutralised or co-opted but turned into changes that actually expand the power of political representation. For example, given the territorial codes of representation sustaining the patriarchal culture of indigenous life in Chiapas, the EZLN made a very specific intervention at the limits of this coding process: the creation of the Women's Revolutionary Law. By allowing women (regardless of race) to join the resistance, to work and receive fair wages, to be educated, to choose their partner, to choose the number of children they have, to be free from sexual violence and so on (EZLN 1994), they were able to deterritorialise the coded lines of patriarchal filiation and forced marriage alliance (to some degree). However, in doing so they faced the danger of merely deploying a relative negative deterritorialisation that only strengthened the vanguard military apparatus (EZLN) and initiated a new hierarchical line of filiation and military order still dominated to some degree by men and male values. As Marcos says of the EZLN,

> Accompaniment has sometimes turned into management, advice into orders and support into a hindrance. I've already spoken previously about

the fact that the hierarchical, pyramid structure is not characteristic of the indigenous communities. The fact that the EZLN is a political-military and clandestine organization still corrupts processes that should and must be democratic. (Marcos 2004a)

The Zapatistas also risked a relative negative deterritorialisation with their intervention into the overcoding state apparatus in their early attempts from 1994 to 1996 to negotiate a peaceful settlement with the Mexican government.

In the [San Andrés] agreements the government promised to recognize the right to autonomy of Indian peoples in the constitution, to broaden their political representation, to guarantee full access to the justice system, and to build a new legal framework that guaranteed political rights, legal rights and cultural rights. The government promised also to recognize indigenous people as subjects of public rights. (Ramírez 2008: 138)

But it was not only the negotiation with the Mexican government that made the Zapatistas' intervention a relative negative one (although winning these rights would have been a meaningful victory to some degree, even if it was through a state juridical process). What also made them relatively negative was the fact that the government negotiated and agreed to the San Andrés Accords but never followed through with them. During these years of negotiation the Zapatistas tried not to take any risky or radical actions or retaliations that might jeopardise the peace accords. Meanwhile, however, paramilitary forces, permitted by the government, as well as military troops and local police escalated their attacks on Zapatista and indigenous communities in Chiapas (including murder, assassination, harassment and military relocation). The entire peace accords process was nothing but a temporary deterritorialisation that allowed for the Mexican state's paranoid and impotent attempt at extermination and total capture.

Finally, after being harassed and relocated, the Zapatistas were forced further and further back into the Lacandón Jungle. As food, building materials and water became scarce, the Zapatistas increasingly entered into a mutual deterritorialisation with the jungle: they relied more on their traditional knowledge of the forest, wild plants and animals, while they ultimately ate less and tried not to damage the jungle ecosystem. But this deterritorialisation was soon transformed into a relatively negative one as the indigenous people were accused by the government and non-governmental organisations (NGOs) of 'exacerbat[ing] already existing deforestation pressures in the Lacandón jungle' (O'Brien 2000). Police, military and environmental conservationists were brought in, not just to secure the jungle from the indigenous people but to protect the increasing private axiomatisation of the newly deterritorialised 'biopolitical market' of indigenous knowledge, plants, animals and tourism that had been opened up both by state and NGO protection and by the actions of the indigenous people themselves, whose environmental 'damage' needed 'repairing' by conservation scientists and/or bioprospectors.

Relative Positive Deterritorialisation: The First Declaration of the Lacandón Jungle

It is also possible, however, that revolutionary interventions really split political life down the middle and force people to take action or not. For example, the Zapatista Uprising of 1 January 1994 marked out the real limits of political life in Mexico. The day that the North American Free Trade Agreement (NAFTA) went into effect, the Zapatistas 'burst upon a world that denied their existence', as Zapatista scholar John Holloway says. Armed men and women from the indigenous communities took by force seven towns and over 500 privately owned ranches in the state of Chiapas (Holloway and Peláez 1998: 1). From the perspective of Mexican politics and the dominant referents of politicians, corporations, voting citizens and so on, the Zapatistas surely 'appeared' to 'burst onto the scene' from nowhere. The existence of the Zapatistas was thus definitely at the borderline of popular political intelligibility. Who are 'the Zapatistas', and what is the meaning of their call to 'revolutionary war on the Mexican government'? The First Declaration of the Lacandón Jungle was this first call for the radical deterritorialisation of Mexican politics.

> To the People of Mexico:
> We, the men and women, full and free, are conscious that the war that we have declared is our last resort, but also a just one. The dictators are applying an undeclared genocidal war against our people for many years. Therefore we ask for your participation, your decision to support this plan that struggles for work, land, housing, food, health care, education, independence, freedom, democracy, justice and peace. We declare that we will not stop fighting until the basic demands of our people have been met by forming a government of our country that is free and democratic. JOIN THE INSURGENT FORCES OF THE ZAPATISTA ARMY OF NATIONAL LIBERATION.
> – General Command of the EZLN, 31 December 1993
> (Marcos 2004b: 642)

This evental call to popular revolutionary war split political reality in two. On the one side it is still possible to see the January Uprising as a temporary anomalous (although not immediately recuperable) blip of resistance in the prevailing political world; on the other side it is also the first visible manifestation of what will have been the beginning of a revolutionary war for popular and direct democracy[11] across Mexico. But what clearly marks this event as a relative positive deterritorialisation is that when confronted with this evental splitting of the situation, the Mexican people (for the most part) chose to both support the Zapatistas' struggle and tolerate the Mexican government's continued existence as a negotiator in the peace accords. Thus without a sufficient popular mobilisation of deterritorialised connections across Mexico, the event remained mostly affirmed in name without a large-scale connection of increasingly deterritorialised elements or building of alternative institutions. This type of political intervention is perhaps best exemplified in the creation of counter-institutions: institutions that affirm revolutionary struggles like the Zapatistas' and want to protect it, but that also do so through the struggle for rights, peace accords, negotiations and legal reforms within representational politics. In this case, the possibility of a specific revolution is acknowledged but ultimately staved off through mediating forms of compromise and representation.

Absolute Negative Deterritorialisation: A War Against the Mexican Government?

But these kinds of revolutionary failures are not the worst thing that can happen. In addition to failing to connect to other vectors of deterritorialisation sufficient to sustain a revolutionary struggle, interventions can also become suicidal. For example, the EZLN no doubt had to seriously assess the Mexican people's degree of support for the First Declaration of the Lacandón Jungle in relation to the Mexican military and paramilitary power. Who are the 'Mexican people'? What is the minimal support needed for a successful 'advance to the capital of the country, overcoming the Mexican federal army, protecting in our advance the civilian population and permitting the people in the liberated area the right to freely and democratically elect their own administrative authorities' (Marcos 2004b: 642)? What is the strength of our army? Are we prepared for death in combat?

When popular support turned out to be largely against

revolutionary war, the EZLN had to decide to either continue a prolonged guerrilla war (something for which they had been training for the past ten years), surrender or proceed by other means. Had they chosen to fight an unpopular military war against the Mexican government, knowing that they would likely lose, there is clearly a potential for revolutionary fascism and self-destruction.[12]

Thus we can see in the Zapatistas' Second Declaration (June 1994) the adherence to an 'offensive cease-fire' and a call-out for a 'peaceful and civic mobilization effort' by the Mexican people against the government. This begins a new long-term strategy of popular mobilisation efforts across Mexico and around the world. Clearly aware of the potential fascism that any revolutionary movement faces, Marcos writes:

> We don't want to impose our solutions by force, we want to create a democratic space. We don't see armed struggle in the classic sense of previous guerrilla wars, that is, as the only way and the only all-powerful truth around which everything is organized. In a war, the decisive thing is not the military confrontation but the politics at stake in the confrontation. We didn't go to war to kill or be killed. We went to war in order to be heard. (Marcos 2009)

Absolute Positive Deterritorialisation: Prefiguration and the Juntas de Buen Gobierno

Perhaps most interesting, however, is when political interventions not only escape the secondary reterritorialisations of power but manage to connect up with others to transform the dominant political conditions through the creation of a new world. For example, despite their initial failure to incite a revolutionary war against the Mexican government, or perhaps because of this failure, the Zapatistas proceeded to initiate another kind of warfare no less revolutionary, or perhaps more so: the popular organisation of civil society and the creation of the *Juntas de Buen Gobierno* (Councils of Good Government). In addition to many countrywide tours in previous years (to mobilise popular solidarity), in 2006 the Zapatistas began a concerted national effort to meet with and mobilise a popular unity of Left forces in Mexico around the upcoming electoral campaign: they called it *La Otra Campaña*.

The purpose was not to form a party or select a candidate but to build connections and networks between Left and radical groups across Mexico: to strengthen their shared deterritorialisations. Along with the sustained use of Internet communiqués, calls and responses for global grassroots support, the Zapatistas began holding large annual international events (Intercontinental *Encuentros* for Humanity and against Neoliberalism) and participating in annual Peoples' Global Action and World Social Forum events in order to further increase their connections and solidarities with other deterritorialised groups around the world. What remains so unique about the Zapatistas as a revolutionary movement is the degree to which they have increasingly broadened their struggle beyond their own indigenous territorial situation and taken on others' struggles as their own (against racism, homophobia, sexism, imperialism, neoliberalism and environmental destruction). Many Marxists had previously denied the possibility of a non-industrial working-class revolution, much less one specifically focusing on indigenous autonomy. But through a much more radical form of mutual deterritorialisation, the Zapatistas continue to participate in a whole new type of revolutionary sequence distinct from Marxism.

Secondly, the Zapatistas have also deployed a prefigurative revolutionary intervention in two ways. First, the only way one could possibly say that the Zapatistas 'burst onto the scene of Mexican politics out of nowhere' is if they had not been aware of the ten years of revolutionary activity, training and indigenous mobilisations sustained in the jungles of the Lacandón since 1983. Marcos and three others began as Che-inspired military vanguardists living outside indigenous communities slowly earning the trust of, and radicalising, the indigenous population. Far from appearing out of nowhere, there was a long and ultimately collective decision by the assembly of indigenous *campesin@s* to go to war. During this time the event of Zapatismo certainly existed as a new present that had constructed a past (based on the justice of Emiliano Zapata's peasant revolution) and a future (of directly democratic autonomous communes). 'In our dreams we have seen another world ... This world is not a dream from the past, it was not something that came to us from our ancestors. It came from ahead, from the next steps we are going to take' (Marcos 1994).

Both the past of Zapata and the future of the communes, although technically non-existent, acted directly on the new present of Zapatismo. During these ten years Zapatismo existed as a form of invisibility that will have been visible. The future anterior of Zapatismo is thus the revolutionary belief that the past (Zapata) can be resurrected and requires us to follow out its consequences against the Mexican government and towards the creation of a federated network of autonomous communes. Despite 'factual' evidence to the contrary, a Zapatista believes that Zapatismo *will have been* a revolutionary event. There is no objectivity or science of the revolution, only committed experimentation.

The second example, and perhaps the most original one, is the scale on which the Zapatistas have refused to 'take power' and have instead continued their revolution by creating in the present the world they want to see in their own autonomous municipalities. They began in August 2003 to create the *Juntas de Buen Gobierno*: directly democratic institutional frameworks for collective and autonomous decision-making. One JBG was created in each of the *caracoles* (regional communities, or 'snail shells') to

> promote and approve the participation of *compañeros* and *compañeras* ... to mediate conflicts which might arise between Autonomous Municipalities ... to monitor the implementation of projects and community work in the Rebel Zapatista Autonomous Municipalities ... to serve and guide national and international civil society so that they can visit communities, carry out productive projects, set up peace camps, carry out research, etc. (Marcos 2004b: 619)

Currently over 2,200 communities (over 200,000 people) are federated into thirty-eight autonomous municipalities, each grouped into five local self-governments (JBGs). Today the Zapatistas remain committed to, among other things, autonomy, participatory self-government, consensus decision-making, respect for nature and life without the use of pesticides, and the inclusion of 'everybody without distinctions of party, religion, sex, or color' (Marcos 2006).

By forming a specific block of becoming through rotational self-government, the federation of their communes and ultimately their solidarity with an international network of shared social struggle, the Zapatistas continue to make political interventions and alternative institutions that prefigure the kind of democratic and equalitarian world they and their allies want to live in. Opposed to directly declaring war on the Mexican government and instituting a regime change in the state, or simply affirming the radical possibility that 'another world is possible', the Zapatistas are building, to what degree they can, another world within and alongside the old.

The determination, including my own, that Zapatismo 'will have been' a revolutionary event, however, has no objective status, only a conditional and experimental one: if you believe that Zapatismo is an event, then that belief functions in the future anterior and can be supported by the network of evidence I have outlined above. If not, then Zapatismo is an inconsequential moment in the history of state-capitalism to be co-opted or crushed. Further, 'positive' and 'negative' deterritorialisation should not be understood as an evaluative, qualitative or normative description. 'Positive' merely designates the creation of a new world and 'negative' the mere destruction or reproduction of the old world.

Conclusion

In Chapter 1 I argued that the problem of history and revolution should not be understood as a universal history of either succession or contingency but rather as a diagnostic strategy that examines several specific types of coexistent political processes at once in order to assess the risks and dangers of a given revolutionary struggle. But in the process of this diagnostic practice we were confronted with the problem of intervention and political transformation. In the practice of diagnosing, where and how have we already intervened? How and where will we direct our future interventions based on a given intersectional analysis of power, and what new political world are we creating within the old, if any? In this chapter, I responded to this problem of revolutionary intervention by arguing that contemporary revolutionary intervention is defined primarily by its prefigurative connections and constructions in the future anterior. Drawing on Deleuze and Guattari's concepts of the future anterior (Aiôn) and deterritorialisation in *A Thousand Plateaus*, I supported this argument by showing that future anterior intervention can be distinguished from three other types of political transformation: relative negative, relative positive and absolute negative deterritorialisations. These types of transformation remain insufficient to support a revolutionary political transformation of the plane of organisation into a plane of consistency.

But while the strategy of prefigurative political intervention and deterritorialisation developed in this chapter may provide an account of how political change occurs and begins to connect up with other deterritorialised elements, it remains radically insufficient for understanding how it is that such prefigurative elements are able to cohere and organise themselves into distinctly non-representational kinds of political bodies. Revolutionary organisations constantly risk falling back into patterns of political representation on the one hand, and embracing the unrepresentable conditions for transformation as such on the other. Thus the task of Chapter 3 is to avoid both of these dangers and propose a theory of political participation drawn from Deleuze and Guattari's concept of 'consistency' and the Zapatistas' participatory practice of 'leading by obeying' (*mandar obedeciendo*).

Notes

1. This is precisely why Deleuze cannot offer a theory of concrete political topology in *Difference and Repetition*.
2. 'By removing the abyss from between being and event, [Deleuze's] ontology opens the way for the *event of being* from within what presents itself in actual situations' (Egyed 2006: 83).
3. For example, what would it mean to 'affirm Difference in the state of permanent revolution' (Deleuze 1994: 53) without an analysis of how this same 'continual revolution' is also valorised by capitalist deterritorialisation and axiomatisation? Or, in *The Logic of Sense*, what would it mean to argue that '*Counter-actualisation* is revolutionary' (Egyed 2006: 83) without the warnings found in *A Thousand Plateaus* of 'self-destruction' and 'fascism' that temper the process of political transformation?
4.
   > First of all, it is necessary to point out that as far as its material is concerned, the event is not a miracle. What I mean is that what composes an event is always extracted from a situation, always related back to a singular multiplicity, to its state, to the language connected to it, etc. In fact if we want to avoid lapsing into an obscurantist theory of creation *ex nihilo*, we must accept that an event is nothing but a part of a given situation, nothing but a fragment of being. (Badiou 2004b: 98)

   > In other words, the issue of the singular assemblages of enunciation does not emerege *ex nihilo* from a chaotic reality: there are thousands of outlines, thousands of catalyzing elements, highly differentiated and capable of being articulated to one another or being engaged in a creative process, or entering into phenomena of implosion, self-destruction, or microfascism – which, even then, does not transform them into chaos. (Guattari 2008: 317)

5. Husserl proposes a similar notion in his theory of time consciousness. But this is not nearly radical enough since for Husserl time consciousness is immanent to something else outside time. What I am proposing instead is that revolutionary political events themselves establish new truly immanent space-times that do not transcend the matrix of political representation but are equally immanent to it. Here I am in agreement with Deleuze and Guattari when they say that Husserl discovers

   > the mole of the transcendent within immanence itself. Husserl conceives of immanence as that of the flux lived by subjectivity. But since all this pure and

even untamed lived does not belong completely to the self that represents it to itself, something transcendent is reestablished . . . first, in the form of an 'immanent or primordial transcendence' of a world populated by intentional objects; second, as the privileged transcendence of an intersubjective world populated by other selves; and third, as objective transcendence of an ideal world populated by cultural formations and the human community. (Deleuze and Guattari 1994: 48/46)

6. Deleuze and Guattari refer to *Anti-Oedipus* as a constructivist work only retroactively. *Anti-Oedipus* may have introduced the concept of schizoanalysis that Deleuze and Guattari equate to constructivism in *A Thousand Plateaus*, but *Anti-Oedipus* also lacks a fully developed theory of revolutionary 'consistency' and 'nomadism'. 'Desire has always been a constructivism,' Deleuze and Guattari say (Stivale 2004).

7. The concept of the future anterior is not present in *Difference and Repetition*.

8. 'It axiomatizes with one hand what it decodes with the other' (Deleuze and Guattari 1983: 294/247).

9. Absolute deterritorialisation, though, does not simply come after relative deterritorialisation. Rather, 'relative Deterritorialization itself requires an absolute for its operation' and 'conversely, absolute Deterritorialization necessarily proceeds by way of relative Deterritorialization, precisely because it is not transcendent' (Deleuze and Guattari 1987: 636/510).

10. Deleuze and Guattari are not referring to the merely historical phenomenon of fascism. Rather, they are extracting a concept from it strictly defined as a 'war machine of self abolition' that may apply to some historical situations in some ways and not in others. Nazi Germany was a totalitarian state with an impulse for war and national self-destruction (the murder of its own people and the liquidation of industry for the sake of the war effort). Nick Land thus misunderstands Deleuze and Guattari's concept of fascism when he asks 'does anyone think Nazism is like letting go?' (Land 1993: 76).

11. The meaning of this direct democracy is further developed in Chapter 3.

12. Like the revolutionary fascism of militant terrorist groups of the 1960s and 1970s: the Red Army Faction, the Weather Underground Organization and so on.

3

The Body Politic and the Process of Participation

It's not a question of worrying or of hoping for the best, but of finding new weapons.

(Deleuze 1995: 242/178)

Introduction

While the strategy of political prefiguration developed in Chapter 2 may have provided an account of how different types of political transformation occur within several different representational processes (coding, overcoding and axiomatisation), it remained radically insufficient for understanding how revolutionary prefigurative strategies, in particular, are able to cohere and distribute themselves into distinctly non-representational kinds of political bodies. How is it possible, for instance, to carry out and sustain the consequences of a non-representational revolution? Is there a new type of body politic that would no longer be predicated on the party-body of the nation-state, the market-body of capital, or the territorial-body of the vanguard? Under what conditions would such a political body operate? How might one determine the relative benefits or detriments of the practices within its domain? And how might we understand the efficacy of different forms of agency without the reflection, contemplation and communication of self-knowing (that is, representational) subjects?

This chapter answers these questions.[1] Non-representational revolutions, I argue, do not simply establish new conditions for political life based on a 'more just' sphere of political action whose foundational principles are controlled by political representatives.[2] Nor do such revolutions merely aim to establish counter-institutions, whose sole purpose is to undermine all forms of representation and await the possibility that something new, and hopefully better, may emerge. Rather, a non-representational revolutionary body politic is built and sustained through an expressive and participatory process whose founding conditions are constantly undergoing direct and

110

immanent transformation by the various practices and people who are affected by them to varying degrees.³

This chapter thus poses three responses to the problem of creating a new revolutionary body politic. I first argue that the return to revolution located in Deleuze, Guattari and the Zapatistas is not based on creating a new process of political representation, nor is it based on a mere rejection of all forms of representation as such. Secondly, I argue that, opposed to these two dangers of representation and anti-representation, the body politic of this return to revolution is defined instead by its participatory mutability: the degree to which its conditions are transformed by the participation of the elements and subjects affected by such conditions. I further argue that in order to understand the structure and function of participation in this revolutionary body politic we need to understand the unique relationship it articulates between three different dimensions of its political body: its conditions, elements and kinds of subjects. Representational, anti-representational and participatory political bodies each express a different type of relationship between these three dimensions. In order to develop a theory of a specifically revolutionary and participatory political body I draw on Deleuze and Guattari's concept of consistency, found in *A Thousand Plateaus* and *What Is Philosophy?*, but expand its application to the issue of revolutionary politics. Thirdly, I argue that the Zapatistas have created a similar revolutionary and participatory body politic based on what they call 'leading by obeying' (*mandar obedeciendo*). Together, Deleuze, Guattari and the Zapatistas create a strategy of revolutionary political participation.

I. The Body Politic

THE REPRESENTATIONAL BODY POLITIC

If the crisis of identity and representational politics poses such an enormous problem for us today, it is because identity has for so long provided the philosophical foundation for, and definition of, Western politics as such. With few exceptions, politics has aimed at securing bodies of collective 'capture' that ground and legitimate action through the presupposition of a political unity and identity of the governed: the identity of natural, ethnic or territorial bodies; the identity of God, king, social contract or modern state bodies; or the identity of the money-body of capital. While each of these bodies may be different in operation, each attempts to sustain a political

distribution that can classify and organise various political differences as different from something that stands in for or represents
people's desires in advance.

Representational political bodies are thus made possible, in these
cases, through the presupposition and subsequent repetition of an
identity in the grounding body itself. This representational body
thus establishes a political domain in advance of the differential
expressions that come to populate and repeat it, and whose political elements differentially represent and repeat the generality of this
prior domain. Each 'different' political element that strengthens or
weakens a given domain does so only in relation to the pre-given
criteria for their general equality and exchangeability. These processes of representation were discussed at length in Chapter 1 as the
body of the earth, the body of the state and the body of capital. Their
subjective formations are no exception. Subjects take place only
within the pre-given scope of these conditions and elements representing, recognising, reflecting and communicating to and between
themselves within the generally redundant parameters of a prior field
of shared identity. This unifying process allows conflicting differences to be held together and mediated by a territorially shared 'way
of life', a governmentally enforced system of 'rights/contracts' or a
profit-driven world 'market'. Self-consciousness, reason and subjectivity presuppose these political models of identity when thinking
represents to itself different choices, thoughts, voices and desires on
a pre-given plane of political organisation. For example, we are 'free'
to buy and sell, but we are not free to end private property.

We can even see this type of representational body politic at work
in the notion of vanguardism as it expresses: (1) the historical unity
and necessity of the relevant conditions of historico-political action:
the factory site, the class struggle, labour power and the overthrow of
the state; (2) the practical diversity of elements conditioned on aiding
or hindering this unified class struggle: 'how does x represent the class
struggle?', 'how does x repeat the identity of its body? Favourably?
Poorly?'; and (3) the unity of a revolutionary subjectivity, a prole-
tarian-consciousness of the real historical-material conditions and
the epistemological certitude of intervention: the seizer of the state
apparatus and the dictatorship of the working class. The vanguard
speaks for its class, as a historical identity determined in advance by
the science of political economy, just as democratically elected representatives speak for their citizenry, determined in advance by the
protection of rights, the tally of votes and so on, and money speaks

for the world's consumer desires, determined by a prior axiomatic conjunction of labour and capital. Political differences, according to the politics of representation, are always differences from the same and within the identical.

But there are three conditions of representational political bodies:

(1) Representational political bodies are necessarily exclusionary insofar as their founding principles are excluded from radical modification in the political sphere they constitute. For example, the institution of state law by definition cannot be a legal act in itself since there was no system of law that preceded its institution. The creation of a political domain based on the identity and sameness of its conditions is not only paradoxical, insofar as the creation of law is non-legal, it necessarily excludes certain people from political participation to the extent the state is unable to change its founding conditions of territorial inclusion.[4]

(2) Accordingly, if representational political bodies succeed in securing the evaluative criteria for relatively beneficial and detrimental political elements, they do so only on the precondition of a hierarchy of these elements, no matter what their egalitarian pretensions.[5] Since political differences are always different from the initial identity of their grounding body, elements more or less resemble its general measure of recognition: the filiation of its territory, the laws of its state, the market value of its capital.

(3) Finally, representational political bodies produce subjects of deliberation only by creating an inability for the subject itself to change what it is. The subject of identity is able to reason and deliberate on political actions and decisions only insofar as it presupposes the identity of an undifferentiated body that such decisions or actions are distinguished from. One is free to vote for x representative or y representative, but one is not free to have participatory democracy instead of representational democracy. The political subject then either asserts its positive freedom based on what it 'self-transparently' desires or asserts its negative freedom from others who would curtail such reflectively known desires. In either case the subject is allowed change or difference only on the precondition of the initial unchanging transparency of what it is and wants.[6]

THE ANTI-REPRESENTATIONAL BODY POLITIC

In the wake of the above crisis of representation and the so-called death of the liberal subject, political counter-institutions and strategies based on the rejection of all forms of representation have proliferated. Instead of positing identity as primary, and organising political bodies based on their accurate representation of this identity, anti-representational political bodies presuppose difference as primary, and affirm it as a political condition radically exterior to all pre-given identities. Instead of political differences being different *from* a prior identity, they are instead conceived of as different *in-themselves*. Rather than the violent establishment of an exclusionary political domain posited in advance of the different political elements that would come to populate it, anti-representational political bodies leave the political domain radically open to potential political transformations and peoples yet 'to come'. Revolution can thus be reconceived as a 'becoming revolutionary without the [actual] revolution' (Read 2009: 98).

The anti-representational body politic thus understands difference-in-itself as the condition for all political transformation. 'The political' is thus perpetually open to all those who potentially participate in its non-exclusive community: the community of singularities. The various different political elements that would then assay the strengths and weaknesses, the health and dangers of this community, without an identity or representational condition to be defined against hierarchically, are instead understood as so many heterogeneous elements. All of these elements are equally tied to one another in nested relations that at each level signal the impossibility of political closure and open us up to the potentiality of further transformation.

Instead of subjective transformations taking place solely within the pre-given identity-political domains of territorial, state and capitalist representation, the subject itself is, according to this body politic, part of a larger 'undefined work of freedom' (Foucault 1984: 46): its own transformation beyond 'self-evident' desires *for* something or *from* something. Rather than forming a unified plane on which to evaluate, deliberate and decide different political actions, the differential subject is a fragmented, partial and impersonal process of becoming, composed of multiple drives and conflicting desires that produce the subject more as an effect or partial remainder than as a unified 'self'.

But how is one to put into practice a politics of 'the potentiality of transformation as such'? Or is it the case, as Thomas McCarthy and others have argued (McCarthy 1991; Fraser 1989), that the politics of difference has only a critical function *contra* the politics of identity and no coherent alternative of its own? There are thus three dangers of the anti-representational body politic:

(1) Since transformation as such cannot be delimited by any political domain in particular, it risks affirming an ambivalent condition for participation. Anything can happen. A political commitment to ambivalence, however, does not seem very different from the latent cynicism already pervading capitalist social life (Deleuze and Guattari 1983: 266–7/225).

(2) Anti-representational political bodies may also be able to avoid the great hierarchical 'chain of being' assumed by a politics of elements more or less identical to their original condition, but only at the cost of a latent hierarchy of 'transformative potential' among the elements and the potential they express. While one may affirm their 'equality' qua elements that may become otherwise than they are, it is also the case that in the particularity of their concrete being, some elements undergo transformation more or less so than others. This is roughly the criticism that Badiou, originally in *Deleuze: The Clamor of Being*, levelled against Deleuze's pre-constructivist works *Difference and Repetition* and *The Logic of Sense*, and that Peter Hallward and Slavoj Žižek have taken up in their own monographs against Deleuze (also citing, almost exclusively, Deleuze's pre-constructivist works).[7]

(3) Similarly, the anti-representational body politic avoids the static character of the representational subject who can never change the nature of its 'self', but only by diffusing the self into an endless multiplicity of impersonal drives: a self in perpetual transformation. But without a pre-given unity of subjectivity, how do agents/multiplicities deliberate between and distinguish between different political decisions? The radically ambivalent and unlocalisable processes of subjective potentiality seem then to have nothing to contribute to an analysis of the basic function of participatory democracy at the core of many contemporary resistance movements (see Notes from Nowhere 2003). Insofar as a theory of subjectivity is defined only by its potential for transformation, it is stuck in a kind of paralysis of endless potential change no less disempowering than the politics of identity. Or as Hallward frames this criticism against Deleuze, 'he abandons the decisive subject in favor of our more immediate subjection to the imperative of creative life' (2006: 163).

II. The Revolutionary Body Politic

Given the challenge of these problems, I argue instead in this next section that the return to revolution influenced by Deleuze and

Guattari can be defined by its creation of a participatory political body. By participatory political body I mean a set of political practices constitutive of a social order that incorporates a maximal degree of mutual and conflictual transformation. A participatory body politic is a social order that both transforms the subjects[8] and objects that constitute it and is equally transformed by them. It is a new kind of participatory democracy or political self-management.[9]

In order to further develop the strategy of participation, in this section I draw on the concept of consistency in Deleuze and Guattari's political philosophy and expand its implications for revolutionary politics. I find Deleuze and Guattari's concept of consistency particularly useful because it allows us to conceive of a non-representational social organisation based on more than the mere rejection of representation. Even as early as *Difference and Repetition* Deleuze had formulated a similar philosophical concept of self-management. 'We remain slaves', Deleuze says, 'so long as we do not control the problems themselves, so long as we do not possess a right to the problems, to a participation in and management of the problems' (Deleuze 1994: 206/158). It is, however, not until *A Thousand Plateaus* and *What Is Philosophy?* that the theory of consistency is fully developed and politicised. But even then it is not developed as a theory of a revolutionary body politic. The aim of this section is thus to expand this concept in order to develop such a theory.

But consistency is not just another word for static predictability; it is precisely the opposite. A revolutionary body politic is consistent insofar as it (1) sustains a constructive rupture or break from the intersection of representational processes; (2) connects or consolidates a block of collective practices or capacities for action that have all been similarly deterritorialised; and (3) is continually transformed by the various elements and agents that compose it. Thus, what makes a revolutionary body politic consistent is precisely its participatory mutability around a locally determinate event. While the first of these three characteristics was argued for at length in Chapter 2, the last two will be argued in the present section, drawing on the work of Deleuze and Guattari. In particular, I draw on their concept of consistency and its three component concepts – the abstract machine, the concrete assemblage and the machinic persona – to understand how a non-representational political body functions.[10]

Other scholars of radical political theory have also posed the problem of defining a distinctly non-representational social order. Revolutionary politics requires, according to Bruno Bosteels, a 'consistency and durability' (2005a: 594), that is, 'the putting to work of an event' (2004: 104), based on a careful 'study [of] the consequences of an event within the situation, not [the] elevat[ion of] the event into a wholly other dimension beyond being' (2004: 104). Or, as Alberto Toscano frames it, to 'articulate what the parameters and modalities for the consistency of reality may be, [and] how this consistency might find itself regulated and stabilised' (Toscano 2004: 215), without, that is, being represented. Here, I am certainly in agreement with Bosteels and Toscano, except that I think we can locate such a theory in Deleuze and Guattari.[11]

Even Antonio Negri is sympathetic to such a task. In an interview with Cesare Casarino, Negri claims that Deleuze's political philosophy is still unable to translate the ontological theory of the event, as the revolutionary potentiality of transformation, into 'a logic of collective action' (Casarino and Negri 2004: 157) that would 'adequately describe the positive recomposition of power' (2004: 152). 'In Deleuze', Negri says,

> – and even in his last works – there is always a sense of astonished stupor in the face of Singularity, there is always an inability to translate the ontological Event into a prefiguration or schematism of reason, into a constitution, or even into a merely virtual constitution that would nonetheless contain a constructive element. There is always surprise and chance. (2004: 155)

For Negri, the question remains, 'how can we translate the ontological substratum into logical dimensions?' (155), that is, into 'the discovery of the logic of collective actions, the constitution of such a logic in that moment of Singularity' (157).

Whether Negri's criticisms are fair to Deleuze or not, his concerns articulate well the aim and challenge of the present work, and in particular this chapter; that is, to advance, in spite of certain limitations in Deleuze and Guattari's political philosophy and those of their critics, a 'logic of collective action' or consistency drawn from their political philosophy and placed alongside the revolutionary practices of Zapatismo. The aim of this is to discover an alternative political practice to the representational politics of territory, state and capital, as well as the merely anti-representational politics of speculative or spontaneous leftism (see Bosteels 2005b). In order to develop the concept of what I am calling a revolutionary body politic, I examine each of its constitutive components in turn: (1) the *conditions* under which this body politic emerges and determines who counts as part of it; (2) the distribution of concrete *elements* that express and constitute its body; and (3) the kinds of *subjects* who act and transform its body. Or, as Deleuze and Guattari name these components, the abstract machine, the concrete assemblage and the machinic persona.

THE REVOLUTIONARY ABSTRACT MACHINE

What are the conditions under which a revolutionary political body can emerge and sustain itself? Is there such a thing as a body politic that would no longer be conditioned by the old models of territorial, state and capitalist representation?

In this section I propose an alternative kind of political condition that is neither limited, representational, nor merely open, but is flexibly open and transformable by its membership. This kind of determinate but flexible political condition for inclusion in a body politic is what Deleuze and Guattari call a revolutionary abstract machine. A revolutionary abstract machine, they say, is characterised by four distinct features, each of which I argue can help us understand the conditions for a revolutionary body politic.

(1) A Revolutionary Abstract Machine is Both Singular and Absolute

> In historical phenomena such as the revolution of 1789, the Commune, the revolution of 1917, there is always one part of the event that is irreducible to any social determinism, or to causal chains. Historians are not very fond of this point: they restore causality after the fact. Yet the event itself is a splitting off from [*décrochage*], a breaking with causality; it is a bifurcation, a lawless deviation, an unstable condition that opens up a new field of the possible. (Deleuze 2006: 215/233)

The emergence of the conditions for a revolutionary body politic, according to Deleuze and Guattari, do not resemble any recognisable legal or legitimate thing within the present state of affairs. In this sense the conditions for a revolutionary body politic mark a 'singular' event. As an abstract machine this condition is 'free from all normal or normative causalities' deduced or derived from the known possibilities of what a political body is capable of doing. A revolutionary body politic does not just establish another cultural identity, subject of rights or commodity in circulation, it creates a new condition for inclusion that is both contingent and heterogeneous to the topology of representational power. But this new condition is not the

118

mere rejection of all conditionality as such. Rather, the revolutionary abstract machine creates a unique and '*unstable condition* that opens up a new field of the possible' (Deleuze 2006: 215/233) alongside the state of affairs that supports a whole 'series of amplified instabilities and fluctuations' (Deleuze and Guattari 1987: 127/100) that constitute the localised struggle of the body politic itself. Insofar as Lenin, the Paris Commune and May 1968 were all contingent and heterogeneous ruptures in the processes of political representation, that is, singular, Deleuze and Guattari argue that they were all, to some degree, revolutionary abstract machines.

But the condition for a revolution works like an abstract machine not only in the sense that it is singular, but also in the sense that it is the self-referential basis by which the body politic legitimates its own existence. Without reference to a transcendent political power (God, social contract, natural right, profit and so on) to justify its emergence, the condition for a revolutionary body refers only to itself as the guarantor of its own existence and must be continually reaffirmed. 'As concept and as event,' Deleuze and Guattari say, 'revolution is self-referential or enjoys a self-positing [*auto-référentielle ou jouit d'une auto-position*] that enables it to be apprehended in an immanent enthusiasm without anything in states of affairs or lived experience being able to tone it down' (1994: 97/101). While representational political bodies stand in for the unity of their social bodies, revolutionary political conditions, as contingent and self-referential, change in nature each time a new kind of element or agency effects a 'redeployment' of them, like a perpetually remade political feedback loop.[12] 'The possible', contrary to the identical, Deleuze says, 'does not pre-exist, it is created by the event. It is a matter of life. The event creates a new existence, it produces a new subjectivity (new relations with the body, with time, sexuality, the immediate surroundings, with culture, work)' (2006: 216/234).

But the condition for a revolutionary body politic is also 'a *local absolute*'; that is, 'an absolute that is manifested locally, and engendered in a series of local operations of varying orientations', as Deleuze and Guattari say of revolutionary abstract machines. It is a singular-universal (1987: 474/382) or point of 'absolute survey' [*survol absolu*] (1994: 96/100) whose origins are contingent and local but whose consequences are potentially infinite. As such, a revolutionary body politic is radically inclusive of anyone who wants to participate under its mutable and reinterpretable conditions, but only insofar as such participation changes the nature of the entire assemblage.[13] The absolute of this abstract machine, then, should not be confused with the absolutes or universals of identity that remain the same (and pre-given) while only adding on an increasing number of axioms or elements to be represented as in representational democracies and market economies. Rather, when Deleuze and Guattari speak of a 'becoming-everybody/everything' [*devenir tout le monde*] of revolution (1987: 588/470), what this means is that everybody and everything may participate in an effectuation and transformation of a revolution to the extent that they are also transformed by it and as they 'respond to the demands of the event' (Deleuze 2006: 216/234).

Thus, the condition for participation in a revolutionary body politic is like an abstract machine in the sense that it is singular, self-referential, inclusive and absolute. Its contingent and local emergence can, with only itself as its support, bring about inclusive and infinite consequences without representation or pre-given criteria or exclusion like a territory, state or market and so on. A condition for participation thus does not merely allow for the possibility that everyone may become other than they are, it names a singular and absolute condition under which everyone can participate in and shape the creation of another world alongside the old. It 'posit[s] revolution as a plane of immanence,' Deleuze and Guattari say, 'infinite movement and absolute survey, but [only] to the extent that [its] features connect up with what is real here and now in the struggle against capitalism, relaunching new struggles whenever the earlier one is betrayed' (1994: 96/100).

(2) A Revolutionary Abstract Machine is the 'Degree Zero' of its Body Politic

The condition of a revolutionary body politic, or what Deleuze and Guattari call a revolutionary abstract machine, also marks the most minimal degree of existence within the body politic. In the sense that an emerging revolutionary condition or event is singular, it is not representable within the normal state of affairs. Because of this relative invisibility Deleuze and Guattari say that such an abstract machine marks a 'degree zero' (1987: 190/157) or is the 'most deterritorialized element' in the political arrangement (1987: 177/142). But this condition does not indicate a mere potential for transformation as such that cannot be realised in any particular transformation or whose realisations are only betrayals or ironies. This 'zero degree' bears a particular name such that a political field can begin to gain consistency around it, creating a 'vortex' or site of 'circulating reference' (Latour 1999), like the name of 'Lenin' or the 'Paris Commune' and so on.

Political consistency, according to Deleuze and Guattari, thus not only requires a self-referential condition for its beginning, but it also requires this beginning point to bear some sort of marker to indicate its non-appearance from the perspective of the dominant political arrangement of laws and markets. Further, the abstract machine is also invisible from within its own political arrangement. No one knows entirely what it is or what it is capable of doing. This is why Deleuze and Guattari call it an 'abstract' machine. A revolutionary condition is similarly 'abstract' in the sense that it does not appear as a concrete 'thing'. May 1968 was not a thing. From the perspective of the state, May 1968 did not mark the necessity of a new non-statist, non-capitalist politics. It was a problem to be resolved into the state. Even from the perspective of those who were committed to the event, May 1968 was not a thing that ever appeared in full light. It was a real and contested moment whose name brought together a host of previously marginalised political desires. It is in this sense that Deleuze and Guattari say that the abstract machine is that 'which at every instant causes the given to be given, in this or that state, at this or that moment. But . . . itself is not given' (1987: 324/265), not, however, as in 'a dream, something that is not realized or that is only realized by betraying itself', but rather as a 'Real-Abstract . . . that is neither undifferentiated nor transcendent (1987: 179/142).

(3) A Revolutionary Abstract Machine Supports a Conjunction of Concrete Elements

So far I have argued that the conditions of sustaining a revolutionary political body, following Deleuze and Guattari's theory of the consistent abstract machine, are (1) that its emergence be contingent and heterogeneous to all forms of political representation; (2) that it legitimate its emergence with reference only to itself; and (3) that it indicate a degree of real non-appearance within the concrete situation.[14] But the abstract machine of a consistent revolutionary body also supports a 'conjunction, combination, and continuum' of all the concrete 'degrees of deterritorialisation'[15] that it conditions.[16] An abstract machine does not represent the concrete elements or degrees of deterritorialisation that it conditions. It does not stand in for or speak for them, nor does it indicate their pure becoming. Rather, the abstract machine has no existence independent of the concrete degrees of positive deterritorialisation that it combines together. The abstract machine acts not as a cause but as an attractor or horizon around which concrete actions and agents circulate, contest and transform each other.[17] Where there is a whole swarm of heterogeneous political grievances, problems and crises in power (kinds of deterritorialised elements), a revolutionary political body, like an abstract machine, acts as a mobile and flexible point or proper name like 'Zapatismo', 'Peoples' Global Action' or 'Occupy', around which diverse groups and grievances can coalesce and take collective action.

As such, Deleuze and Guattari say, the abstract machine 'causes the other element[s it conditions] to cross a threshold enabling a conjunction of their respective deterritorializations, a shared acceleration. This is the abstract machine's absolute, positive deterritorialization' (1987: 177/142). A conjunction of deterritorialisation for Deleuze and Guattari simply means an intercalation or 'ordering without hierarchy' of heterogeneous elements within a consistent political arrangement (1994: 87/90).[18] It is what allows radically heterogeneous political elements to all be equally constitutive of an event even if that event is changed by this variable constitution. Similarly, what revolutionary practices have 'in common' is only their relative differentiation from the condition they continue to transform. The conjunction of a revolutionary condition, like an abstract machine, is thus what 'transforms the respective indexes into absolute values' (Deleuze and Guattari 1987: 91/71) and gives multiple concrete elements a specific field of immanent practice without external reference to territory, state or capital. A revolutionary body politic does not represent anything, it acts as a mutable and contested marker around which various deterritorialised elements combine and take on consistency.

(4) A Revolutionary Abstract Machine has a Proper Name and Date

Finally, the condition for a revolutionary body politic has a proper name and date that acts as a shared and contested common ground for diverse struggles. We can see this in Deleuze and Guattari's description of this kind of abstract machine:

> The abstract machine is always singular, designated by the proper name of a group or individual, while the assemblage of enunciation is always collective, in the individual as in the group. The Lenin abstract machine, and the Bolshevik collective assemblage. (1987: 127/100)

And, further,

> Abstract, singular, and creative, here and now, real yet nonconcrete, actual yet noneffectuated – that is why abstract machines are dated and named (the Einstein abstract machine, the Webern abstract machine, but also the Galileo, the Bach, or the Beethoven, etc.). (1987: 637/511)

The abstract machine, according to Deleuze and Guattari, is an 'asignifying proper name' [*noms propres asignifiants*] (1987: 40/28) that works within a logic of collective action to 'designate something that is of the order of the event, of becoming or of the haecceity' (1987: 322–3/264), like the name of a military operation or the name of a hurricane. Proper names do not 'represent' or stand in for something else; they are instead the markers of a real yet non-concrete, actual yet non-effectuated event whose being is nothing more than all of the affects, elements and agencies that constitute it. 'The theory of proper names should not be conceived of in terms of representation; it refers instead to the class of "effects"', Deleuze and Guattari say, 'that are not a mere dependence on causes, but the occupation of a domain, and the operation of a system of signs' (1983: 103/86).

This is why Deleuze and Guattari write *A Thousand Plateaus* as a series of abstract machines, planes or plateaus instead of chapters; each chapter/plateau is given a name, a date and an image or placard at the beginning to mark its distribution of 'asignification'. The subsequent pages of the plateau are then the concrete assemblages that effectuate this proper name. But all this only raises the question of how such a real non-concrete revolutionary machine is concretely effectuated.

THE REVOLUTIONARY CONCRETE MACHINIC ASSEMBLAGE

In the previous section I showed how it is possible to conceive of a political condition for a revolutionary body politic that is based on neither representation nor anti-representation but upon what Deleuze and Guattari call consistency, and what I am arguing is part of a participatory political strategy. If we are to truly return to the concept of revolution today, the conditions of a revolutionary body politic can no longer be the static and relatively immutable ones of territorial borders, contracts and rights of the sovereign state, or even the unpredictable fluctuations of the world market. Nor should we simply reject all political conditions outright. Rather, what I am proposing is that we conceive of an alternative social order or revolutionary body politic based on a maximum degree of feedback and mutual transformation between the conditions, elements and agencies that constitute it. This body would not be constrained by representation (that often blocks the direct transformation of political conditions when one person stands in for another) because a consistent body politic is open to direct transformation by the people. On the other hand, this body is also not so open and mutable that it becomes everything and thus ambivalent. In other words, political consistency is more mutable than representation but less mutable than a political ontology of difference-in-itself.

Thus in order to understand how a revolutionary body politic works we need to understand not only how its conditions work but also how the concrete elements that articulate and realise these conditions work. This is the task of the present section. By 'elements' I mean all the actions, weapons, tools, interventions, slogans, demands and occupations that come together to create a revolutionary sequence. A revolutionary body politic has no existence independent of these concrete deployments.

Given the previously argued dangers confronting representational and anti-representational body politics, I propose instead in this section an alternative concept of political elements that is non-hierarchical but is still ordered and mutually transformative of the body politic. This kind of determinate but flexible political effectuation in a body politic is what Deleuze and Guattari call a revolutionary concrete assemblage. A revolutionary concrete assemblage, they say, is characterised by three distinct features, each of which I argue can help us understand the elements of a revolutionary body politic.

(1) A Revolutionary Concrete Assemblage Effectuates an Abstract Machine

A revolutionary body politic has a real but abstract condition that does not appear as a concrete thing within the dominant matrix of political power or even within the revolutionary body itself. Thus, what still needs to be explained is how a revolutionary body politic is effectuated in a variety of different concrete expressions (practices, slogans, actions, institutions and so on). But these concrete effectuations are not ordered in a hierarchy with either an identity (territory, state or market) at the top or a radical difference at the bottom. Rather, following Deleuze and Guattari, the concrete elements that effectuate a revolutionary condition are deployed in various degrees of intensity that react back on their own conditions for effectua-

tion. Thus the body politic is always undergoing a continual transformation: a participatory feedback loop. But we should not let
this feedback loop obscure the difference between the abstract and
concrete machinic assemblage. 'The *machinic assemblage*', Deleuze
and Guattari say, 'is something entirely different from the abstract
machine.' But there is still a 'coadaptation' (1987: 91/71) or reciprocal presupposition of the two (1994: 74/77) that allows for an
acentered and non-hierarchical, participatory transformation (1987:
31–2/21).

> In every respect, machinic assemblages *effectuate* the abstract machine
> insofar as it is developed on the plane of consistency or enveloped in a
> stratum. The most important problem of all: given a certain machinic
> assemblage, what is its relation of effectuation with the abstract machine?
> How does it effectuate it, with what adequation? Classify assemblages.
> (Deleuze and Guattari 1987: 91/71)

It is never possible to decide once and for all, or in advance, given a
certain machinic assemblage, who is and who is not an ally or enemy
of the revolution or what relation they have to the abstract machine.
This is because a revolutionary political body is continually undergoing a transformation in its abstract condition and its concrete elements, hence Deleuze and Guattari's insistence that determining their
relationship is the most important problem of all. It is a question that
must be continually answered, transformed and reanswered. What
are the aims of the revolution in the short term, mid term and long
term? How should we effectuate it in a certain situation? What supports the revolution, what is hindering it and what is irrelevant to it?

Unlike 'arbitrary or inconsistent [elements]', Deleuze and Guattari
say, '[that] do not hold up for an instant', 'concrete assemblages
[are] like the configurations of a machine' that give it its degrees of
consistency (1994: 39/36). 'The plane [of immanence]' then 'is the
abstract machine of which these assemblages are the working parts'
(1994: 39/36). To expand this concept to revolutionary praxis, the
concrete elements of a revolutionary political body like its slogans,
demonstrations, demands, actions and occupations are transformed
by their condition no less than they transform that condition.[19] Thus,
they cannot be understood as 'normative' or 'goal-driven' effectuations that merely follow out prescriptive conditions (laws, demands
for profit and so on). But neither should such mutual transformations
be mistaken for a kind of pragmatic 'revisionism' where a hypothesis is 'tested', found to work or not work, and then rationally (or

otherwise) revised accordingly, thus grounding a narrative of political 'progress'.[20]

Rather, the politics of consistency is revolutionary in the sense that instead of applying solutions to pre-given problems (how to make sure everyone is represented fairly in a presupposed state, for example), or simply affirming that 'other problems are possible', particular problems are themselves transformed directly by those who effectuate them and who are affected by them. 'When people demand to formulate their problems themselves', Deleuze and Guattari say, 'and to determine at least the particular conditions under which they can receive a more general solution', there is a politics of consistency: a direct participation without representation or mediation (1987: 588/471). This kind of participation and self-management thus offers a political alternative absolutely incompatible with territorial hierarchies based on ethnic lineage, state hierarchies (both liberal and socialist) based on sovereign right, and capitalist hierarchies based on wealth and private property.

(2) A Revolutionary Concrete Assemblage Creates an Endoconsistency

A revolutionary body politic marks a break with representational power and creates an evental condition that combines a new set of concrete practices. These practices then turn back on and transform their condition in a social order of participatory feedback. But according to Deleuze and Guattari, these machinic assemblages, or what I am arguing are the concrete practices of a revolutionary body, also create an internal consistency of their own within this revolutionary body. How do we determine which concrete practices are more or less part of the same struggle, sequence, alliance and so on? And in what sense do they function in a political 'ordering without hierarchy' or an 'equality without homogenization', as Deleuze and Guattari say?

The concrete machinic assemblage, according to Deleuze and Guattari, has an internal or endoconsistency that 'renders components inseparable within itself'. 'There is', they say, 'an area ab that belongs to both a and b, where a and b "become" indiscernible. These zones, thresholds, or becomings, this inseparability defines the internal consistency' of the arrangement (Deleuze and Guattari 1994: 25/20). In terms of a revolutionary political body, this simply means that its concrete practices are dependent and inseparable in varying relations and to greater or lesser degrees. Thus, no concrete practice

126

acts independently without affecting certain others. Since, as was previously argued, there is no transcendent or external guarantee in historical necessity, God, reason, the state and so on for the legitimacy of such a revolutionary body, and the abstract machine has no existence outside its concrete effectuations, then these concrete effectuations are bound to the body politic only by their immanent relationship: their internal consistency. 'As fragmentary totalities', Deleuze and Guattari say, concrete machines 'are not even the pieces of a puzzle, for their irregular contours do not correspond to each other'. They do, however, 'form a wall, but it is a dry-stone wall, and everything holds together only along diverging lines' (Deleuze and Guattari 1994: 28/23). Accordingly, Deleuze and Guattari say, the concrete machine 'has no reference; it is self-referential; it posits itself and its object at the same time as it is created' (1994: 27/22).

It is one thing to evade the hierarchy of representational political bodies by creating an inseparability, becoming or generic equality of elements within a political event, but such an affirmation, while important, is not sufficient for elucidating the ordered relationship between such elements. Similarly, within a revolutionary political body not all of its concrete practices will be equally important. Political revolution may be 'a question *of consistency*: the "holding together" of heterogeneous elements' but it is also a question of creating a variable social order (Deleuze and Guattari 1987: 398/323).

Thus, Deleuze and Guattari say of the concrete assemblage that it is 'a synthesis of disparate elements, defined only by a degree of consistency that makes it possible to distinguish the disparate elements constituting that aggregate (discernibility)' (1987: 424/344). These discernible degrees or 'individuals' can then 'enter into composition with other degrees, other intensities, to form another individual' (1987: 310/253), all of which are arranged 'according to this or that degree of deterritorialization' (1987: 127/100), whose orderings can be consistently discerned within the arrangement (1994: 87/90). The more positively deterritorialised or differentiated a concrete element is, the less strongly it appears or consists in the political arrangement and the closer to the zero degree or abstract machine it becomes. The less deterritorialised it is, the more strongly it appears and consists in the dominant political arrangement and the closer it comes to creating a political unity.[21] Similarly, a revolutionary body politic creates a non-hierarchical order in the sense that it is not a causal order, or an order of power over anyone or anything, but in the sense that some practices in the social body are more important or are at greater risk of co-optation by power. A revolutionary body aims to increase its degrees of deterritorialisation against power while also connecting, sustaining and defending the greater degrees that have already been liberated.

These degrees of deterritorialised consistency, according to Deleuze and Guattari, are then bounded by two limits: a pessimal threshold, or degree zero, after which consistency is broken down or dissipated into inconsistency; and a maximal limit, after which it is exploded or totalised under something else like a form of representation. In between inconsistency and representation there is thus the consistency of degrees of positive deterritorialisation. Just as a tick's power, Deleuze and Guattari say, is 'bounded by two limits: the optimal limit of the feast after which it dies, and the pessimal limit of the fast as it waits', there is a minimal threshold of revolution where popular support, enthusiasm or commitment wane to such a degree that its consistency is lost, and there is a maximal limit after which it becomes deterritorialised into the party or state apparatus (Deleuze and Guattari 1987: 314/257). The aim of a revolutionary consistency is accordingly to occupy and populate the middle with new elements, institutions and agencies. There is thus a non-hierarchical equality of elements (*qua* effectuations of the event) and a non-homogeneous diversity of elements (*qua* the degree to which they consist in an arrangement). Elements are not ranked by how they affirm a presupposed identity or difference-in-itself, but are locally and non-hierarchically ordered to the extent that they create a strong or weak consistency of a specific event.

(3) A Revolutionary Concrete Assemblage Creates an Exoconsistency

A revolutionary political body not only creates an internal consistency of its concrete practices but also creates an external consistency that connects it to other elements outside itself. Deleuze and Guattari call this the exoconsistency of the concrete assemblage:

> Its internal neighborhood or consistency is secured by the connection of its components in zones of indiscernibility; its external neighborhood or exoconsistency is secured by the bridges thrown from one [machine] to another when the components of one of them are saturated . . . [but] we can no longer add or withdraw a component without changing the nature of the [assemblage]. (1994: 87/90)

Similarly, a revolutionary body politic of concrete practices not only includes those who participate in its internal transformation but also aims to include others not already part of the struggle. That is, revolution is both inclusive and expansive. It has the capacity for internal transformation and external growth beyond its local construction.

THE REVOLUTIONARY POLITICAL PERSONA

So far I have argued that we use Deleuze and Guattari's concept of consistency, composed of an abstract machine and concrete assemblage, to understand the participatory process that forms the basis of a revolutionary political body distinct from both representational and anti-representational bodies politic. But we have not yet seen how Deleuze and Guattari's concept of personae can be expanded from its limited use in *What Is Philosophy?* and become relevant for revolutionary praxis. This is the task of the present section.

   The concept of a revolutionary subject poses two problems. On the one hand, the subject can be understood as a unified and identical basis from which to exercise a freedom of expression or a freedom from domination. The problem was that such a subject itself cannot change what it is, only act for or against something via the pre-given self of contemplation modelled after various forms of political representation (territory, state, capital).[22] On the other hand, the subject can be understood as a capacity for the transformation of subjectivity as such. But this notion allows for subjectivity only by dispersing its agency into a pure potentiality. In what follows I would like to propose instead a third theory of revolutionary subjectivity drawn from Deleuze and Guattari's concept of conceptual personae.[23]

   Against Peter Hallward's claim that Deleuze and Guattari's concept of subjectivity is 'derivative' or 'dissolved into the imperative of creativity as such' (2006: 163), I argue instead that by expanding their concept of the persona we can articulate a theory of revolutionary subjectivity defined by the 'intervention of a local operator' who connects the conditions of a revolutionary body to its concrete consequences (Deleuze and Guattari 1994: 73/75). Personae are not primarily subjects of experience, rational reflection, discourse, representation or difference/creativity-in-itself (although these can certainly be kinds of subjectivity). They do not transcend political bodies in any way. Rather, they are subjects of and within a political body. They function as the internal process of connection between its abstract conditions and concrete effectuations. A persona, Deleuze and Guattari say, is characterised by three distinct features, each of which I argue can help us understand this new form of revolutionary subjectivity.[24]

(1) A Revolutionary Persona Makes an Immanent Intervention in the Body Politic

A revolutionary body politic is a continually transformed condition and set of concrete practices, but it is the revolutionary subject that connects the two together. The connection between a revolutionary condition and its consequences, however, is a conflictual process because, as Deleuze and Guattari say of personae,

> There are types of persona according to the possibilities of even their hostile encounters on the same plane and in a group. But it is often diffi-cult to determine if it is the same group, the same type, or the same family. (1994: 74/77)

Even within the same body politic there are different types of perso-nae or subjects who contest the order and consequences of its terri-tories, deterritorialisations and reterritorialisations in the social field. These form, Deleuze and Guattari say,

> inextricable knots in which the three movements are mixed up so that, in order to disentangle them, we have to diagnose real types or personae. The merchant buys in a territory, deterritorializes products into com-modities, and is reterritorialized on commercial circuits. In capitalism, capital or property is deterritorialized, ceases to be landed, and is reter-ritorialized on the means of production; whereas labor becomes 'abstract' labor, reterritorialized in wages: this is why Marx not only speaks of capital and labor but feels the need to draw up some true psychosocial types, both antipathetic and sympathetic: the capitalist, the proletarian. (1994: 66–7/68)

According to Deleuze and Guattari, the personae that Marx draws up are not self-knowing subjects, independent from the processes of deterritorialisation and reterritorialisation, who decide what is beneficial or harmful as such outside of larger social bodies. Nor are they entirely absorbed into the pure processes of transformation. Rather, the 'proletarian' and the 'capitalist' are specific personae or '"terminals" of a whole group of social assemblages' that locate, distinguish and connect various political practices to and through the social body (Guattari 2008: 371). That is, their subjectivity is not essentially conscious, rational, emotional, embodied, experiential or grounded in any other transcendental monolith. Rather, personae exist immanent to their social body.

Expanding on Deleuze and Guattari's example of Marxism, we can see the use of this notion for understanding a distinctly revolu-tionary kind of subjectivity. The political persona of the 'proletarian' is Marx's subject of revolutionary praxis. Passing back and forth between the specific (maximally deterritorialised) abstract machine of 'communism' and locating the (deterritorialised degrees) of concrete 'worker-assemblages' composed of various slogans, direct actions, factory reclamations and self-management efforts is the persona of the 'proletarian'. Without reflection, contemplation or communication, a revolutionary subjectivity intervenes within a process of political representation and connects degrees of deter-ritorialised labour to each other (self-management) while warding off the reterritorialisations of private property and capital. Thus the role of political personae, according to Deleuze and Guattari, is to 'make perceptible, in the most insignificant or most important circumstances, the formation of territories, the vectors of deterritori-alization, and the process of reterritorialization' (1994: 66–7/68). A political persona is thus revolutionary insofar as it determines where a political body forms territories, deterritorialises those territories, connects those deterritorialised elements to each other, and avoids reterritorialisation by various forms of political representation.

Like a 'runner, or intercessor' (1994: 62/64), Deleuze and Guattari say, the 'persona is needed to relate concepts on the plane, just as the plane itself needs to be laid out' (1994: 73/75–6). 'But these two operations do not merge in the persona, which itself appears as a distinct operator' (1994: 73/76). Thus, far from being dissolved into an affirmation of pure transformation (or negative deterritorialisa-tion), as Peter Hallward has suggested of Deleuze's earlier theory of agency, Deleuze and Guattari's theory of political personae is based on two specific interventions: the laying out of an abstract machine, and the connection of it to the concrete machines that populate it.

Herein lies the difficulty: one cannot have a revolutionary subjec-tivity without a revolution, but one cannot have a revolution without subjects that bring it about. Deleuze and Guattari's solution to this problem, however, is to suggest that both interventions occur simul-taneously in the mutual presupposition of the other; problem and solution are co-given, they say (1994: 75/78, 79/82). 'Sometimes', Deleuze and Guattari claim, 'the persona seems to precede the plane, sometimes to come after it – that is, it appears twice; it intervenes twice' (1994: 73/75). On the one hand, the political persona extracts the determinations of the abstract machine 'as if it seizes a handful of dice from chance so as to throw them on the table', and on the other hand it establishes a correspondence between each throw of the dice and the components that occupy this or that region of the table (the concrete assemblages) (Deleuze and Guattari 1994: 73/75). Since, for Deleuze and Guattari, 'there are only immanent criteria' in revolutions, the political personae of these movements are also immanent to these criteria in their expression and determination of them (1994: 72/74).

The persona's dedication to these mutually determining criteria thus forms the structure of political 'commitment' or 'belief'. 'Personae concern those who believe in the world,' Deleuze and Guattari say, not in the existence of the world as a thing but in its particular possibilities and intensities, so as once again to give birth to new modes of existence (1994: 72/74). In 'Control and Becoming', an interview with Deleuze, Antonio Negri asks Deleuze what he thinks the political consequences of his conception of the subject will be for a new militant pragmatism. Deleuze responds by saying, 'What we most lack is a belief in the world, we've quite lost the world, it's been taken from us. If you believe in the world you precipitate events, however inconspicuous, that elude control, you engender new space-times however small their surface or volume' (1995: 239/176). Political personae are exactly this immanent belief in a new world that is both 'now-here', in the concrete machines used to effectuate the abstract machine, and 'no-where', in the abstract machine that is continually being transformed. Personae, as revolutionary subjects, are thus committed to the creation of new modes of existence, no matter how small, that will connect up with others to construct a new revolutionary political body.

(2) A Revolutionary Persona has Different Features
Revolutionary political personae do not have psychological or personological traits based on the subjective identity of their consciousness, nor are they merely fractured or dissolved 'egos'. Rather, according to Deleuze and Guattari, they have distinct pathic, relational, dynamic, juridical and existential features. Revolutionary personae thus create specifically different kinds of consistencies and relations among concrete and abstract machines. Deleuze and Guattari discuss, in *What Is Philosophy?*, several different features of some of these personae in the history of philosophy that I would like to expand and explicitly politicise in this section (1994: 68–71/70–3). But before developing each of these features in turn, it is important to note the limitations of this typology as well as clarify the lack of any pretension to an exhaustive universal list of political personae. As Deleuze and Guattari say, 'no list of the features of con-

ceptual personae can be exhaustive, since they are constantly arising and vary with planes of immanence. On a given plane, different kinds of features are mixed together to make up a persona' (1994: 68/70). Personae are not unified static beings without conflict, nor do they fit any exhaustive list made of their types. Accordingly, it is not 'always easy to decide which, at a given moment in a given society, are the good types' (1994: 67/68). Despite the difficulty, the task of articulating them remains an important practice that is more like a creation or participation than a representation.

First, political personae have *pathic* features:

> The Idiot, the one who wants to think for himself and is a persona who can change and take on another meaning. But also the Madman, a cataleptic thinker or 'mummy' who discovers in thought an inability to think; or a great maniac, someone frenzied, who is in search of that which precedes thought, an Already-there, but at the very heart of thought itself. (Deleuze and Guattari 1994: 68–9/70)

These pathic personae have certain passions, dispositions or sufferings in a political domain that affect the kinds of connections they make in it. These can be helpful for understanding the pathic features of revolutionary political personae: the revolutionary *pessimist* who demands only the impossible in order to maintain moral superiority; the *defeatist* who, like a 'mummy', discovers in the revolution the hopelessness of all collective action; or even the frenzied *activist* driven by guilt to constantly be 'taking action'.

Second, political personae have *relational* features:

> 'The Friend,' but a friend who has a relationship with his friend only through the thing loved, which brings rivalry. The 'Claimant' and the 'Rival' quarrel over the thing or the concept. (Deleuze and Guattari 1994: 69/71)

Personae can be defined in terms of their relationships with other personae. Consider the political persona of the '*compa*' (short for *compañer@*, or partner/comrade) that the Zapatistas created to designate a certain type of subjectivity. The *compa* has a relationship with another *compa* only insofar as both are struggling for similar conditions, principles or specific actions. This brings conflict over the 'aims of the revolution' or how best to achieve them. The 'Revolutionary' and the 'Reactionary' then quarrel over the ends or means of the struggle.

Third, personae have *dynamic* features insofar as they undergo transformation or movement:

If moving forward, climbing, and descending are dynamisms of conceptual personae, then leaping like Kierkegaard, dancing like Nietzsche, and diving like Melville are others for philosophical athletes irreducible to one another. (Deleuze and Guattari 1994: 69/71)

In terms of political personae we might consider direct action, sabotage and mass demonstration (among others) as kinds of group-subject dynamisms. Retreating, compromising, occupying, hiding, attacking, defending and organising can all be considered dynamisms of political personae. The subterfuge of Subcomandante Marcos, the negotiations of the San Andrés Accords and the teaching at the Zapatista autonomous schools are all dynamic features of the *compas*.

Fourth, political personae have *juridical* features insofar as collective actions 'lay claim to what belongs to them by right and, from the time of the pre-Socratics, have confronted Justice' (Deleuze and Guattari 1994: 70/72). But Deleuze and Guattari do not have in mind a transcendent conception of judgement by law or values or even the virtue of conscience. Rather, the juridical features of political personae are mergers of judge and innocent where judgement takes place within the purely immanent criterion of evental existence (Deleuze and Guattari 1994: 70/72). Immanent justice may mean beyond good and evil, but it does not mean beyond good and bad. Consider the *caracoles* and people's courts of Zapatista territory. Rather than being informally judged by the juridical army (the EZLN), the village people (as personae of Zapatismo) of these territories have begun rotational participation in people's courts in order to respond to legal issues of drug and human trafficking, non-regional use of forest materials, and various community disputes they lay claim to by their own right: by autonomy. Community members (both men and women) take turns learning how to use these juridical features immanent to the values and laws they have established independently from the Mexican government or corporate interests over the resources of their land.

Finally, political personae have *existential* features: the small aspects of daily life which compose the significance of political struggle. Deleuze and Guattari provide an example from the history of philosophy: 'is not Kant's stocking-suspender a vital anecdote appropriate to the system of Reason?' they suggest. And Spinoza's liking for battles between spiders due to the relations of the modes in *Ethics* (Deleuze and Guattari 1994: 71–2/72–3)? Might we also consider the importance of Lenin's taste in music, Marcos's use of poetry and art, or Marx's health problems, or the *compas*' taste for *pozol* (a fermented maize porridge) and so on? How do these features contribute to the functioning of the personae and the effectuation of the event?

While there are certainly many more features to political personae, it remains an important part of a theory of revolutionary subjectivity to be able to articulate how and to what degree the different kinds of personae work and relate to each other within a particular domain, rather than simply affirming their capacity to become other.

> No rule, and above all no discussion, will say in advance whether this is the good plane, the good persona, or the good concept; for each of them determines if the other two have succeeded or not, but each must be constructed on its own account – one created, one invented, and the other laid out. Problems and solutions are constructed about which we can say, 'Failure . . . Success ...' but only as we go along and on the basis of their coadaptations. (Deleuze and Guattari 1994: 79/82)

(3) A Revolutionary Persona Operates in the Third Person

A revolutionary body politic has various types of subjectivity that contest and participate in the direct transformation of its conditions and consequences. But these personae do not act or speak from the perspective of an autonomous self in the first person, they operate as agents immanent to a revolutionary body politic in the third person (he, she, they) and the indefinite (one, everyone, anyone and so on). While the first person generally indicates a self-conscious subject of enunciation who makes decisions on a political arrangement independent from it, and the second person designates the projection of the first, the third person persona indicates an indefinite group-subject always in co-adaptation with the body politic. In *A Thousand Plateaus* Deleuze and Guattari say,

> We believe . . . that the third person indefinite, HE, THEY, implies no indetermination from this point of view; it ties the statement to a collective *agencement*, as its necessary condition, rather than to a subject of the enunciation. Blanchot is correct in saying that ONE and HE – *one* is dying, *he* is unhappy – in no way take the place of the subject, but instead do away with any subject in favor of an *agencement* of the haecceity type that carries or brings out the event insofar as it is unformed and incapable of being effectuated by persons ('something happens to them that they can only get a grip on again by letting go of their ability to say I'). The HE does not represent a subject but rather makes a diagram of an *agencement*. (1987: 324/265)

Thus, opposed to the 'indetermination' of a pure potential for transformation, or the representational first person of enunciation (based on contemplation, reflection and communication), the third person effectuates or makes a diagram of the event, immanent only to the collective assemblage. Personae are 'indefinite' in the sense that they are not persons independent from the event who look on, judge and make decisions about how it should proceed, but they are 'determinate' in the sense that they are indicated by a third person that is tied to a collective *agencement*. The persona is thus never a person or consciousness but rather an inseparable 'they' or 'everyone' effecting a becoming, folding or co-adaptation of the abstract and concrete machines.

'I won't say *I* anymore' [*je ne dirai plus moi*], Deleuze and Guattari say in *Anti-Oedipus*. 'I'll never utter the word again; it's just too damn stupid. Every time I hear it, I'll use the third person instead' (1983: 30/23). The important and ironic point is that it is not a matter of never using the first person pronoun again, but that the speech acts of personae always be considered as most primarily 'speech act[s] in the third person where it is always the conceptual persona who says "I"' (Deleuze and Guattari 1994: 63/64). It is not the case that the first and second person pronouns 'I' and 'you' have no meaning; rather, the point is that they are derived or conditioned on a more primary third persona of the event. 'I' and 'you' function as different features of political events that engage in negotiation and conflict immanent to the collective assemblage at hand, not as features of an independent consciousness, ego, radical alterity or transcendence *outside* the assemblage.

Rather than representing or speaking about a political event, the persona or avatar is always the immanent agent of an operation and locally determinate in relation to the abstract and concrete machines it helps create and connect (see Deleuze and Guattari 1983: 22–3/16). For Deleuze and Guattari, the revolutionary political 'subject' is not simply 'de-centered'; it is a co-adaptive component of a particular collective enunciation or political consistency. Having expanded and explicitly politicised Deleuze and Guattari's concept of the persona, we can see how it accounts for a new kind of revolutionary political subject different from both representational and anti-representational types. Along with the return of the theory and practice of revolution found in Deleuze and Guattari is the return of the concept of a revolutionary subject. This subject is not structured by an identity based on static and pre-given political conditions (territory, state and capital), or merely dispersed, but is rather a third person part of a consistent and participatory political body.

III. *Zapatismo and the Creation of a Participatory Body Politic*

In the last section I argued that, opposed to the two dangers of representation and anti-representation, there exists a third type: the participatory body politic. This new body politic is defined by its participatory mutability: the degree to which its conditions are transformed by the participation of the elements and subjects affected by it. I further argued that in order to understand the structure and function of this participatory and revolutionary body politic we need to understand the unique relationship it articulates between three different dimensions: its conditions, elements and kinds of subjects. Representational, anti-representational and participatory political bodies each express a different type of relationship between these three dimensions. But this has only been a theoretical development.

In this next section I argue that the Zapatistas have created a revolutionary and participatory body politic in practice. The two sides of theory and practice thus constitute the strategy I am calling revolutionary participation. Zapatismo presents an interesting case in political theory and practice because it cannot be understood by the political philosophies of liberalism or Marxism. Zapatismo abandons both the notions of sovereign power based on political and juridical representation and the basic tenets of Marxist science, vanguardism, state capture, class struggle and the determination of the economy 'in the last instance'. Marcos and the early EZLN, upon arriving in Chiapas, found that their Marxist, Leninist and Maoist preconceptions were 'totally inadequate for communicating with the local population' and eventually concluded that their original plans for struggle were 'undemocratic and authoritarian' (Ross 2006: 14). But the Zapatistas are not a 'postmodern' revolution in the sense that they merely reject these forms of representation in favour of a spontaneous or speculative leftism. Instead, they have constructed a new kind of body politic based on participation. They call this process *mandar obedeciendo*, or leading by obeying.[25] But what is leading by obeying, and how does it function as a practice of political participation?

> Perhaps, the new political morality is constructed in a new space which will not be the taking or retention of power, but the counterweight and

opposition which contains and obliges the power to 'rule by obeying' . . . '[R]ule by obedience' is not within the concepts of 'political science' and it is devalued by the morality of 'efficiency' which defines the political activity which we suffer. (Marcos 2004b: 217)

The new body politic the Zapatistas invent is thus one whose conditions for social order and inclusion must obey the concrete elements and subjects obedient to this same social order. Zapatismo is defined by this reciprocal governance, not by the taking of representative power or the rejection of all political organisation. Leading by obeying thus expresses a political vertigo or participatory feedback loop between the leaders who obey the led, and the led who must lead the leaders and obey. *Mandar obedeciendo* breaks the traditional political distinction between means and ends; it 'makes the road by walking'. The process of leading by obeying can be understood as the mutual transformation of three different dimensions: a revolutionary condition, its concrete practices and its form of revolutionary subjectivity.

THE REVOLUTIONARY CONDITION: 'ZAPATISMO, 1994'

As a body politic, Zapatismo invents a new condition for social order and inclusion. Like the phenomena of the revolution of 1789, the Paris Commune and the revolution of 1917, Zapatismo is a singular event in the sense that it is irreducible to historically necessary causal chains. In 1994, in Mexico, Zapatismo held no resemblance to any recognisable legal or legitimate political thing within the present 'state of affairs', that is, no political representation (party), market representation, linguistic representation (their languages are not spoken or recognised by political representatives) or representation by the local indigenous leaders (*caciques*). There was no causal necessity that Zapatismo should have existed, no way it could have been deduced from the domains of 'rights', 'commodities' or 'class struggle' from which it emerged. From the representational point of view of Mexican politics, the marginalised and unrepresented Zapatistas of Chiapas have no 'legitimate' existence and yet they coexist immanently and heterogeneously within the political arrangement anyway. The singular event of Zapatismo is thus not conditioned on requests for representation like 'rights', the overthrow of the state, a new market economy or a new ethnic nationalism, but instead takes on its own self-reference or autonomy from within the situation.

But the condition of the Zapatistas' body politic is also universal in the sense that it is both inclusive and infinite in its consequences. 'To be Zapatista' does not mean that you must be represented by the EZLN or that you must be indigenous, or even from Mexico. But Zapatismo cannot mean anything one wants. Zapatismo means participating in a struggle against neoliberalism and for direct self-management wherever one is and to whatever degree one is capable of. Without a prior or immutable condition for exclusion, the Zapatistas have made it clear that anyone can become a Zapatista to the degree that they share their struggle.[26] Many around the world have subsequently taken up this universal event where they are (Europe, Asia, North America and so on). So rather than simply affirming their difference and unrepresentability, the Zapatistas have created a *singular-absolute* event/intervention and given it a specific consistency of its own, heterogeneous to the regimes of political representation. This singular-universality is practically constituted through the creation of *Encuentros* (international gatherings)[27] that aim to include others that will change the nature of Zapatismo as a social body each time they meet (see Chatterton 2007).

But Zapatismo does not represent anyone. Rather, as a condition for a revolutionary body politic, Zapatismo mobilises a proper name or marker that acts as an attractor or horizon for all those elements in Chiapas that did not legally 'exist', who were politically 'invisible', who were marginalised or had disappeared or been killed by the government (the underpaid, landless, non-Spanish-speaking, indigenous *campesin@s*).[28] In 1994 the proper name 'Zapatismo' was brought into popular existence, not to represent these people, but to mark the visibility of their invisibility within Mexican politics. The proper name 'Zapatismo' provides a sign of something through which people can speak. Thus when Marcos speaks to the Mexican government, he does not represent the Zapatistas, he is instead named 'Delegate Zero' of the 'Other Campaign'.[29] Where a normal delegate represents or stands in for its people, 'Delegate Zero' instead expresses a positive marker of what does not appear as legitimate political being in Mexico. This zero is a positive indication of what is being spoken *through*, without referent or representation. It indicates the condition of an 'Other politics'.

This conditional marker 'Zapatismo' does not represent Emiliano Zapata, Marcos or the sum total of denumerable Zapatistas, but is like a pure infinitive 'to Zapatista' in a concrete field of collective actions that circulate and transform the body politic marked by this name. Zapatismo thus has no existence outside of the concrete practices that effectuate and mutually transform it. As a condition for collective action it must be elaborated step by step and is always changing. The slogan '*Todos somos Zapatistas!*' ('We are all Zapatistas!') demonstrates the universality of this process. This slogan creates an incorporeal transformation, that is, a real change in the world that is not necessarily or immediately physical or corporeal. As a speech act tied to the conditions of a revolutionary body politic it brings together all of the solidarity actions, demonstrations and celebrations of 'inexistent' and marginalised people around the world. Each time someone or something new is included in this 'we', the meaning of Zapatismo changes and grows stronger, like the differential repetition of a festival.[30] This is a feature of the participatory body politic I am arguing takes place both in Deleuze and Guattari's philosophy and in the Zapatistas' political practice. This is why the Zapatistas have so many celebrations and Intercontinental *Encuentros*: not to provide new laws or programmes, but to 'redeploy' and transform the nature of Zapatismo itself each year. 'They do not add a second and a third time to the first, they carry the first time to the "nth" power,' as Deleuze says (1994: 8/1).

Zapatismo also creates and combines various concrete practices of different degrees of importance, proximity and intensity. For example, environmentalists, feminists and labour activists may all equally be considered Zapatistas if they take up and follow out its consequences: the struggle for direct democracy against neoliberalism. They all do so to different degrees of significance and intensity that are all ordered but not by a hierarchy of power and control.

The Revolutionary Concrete Practices: the Zapatista Autonomous Municipalities

The body politic created by the Zapatistas not only establishes a singular-universal condition by which to combine and include various concrete practices within its social order but also creates a variety of concrete practices that effectuate and react back on their conditions. These concrete practices 'obey' in the sense that they are politically conditioned by the singular-universal event of Zapatismo but also 'lead' in the sense that they are able to transform this condition through direct participation.

For example, the Zapatistas have created thirty-eight autonomous municipalities covering more than a third of the state of

Chiapas in order to concretely actualise the real but 'invisible and abstract' conditions of their body politic (Ross 1995). These autonomous municipalities are the Zapatistas' implementation of the 1996 San Andrés Accords, which the government abandoned in December 1996 after refusing to carry them out. The Accords guarantee the right of indigenous peoples to form and govern their own municipalities. In forming the municipalities, residents reject the representation of official authorities and elect their own rotating and recallable administrators. They name their 'local health promoters [and] indigenous parliaments, and elaborate their own laws based on social, economic, political and gender equality among the inhabitants of diverse ethnic communities' (Mora 1998). The municipalities make their own decisions based on the participatory, direct consensus of its constituents and through the rotational governance of the *Juntas* (councils or cabinets that adjudicate disputes, distribute funds and register workers' cooperatives) and the Clandestine Revolutionary Indigenous Committee (Comité Clandestino Revolucionario Indígena, or CCRI). But this participation is not only political participation. The Zapatistas also effectuate their political body in the concrete practices of workers' cooperatives based on collective ownership, worker control and self-management. There are no bosses, landowners or capitalists, but instead a participatory economics based on shared prosperity. These concrete effectuations of their condition are not perfect by any stretch of the imagination, but the aim of their creation of these concrete expressions is, as Guattari would say,

> to set up structures and devices that establish a totally different kind of contact: a kind of self-management or self-organisation of a set of problems which does not start from a central point that arranges elements, inserts them into a control grid or establishes an agenda, but that, on the contrary, allows the various singular processes to attempt a rhizomatic unfolding. This is very important, even if it doesn't work. (Guattari 2008: 178)

The Zapatistas' concrete effectuation of their body politic is their struggle for a maximum of participation and 'self-management conceived outside the criteria of a formal democracy that has proven to be sterile' (Guattari 2008: 391).

The Zapatistas have created a whole host of various concrete articulations of their event: abolishing alcohol, having a rotational form of participatory self-government in the *Juntas*, harvesting coffee and honey, weaving and working in cooperatives, receiving aid from international NGOs, participating in the horizontal cooperative economy that 'fair trades' with them around the world, using the slogan 'We are all Zapatistas!'. As Marcos says, 'The kids, the chickens, the stones, everything here is Zapatista.'[31] Zapatismo, according to Marcos, is not a political ideology; it has no normative prescriptions, or necessary consequences given in advance of its expression. It is neither party nor vanguard. Rather, it creates a new type and concrete distribution of existence: kids, chickens and stones all become the concrete body of Zapatismo.

But this does not mean that all these concrete elements are exactly the same. The *campesin@s* who grow, produce, eat, sell, teach, learn and govern as 'Zapatista' as they can should not, of course, be confused with those in Europe, America or elsewhere who are in solidarity with them, write academic articles about them, give them aid and so on. Each element of Zapatismo functions in a different way and with a different degree of risk and privilege at stake, even though each helps constitute the other. These elements, however, do not exist in a hierarchy of power and knowledge. They are ordered based on their intensity and importance, but not on their hierarchy. No one person or programme stands at the top to order such a hierarchy.

Even within Zapatista territory there are degrees of intensity in relation to Zapatismo. The 'First of January Boot Cooperative' in the *caracol* Oventic has to import its boot soles from Asia, but the Yachil Coffee co-op is entirely Zapatista owned and managed. Importing boot soles may demonstrate a lesser degree of intensity of Zapatismo (in relation to the goals of local production, self-management and economic justice), whereas the local production of the coffee co-op would demonstrate a greater degree of Zapatismo's intensity or strength. Such degrees of deployment in Zapatismo are in constant mutation, growing greater when a Canadian anarchist boot co-op opens up to sell the Zapatistas' boot soles, for example, or becoming weaker when cooperative cafés that sell Zapatista coffee go out of business because a Starbucks moves in. There are thus a variety of elements and degrees in which Zapatismo is effectuated and whose degrees of consistency do not constitute a hierarchy of power, but rather an order of relation to and within the event.

But the participatory body politic created by the Zapatistas not only creates an internal consistency of the concrete practices that constitute it to various degrees, as we have seen, it also connects these concrete practices up to those outside of this internal consistency. The Zapatistas have concretely expanded their struggle beyond their locality and to the world at large. Had the Zapatistas created an exclusively indigenous, ethnic or nationalistic revolt, it would have risked becoming a limited and locally saturated struggle within the borders of Chiapas or Mexico alone. It became clear after 1994, however, that the Zapatistas could rebel but they could not compete with the Mexican military without national and international popular support from those outside their territory. Thus, the Zapatistas asked the world to see Zapatismo as everyone's struggle. They said '*Detrás de nosotros estamos ustedes*' ('Behind us we are you') and '*Todos somos Marcos*' ('We are all Marcos').

Without media attention and human rights watches that kept paramilitary forces at bay, without the monetary support, cooperative networks, first aid and supplies of the global community, Zapatismo risked an internal saturation in several regards. It risked running out of supplies and being forced into desperate acts of violence against the Mexican army; it risked becoming a reformist movement out of desperation for any kind of political amelioration; it risked becoming a sectarian, nationalist or indigenous movement without any global vision; and it even risked falling back on military vanguard and patriarchal hierarchies within its communities.

The concrete practices that have created this external and expansive connection include the way that Zapatistas take on refugees from all over Chiapas, hold Intercontinental *Encuentros* around the world, assist the struggles of many Left social movements around Mexico, and provide medical and legal aid to non-Zapatistas and even to anti-Zapatistas within their own communities. Despite the fact that the Zapatistas may not be in complete agreement with all the groups or individuals with whom they share certain campaigns or resources, the Zapatistas can at least form bridges where their interests are common. Beyond ideology, geography, identity and certainly beyond an affirmation of difference-in-itself, the Zapatistas have created a vast global network of external consistency piece by piece.

The Revolutionary Political Subject: The *Compa*

Leading by obeying not only means creating a revolutionary political body and effectuating a set of concrete practices that sustain it and follow out its consequences, it also means inventing a new form of subjectivity that connects the two with each other in a mutual transformation. For this purpose the Zapatistas have invented the revolutionary subject of the *compa*. The Zapatista *compa* has a strange double existence. For the event of Zapatismo to be brought about there must be *compas* to do so, but for there to be Zapatista *compas*, Zapatismo must already exist. The emergence of each presupposes the other; thus both emerged at the same time: 1 January 1994.[32]

The purpose of the *compas*, as the revolutionary subjects of Zapatismo, is to articulate and determine the various processes of Zapatismo: where are its dangers, where are its opportunities, where are its points of antagonism and conflict, and so on. For example, the *compas*, as the subjects who connect the evental condition 'Zapatismo' to its concrete consequences, have to decide how many trees may be taken from the jungle to avoid deforestation, what the penalty for taking too many is (planting two more and caring for them), or whether or not a consequence of Zapatismo is intervening against forty state troopers arresting environmental activists for protesting against the destruction of a forest of 200-year-old trees to make way for a shopping mall in Morelos.[33] Piece by piece the *compas* show Zapatismo's concrete consequences by effectuating some actions, some slogans, some demonstrations and not others. But these effected elements, as processes of leading by obeying, in turn transform Zapatismo. It has no existence outside of its effectuations. This transformation of the condition 'Zapatismo' then transforms the *compas*, who must then redeploy new concrete effectuations based on this change. Zapatismo thus leads itself by obeying itself in a kind of feedback loop with no vanguard at the helm. It is in this sense a process of participation where event, consequence and subject all enter a mutual transformation.

The Zapatista *compa* also breaks with a tradition of revolutionary subjectivity based on individualism and self-discipline. Instead, the *compa* acts in the third person and creates a new kind of discipline: the collective discipline of the event. This does not mean, of course, that *compas* never say 'I' or 'you'; it simply means that these features are derivative or secondary to the more primary third person that acts as the agent of a connection between an event and its consequences. Conflicts and agreements still take place between specific 'I's' and 'you's', but only as conflicts and agreements of the event they participate in: not outside it, nor upon it, but within and through it. Like the use of Delegate Zero to replace the political condition of representation and exclusion, or the use of the self-managed autonomous municipalities to replace the concrete practices of private and public

144

property, the Zapatistas create *compas* to replace the representational subject of liberal and capitalist individualism. The *compas* accomplish this practically through the use of black ski masks.

The *compas* use black masks and bandannas to create a collective and 'indefinite' group-subject. 'In order for them to see us, we covered our faces; so that they would call us by name, we gave up our names; we bet the present to have a future; and to live . . . we died' (Marcos 2004b: 115). While Marcos has given several different reasons for the use of these masks over the years, from making sure no one tries to become the leader[34] to portraying Mexico's covering up of its *real* Mexico,[35] the collective practice of masking has produced a very specific kind of revolutionary subjectivity immanent not to a consciousness who represents an 'I' to itself, but to the event: to Zapatismo itself. The practice of collective masking in Zapatismo is hostile to vanguardism insofar as it creates a visual equality between subjects without leaders. It de-individualises first person subjects in favour of third person collective subjects of the event. We might imagine how confusing it would be to try and follow a single person when everyone was wearing the same black ski mask. 'Are you the one leading us? No, I thought you were leading us.' Everyone takes turns leading by obeying (Marcos 2006). The point is to create a locally generic subjectivity of Zapatismo and express it collectively, that is, to lead but to lead by obeying those you are leading. 'Because', as Subcomandante Marcos says, 'here in the EZLN the mistakes are conjugated in the first person singular and the achievements in the third person plural' (Ramírez 2008: 307). Rather than affirm a pure alterity or potential for 'transformation as such' found in 'the face' (Levinas 1979) of a 'Thou' (Buber 1958) against a representational 'I/You' opposition, the Zapatistas propose instead an indefinite but determinate third person of the event. By covering their faces as a political action, the Zapatistas are able to create a unique political anonymity (open to anyone, and yet unambiguously against neoliberalism) that rejects both liberal and critical models of subjectivity in favour of a subject of the event itself. This practice has been taken up by others around the world to achieve a similar collective form of agency (see Thompson 2010).

In this section I have argued that the Zapatistas have created a revolutionary and participatory body politic based on leading by obeying. In particular they have done this by creating the conditions of a singular-universal event with the proper name and date 'Zapatismo, 1994', by sustaining and effectuating its concrete consequences in their autonomous municipalities, and by creating a new form of revolutionary subjectivity that acts in the third person: the masked *compa*. These three dimensions of their revolutionary body politic not only parallel Deleuze and Guattari's political philosophy of consistency, but also express the larger strategy of participation that I have developed throughout this chapter.

Conclusion

In the previous chapter we were left with the problem of how revolutionary interventions could be sustained through the creation of an alternative body politic without becoming either representational or merely anti-representational. This chapter has argued that there is a third way to understand the concept of a body politic today: as a participatory set of conditions, elements and agencies engaged in a maximal degree of mutual and direct transformation. This can be seen in both the political philosophy of Deleuze and Guattari and the practice of the Zapatistas.

Against the exclusionary conditions of political representation defined by a set of pre-given normative criteria for political participation, or the ambivalent conditions of potentiality defined by the general capacity for change as such, I have argued for a concept of political conditions along the lines of what Deleuze and Guattari have called abstract machines. Since the abstract machine is a singular marker of an event (and not a thing) that both conditions and is transformed by the political elements it conditions, it has no pre-given exclusionary criteria, only participatory ones contingent on what/who directly participates. Since the abstract machine marks a locally waged struggle against specific forms of power, it is also an unambivalent commitment to more than just change as such: it is the creation of specific new elements and agencies.

Against the hierarchical ordering of elements found in the politics of representation, defined by their distance from, or reproduction of, pre-given norms or identities, as well as the hierarchical ordering of elements in the politics of potentiality, defined by their distance from the process of pure becoming or a difference-in-itself, I have argued for a concept of political elements based on Deleuze and Guattari's concept of the concrete machinic assemblage. Since concrete machines effectuate their condition in a relation of reciprocal transformation (and not by a reproduction of pre-given criteria) they are participatory and non-hierarchical insofar as every element can change the conditions of the whole. Additionally, since they express 'degrees of consistency' (between pure difference and pure identity), they can also be meaningfully ordered in relation to an abstract machine opposed to affirming a general degree of a 'capacity to become other'.

Similarly, against the paralysis of the subject, created by limiting its transformation to what it may rationally desire to be free *from* or be free *to*, found in the politics of identity, as well as the paralysis created by dispersing subjectivity into a pure form of becoming or transformation as such, I have argued for a concept of political subjectivity based on Deleuze and Guattari's concept of 'personae'. Since political personae are defined by the simultaneity of their immanent intervention as well as their connection between the abstract and concrete machines, they are able to change not only their desires within the political domain of a given event, but also their very nature insofar as their actions transform the initial conditions of their existence. In addition to their localised interventions, personae have specific features that distinguish them from a purely dispersed form of transformational becoming: they combine and conflict, juridically, existentially, relationally and so on. The three concepts of the abstract machine, the concrete assemblage and the political persona thus provide real conceptual alternatives to the representational and anti-representational political bodies, just as Zapatismo provides a practical alternative to them in the practice of leading by obeying.

But while this chapter has been able to show the structure and function of how revolutionary interventions are sustained in a participatory body politic, it has failed to offer much more than a gesture of how such political bodies can connect up with others. It is one thing for a revolutionary event to create an internal consistency between its abstract condition, concrete consequences and subject, or even to connect a few of its consequences outside its local struggle, as we have seen in the case of Zapatismo, but how do radically heterogeneous revolutionary political bodies connect to *one another*, if they can at all? On what new condition? How would we reconcile their potentially mutually exclusive concrete commitments? This is a question of political affinity and universal solidarity and will be addressed in the next and final chapter of this book.

Notes

1. In contrast to the political processes of coding, overcoding and axiomatisation examined in Chapters 1 and 2, the present chapter examines a fourth type of political process: consistency.
2. What counts as 'just' will be highly variable, but cannot include racism, sexism and authoritarianism, because these are all forms of representation (see Chapter 1).
3. This is not a form of ambivalence between representation and anti-representation, because it is defined by its commitment to the construction of a specific event. Just because there is no political programme given in advance, it does not mean that this commitment is ambivalent.
4. While the state can certainly change its laws to abolish slavery, give women and non-landowners the right to vote and so on, it is unable to tolerate autonomy. It must exclude all those who seek political self-management.
5. A 'hierarchy based on the degree of proximity or distance from a principle' (Deleuze 1994: 60/37).
6. The subject of non-representational or direct democracy is different insofar as it derives its identity not from the unity of the condition (which represents the subject's desires) but from the collective mutation of the event which does not represent the subject at all. Rather, it *expresses* a collective subjectivity.
7. See Introduction.
8. A theory of the subject distinct from the previous two outlined above will be offered later on in this chapter.
9. The process of participation, consistency or leading by obeying should not be confused with the process of liberalism or representative democracy. The process of participatory politics is a rejection of majoritarian democracy. Instead, it proposes a more direct and unmediated process of political inclusion and self-transformation much more similar to the Zapatista process of consensus decision-making and rotational self-management found in the political, economic and social life of the autonomous municipalities. Those who are directly affected by it are not represented by it but rather participate directly in its management: 'quod omnes tangit, ab omnibus approbetur/that which touches all, should be decided by all'.
10. Not all abstract or concrete machines are revolutionary. As we saw in Chapter 1 there are four kinds of abstract machines for Deleuze and Guattari, three of which support processes of representation (territory, state and capital). This chapter engages only the fourth type of abstract machine: the revolutionary machine.
11. Eduardo Pellejero too believes that political consistency is possible in Deleuze and Guattari's work. He says, 'for this new [revolutionary]

sensibility to be asserted, it is necessary to create proper assemblages. That creation is, after all, the task that gives consistency to this new militant praxis' (Pellejero 2010: 107).

12. 'In physics, Ilya Prigogine spoke of states in which the slightest differences persist rather than cancel themselves out, and where independent phenomena inter-resonate' (Deleuze 2006: 215/233).

13.
> Contingent holism sees the social world as composed of practices that intersect with and affect one another (although not every practice intersects with every other practice), that change over time, that form the parameters within which we understand ourselves and our world, but that do not offer a foundation from which the world can be exhaustively or indubitably understood. (May 1997: 34)

While it is true that anyone can participate in a revolutionary event, there will certainly be local manifestations and differing interpretations of this event, as we will see later in this chapter in the case of Zapatismo.

14. The condition for a revolutionary political body is not only self-referential, as witnessed in claims of political autonomy like 'we are autonomous because we are autonomous', but it is also minimally marked in its real-abstract non-appearance (cipher or degree zero), as we witness in another Zapatista claim 'we are nowhere, but we are everywhere'.

15. See the next section of this chapter on 'the degrees of deterritorialisation' within the consistency of the concrete machinic assemblage.

16. See Chapter 2.

17. 'It's not a matter of bringing all sorts of things together under a single concept but rather of relating each concept to variables that explain its mutations' (Deleuze 1995: 47/31). As Deleuze and Guattari say, the abstract machine 'crosscuts the chaotic variability and gives it consistency (reality) . . . It refers back to chaos rendered consistent' (Deleuze and Guattari 1994: 196/208).

18. This was explored in depth in Chapter 2.

19. This is the meaning of the body-without-organs. It is not that the body of the abstract machine has no concrete organs at all, it is just that these concrete organs do not come pre-organised. There is no static political image that organises the organs of the political body in advance. The revolutionary body-without-organs is constantly reorganising its organs in a process of continual and participatory transformation.

20.
> Belief, sheer, direct, unmitigated personal belief, reappears as the working hypothesis; action which at once develops and tests belief reappears as experimentation, deduction, demonstration; while the machinery of universals, axioms, *a priori* truths, etc., is the systematization of the way in which men have always worked out, in anticipation of overt action, the implications of their beliefs with a view to revising them in the interests of obviating

the unfavorable, and of securing the welcome consequences. (Dewey 1906: 124)

21. The difference between deterritorialisation as 'the degrees of shared acceleration of heterogeneous components on a plane of consistency', territorialisation as 'the degrees of coding and primitive unity on the plane of organization' and reterritorialisation as 'the degrees of over-coding and axioms on the plane of organization' was developed in Chapter 2. 'With the nomad . . . it is deterritorialization that constitutes the relation to the earth, to such a degree that the nomad reterritorial-izes on deterritorialization itself. It is the earth that deterritorializes itself, in a way that provides the nomad with a territory' (Deleuze and Guattari 1987: 473/381).

22. The existence of representational subjects does not preclude the pos-sibility of revolutionary subjects. Just as we saw in Chapter 2 with the prefigurative emergence of revolutionary struggle, so we can see the pre-figurative emergence of new forms of revolutionary subjectivity. These new forms of subjectivity are defined not by who represents them but by their commitment and direct contributions to the revolutionary event.

23.

> It definitely makes sense to look at the various ways individuals and groups constitute themselves as subjects through processes of subjectification: what counts in such processes is the extent to which, as they take shape, they elude both established forms of knowledge and the dominant forms of power. Even if they in turn engender new forms of power or become assimilated into new forms of knowledge. For a while, though, they have a real rebellious spontaneity. This is nothing to do with going back to 'the subject,' that is, to something invested with duties, power, and knowledge. One might equally well speak of new kinds of event, rather than processes of subjectification: events that can't be explained by the situations that give rise to them, or into which they lead. (Deleuze 1995: 239/176)

24. I use the word 'subjectivity' because there is a real kind of distinct agency at work here. Personae are not equally dispersed (and thus obliterated) into the event. Rather, they are the distinct beings that connect the political condition to its concrete consequences.

25. The Clandestine Revolutionary Indigenous Committee in each region monitors the operations of the Good Government *Juntas* in order to prevent acts of corruption, intolerance, injustice and deviation from the Zapatista principle of 'leading by obeying'.

26. 'We are all Zapatistas!' became a global slogan for solidarity actions with the Zapatistas.

27. The Intercontinental *Encuentros* (Encounters) for Humanity and Against Neoliberalism emerged from the Zapatista movement's engage-ment with individuals and social movements around the world follow-ing the Zapatista uprising.

28. 'We were silenced. We were faceless. We were nameless. We had no future. We did not exist' (Marcos 2001b: 101).
29. Unlike other Zapatista comandantes, Subcomandante Marcos is not an indigenous Mayan.
30. 'Behind our black mask . . . we are you' (Khasnabish 2008: 127).
31.
> For a long time, this place has existed where the men are Zapatistas, the women are Zapatistas, the kids are Zapatistas, the chickens are Zapatistas, the stones are Zapatistas, everything is Zapatista. And in order to wipe out the Zapatista Army of National Liberation, they will have to wipe this piece of territory off the face of the earth, not just destroy it but erase it completely, because there is always the danger of the dead down below . . . (Subcomandante Marcos's letter to *Proceso*, 1994, cited in Ross 2006: 167)

32. See Chapter 2 (this date is complicated by the prefigurative labours that began in 1983).
33. Apparently it does.
34. 'The main reason is that we have to be careful that nobody tries to be the main leader. The masks are meant to prevent this from happening' (Marcos, quoted in Maxwell and Harvey 1999: 6).
35. 'I will take off my ski mask when Mexican society takes off its own mask, the one it uses to cover up the real Mexico' (quote from an interview with Marcos in Katzenberger 1995: 70).

Political Affinity and Singular-Universal Solidarity

Clearly, a revolutionary machine cannot remain satisfied with local and occasional struggles: it has to be at the same time super-centralized and super-desiring. The problem, therefore, concerns the nature of unification, which must function in a transversal way, through multiplicity, and not in a vertical way, so apt to crush the multiplicity proper to desire.

(Deleuze 2004: 278/199)

Introduction

While the theory of a participatory body politic developed in Chapter 3 may have been able to account for the practical and theoretical reality of a third type of political body, it failed to understand on what basis such revolutionary bodies would be able to connect to one another and assemble a larger global alternative to neoliberalism. If the conditions of revolutionary political bodies are singular and non-representational, on what basis can such heterogeneous political conditions share a common affinity or belonging? To what degree can this inclusive model of political participation, argued for in Chapter 3, be practically extended into a worldwide revolutionary movement? Does one condition or body politic simply swallow another in larger and larger spheres of participation, or do they exist in parallel?

Defined as the connection between two or more heterogeneous political conditions, what I am calling revolutionary political affinity confronts two dangers. On the one hand, it risks being synthesised into a single global condition under which heterogeneous conditions can communicate, but only as particular elements under a larger representational condition (the affinity of citizenship within nation-states, the unequal/vertical affinity between allied and axis nations and so on). On the other hand, the affinity between revolutionary political bodies risks becoming dispersed into a multiplicity of unconnected singularities whose only belonging is the universal non-belonging of their radical difference. In this chapter,

I argue that the political solidarity found in what I am calling the contemporary return to revolution is not simply a matter of integrating marginalised demands back into the dominant nation-state apparatus by simply tweaking the criteria for citizenship to include those who are currently excluded. Nor is it a matter of recognising the universal singularity of all beings to become other than they are. Rather, this kind of revolutionary solidarity occurs when the participatory political bodies, defined in Chapter 3, adopt each other's struggles as their own. This solidarity is not a matter of recognition, charity or even radical difference, but rather a federated and transversal connection between multiple singular-universal political bodies.

This chapter thus poses three responses to the problem of creating solidarity between multiple non-representational political bodies. First, I argue against the concepts of citizenship and difference as desirable models of political belonging insofar as the former is structurally exclusionary and the latter is unable to theorise any concrete relations between multiple coexistent conditions. Second, I argue that, opposed to these two dangers of citizenship and difference, the solidarity that defines the contemporary return to revolution is defined instead by the federated connection between multiple singular-universal conditions without totality. In order to develop this third concept of political solidarity I draw on Deleuze and Guattari's concept of nomadism and expand its implications to the issue of revolution. Third, I argue that this strategic use of solidarity is also expressed in the Zapatistas' political practice of global networking and the assembly of Intercontinental Gatherings (*Encuentros Intercontinentales*). Together, the theory of nomadism and the practice of mutual global solidarity in Zapatismo define the strategy of what I am calling singular-universal solidarity.

I. Universal Political Affinity

CITIZENSHIP AND THE TERRITORIAL NATION-STATE

The concept of political affinity in the twentieth century was dominated by the figure of the citizen. Though far from articulating a homogeneous figure of political affinity, the concept of citizenship has been a rich and pivotal site for increasingly divergent contestations over political agency, inclusion and exclusion. Today, however, a century of contestation has escalated into full-on destabilisation, as citizenship has come under siege by three increasingly irreconcilable phenomena:

(1) The increasing frequency of political and economic intervention by trans- and non-national organisations into states by providing many of the affinities, protections, services and goods typically provided by state citizenship. Such organisations include *transnational entities* like the European Union or the Bolivarian Alliance in South America; *international entities* like the United Nations; *global entities* like non-governmental organisations and the growing network of doctors, teachers, journalists, farmers, lawyers and groups 'without borders'; *economic entities* like private corporations and the World Trade Organisation; and *activist entities* like the alter-globalisation movement and the World (and regional) Social Forums.

(2) The growing global movement of economically, politically and environmentally forced migrants (disproportionately from the global south) who are often denied full political status (citizenship) and access to services in their new country. The last decade alone has marked the highest number of migrations worldwide in recorded history. But what is unsettling about this phenomenon is that each year a higher and higher percentage of migrants around the world are becoming irregular or non-status. If citizenship and legal status are the conditions under which nation-states understand the political agency and rights of a people, what does it mean for over fifty million people to be living without status around the world? (United Nations 2008; International Organization for Migration 2008.)[1] Increasing numbers of precarious, criminalised and exploited persons pose a serious challenge to the desirability of citizenship-based political affinity because the increasing population of non-status persons has produced a society where many people cannot vote, whose labour is exploited and who, nonetheless, are required for the economy and nation to function. Many of the benefits of citizenship (equal access to representation and economic goods/property) are predicated on the exploitation and de-politicisation of non-citizens (see Nyers and Rygiel 2011).

(3) The massive internal destabilisation of citizenship brought on by the nation-state itself: the denationalisations during World War I and World War II; the creation of interment, work, refugee and extermination camps throughout the twentieth century; the torture and abuse of prisoners at Abu Ghraib; the suspension of habeas corpus at Guantanamo Bay detention camp and in the Patriot Act, and so on. These demonstrate the increasingly permanent state of

juridico-political exception and executive control into which citizenship has fallen. If states cannot be trusted to guarantee the sole concept of political affinity that only they have given themselves the power to protect, then the legitimacy of such a concept remains permanently in question.

Citizenship, as a form of political affinity or belonging, aims to resolve the relationship between multiple political conditions (territorial, economic, cultural and so on) by capturing them all under a single condition, what Hannah Arendt calls 'the old trinity of state-people-territory' that formed the basis of European civilisation (Arendt 1979: 282). Insofar as multiple political conditions and their agents accept the enforcement of specific criteria for belonging (birth, rights and so on), the state can mediate and identify legitimate forms of political agency (voting, property, family and so on) and illegitimate forms of political agency (revolution, theft, perversion and so on). But it does so only insofar as multiple political conditions are sacrificed to become elements of a single state condition: citizenship.

The problem with the theoretical entrenchment of the territorial nation-state matrix, however, is not that we have yet to find the right balance between them, but rather that all three terms of this trinity are themselves fundamentally exclusionary political concepts. In fact the very philosophical labour of trying to theorise a radically inclusive politics within such a matrix should rightly be considered an 'oxymoron' (Levinson and Tamir 1995). A theory of political affinity delimited by a territorial space necessarily excludes those outside its borders and restricts the free movement of peoples to a logic of political inclusion and exclusion along arbitrary geo-political lines (see Balibar 2002: 2). The territory is the *a priori* condition for migration and its control. Thus, a theory of political affinity based on the particularity of national identity, no matter how 'differentiated' it is, likewise marginalises extra-territorial, extra-national affinities and solidarities that cannot be restricted to the nation.

A political affinity legitimated by the sovereign state also excludes its own power of legitimation from its juridical legislation. Logically, that is, the state cannot include its own condition (the exceptional and executive violence of its foundation) within its own laws. This is why almost all modern state constitutions (democratic, socialist or totalitarian) have paradoxical laws that allow for the suspension of the constitution itself in times of emergency or national security (see Agamben 2005: 11–19). Finally, restricting political analysis to the confines of the territorial nation-state conceals the unquestioned presupposition of liberal multiculturalism: its complicity with mul-tinational capitalism (see Žižek 1997). The argument that modern nation-states should be neutral sites or 'empty universalities' of multicultural representation often simply means that minorities are tolerated as consumer markets or sources of equally exploited wage labour (as an economic exclusion) in a state-protected capitalist economy (Žižek 1997: 44). Despite its pretensions to universality and inclusion, the territorial nation-state is essentially exclusionary, whether it is liberal or socialist.

BIOPOLITICS AND UNIVERSAL SINGULARITY

The inherently exclusionary dilemma of the territorial nation-state that underpins the concept of citizenship-based political affinity is, however, not a new problem, and uncovering its paradox or aporia has not done it any harm. Additionally, the contemporary phenom-ena of extra-national affinity, migration and political states of emer-gency have only exacerbated it. Rather than weakening exclusionary models of power, the logical structure of exceptionalism has only taken on an increasingly multiple, decentralised and permanent for-mulation under modern capitalism – all the more powerful for its sup-pleness and 'contradiction'. The power of political exclusion today 'not only takes place at the territorial borders of the nation-state' but has become diffused into much more flexible border structures that have made life itself (not merely the citizen) the site of multiple inter-secting forms of power (see Balibar 2002: 75–86). Today, invoking juridico-political suspensions of laws and rights towards the ends of increased security against an unidentified enemy (terror), and allow-ing multinational corporations to pass freely across national territo-rial borders while the poor and undesirable are 'refused', states and corporations have mobilised an advanced structural invisibility.[2]

Borders are thus a modern political expression of this mobilised exception. A border excludes and includes less like a barricade or wall than like a passage-way or sieve for capital to pass through a very particular distribution of borders (for profit, control, security and so on) while fortifying others against migrants or terrorists. In the present political climate of terror and securitisation, it has become increasingly apparent that borders no longer exist solely in the geographical space between two sovereign territories; as local police enforcement, fire fighters, hospitals, schools, private compa-nies, airports, banks and individuals begin to independently monitor and strategically report non-status and 'suspicious' persons, 'the border' today is becoming something much more 'self-regulating' and 'self-transmuting' [*modulation, comme d'un déformateur universel*]: what Deleuze calls *les sociétés de contrôle* [control societies] (Deleuze 1995: 243/179). Borders have become multiple modulating constraints not just to block external movement but to regulate and stabilise internal populations to a certain degree or probability within a largely unpredictable milieu or environment (see Balibar 2002: 5).

But if the exclusionary liberalism of the territorial nation-state has been increasingly transformed into the more multiple and heterogeneous exceptionalism of biopolitics and control, what, if any, opportunities does this open up for a new inclusive strategy of political affinity? Giorgio Agamben argues that the decline of nation-state-based citizenship has revealed the figure of the refugee as the starting point for a new theory of political affinity. It is worth quoting him here at length:

> Given the by now unstoppable decline of the Nation-State and the general corrosion of traditional political-juridical categories, the refugee is perhaps the only thinkable figure for the people of our time and the only category in which one may see today – at least until the process of dissolution of the Nation-State and its sovereignty has achieved full completion – the forms and limits of a coming political community. It is even possible that, if we want to be equal to the absolutely new tasks ahead, we will have to abandon decidedly, without reserve, the fundamental concepts through which we have so far represented the subjects of the political (Man, the Citizen and its rights, but also the sovereign people, the worker, and so forth) and build our political philosophy anew starting from the one and only figure of the refugee. (1996: 158–9)

While the 'unstoppable decline of the Nation-State' is far from certain at this point, Agamben's insight here is to highlight the site of such a potential unhinging: the refugee. Insofar as the figure of the refugee 'unhinges the old trinity of State-nation-territory' and expresses the disjunction between the human and the citizen, between nativity and the nation, Agamben argues, 'it brings the originary fiction of sovereignty to crisis' and allows 'the citizen [to] be able to recognize the refugee that he or she is' (Agamben 1996: 164).

If biopolitics has truly created a permanent state of exception and modulated control, everyone has become, at least potentially, a form of bare life, stripped of all particularity. Citizens are no longer the central subjects of political management. It is now environments and populations that are increasingly becoming the focus of a governmental rationality of modulated and flexible control. This form of life or singularity, discernible in the figure of the refugee or the non-status migrant and virtually present in everyone, is internally excluded from the dominant politics of citizenship and the nation-state. Thus, Agamben argues that such singularisation opens up the opportunity for a new radically inclusive form of political affinity based on 'the paradoxical condition of reciprocal extraterritoriality (or, better yet, aterritoriality) that . . . could be generalized as a model of new international relations' (1996: 164). Eugene Holland has expressed similar hopes for the concept of the nomad ('the deterritorialized *par excellence*') found in Deleuze and Guattari's philosophy (2006: 203).

While grounding political affinity in the universal singularity of reciprocal aterritoriality or deterritorialisation may avoid the problem of representation and exclusion inherent in the relation between the universal and the particular found in the nation-state, it remains, however, insufficient for understanding how such singularities organise and connect up with one another or become, in themselves, concretely universal. Singularity, in this theory, seems to remain radically finite, or rather indefinite. While we may agree that universal singularity or absolute deterritorialisation is the condition for 'those who have no "qualification"' to form new networks of non-totalising relations, it does, for all this, fail to theorise how such singularities form immanent relations of greater or lesser consistency (Rancière 2004: 305). For example, if we agree with Agamben that citizenship is inherently exclusionary and that we were all mutually aterritorial refugees, what new practices of political affinity would be desirable to facilitate more or less connection between such singularities? What are the different types of relation between singularities, and what are their dangers? What would such a new model of international relations actually look like? The theory of universal singularity or deterritorialisation fails to provide a theory of political relation and thus to understand political affinity as more than just a finite and ambivalent opening of 'new horizons of possibility previously undreamt of by international state law' (Derrida 2001: 7).

II. Solidarity and the Singular-Universal

In the wake of these problems, I argue in this section that the contemporary return to revolution, of which Deleuze, Guattari and the

Zapatistas are a part, is defined instead by a singular-universal solidarity. By this I mean the degree to which two or more heterogeneous political bodies are united through one or more specific concrete practices. This solidarity, however, is never a complete unity; it is only a *degree of identity* based on the specific number of mutually shared practices. The question of solidarity can thus be formulated in the following way, according to Deleuze: 'How can one uphold the rights of a micro-analysis (diffusion, heterogeneity, fragmentation) and still allow for some kind of principle of unification that will not turn out to be like the State or the Party, a totalization or a representation?' (2006: 120–1/132–3).

The answer to this question requires all of the previous chapters of this book. In Chapter 1, I defined and distinguished between the different dangers of representation facing this kind of unity; in Chapter 2, I defined four types or degrees of change that escape these representational unities; and in Chapter 3, I argued that these degrees of change could be connected together in a participatory body politic defined by its singular-universal conditions, concrete effectuations and immanent subjectivities or personae. But we have yet to see how singular-universal conditions themselves can be connected together to form larger, worldwide revolutionary networks. We have not yet understood the strategy of solidarity: the creation of 'a world where many worlds fit', as Marcos says.

We have so far distinguished between two kinds of universality: the universality of representation (found in the territorial nation-state) and the universality of singularity (found in the potentiality of the deterritorialised refugee or nomad). But the concept of belonging or solidarity I develop in this chapter should also be distanced from four common theories of solidarity:

(1) Solidarity is not a matter of charity. Charity presumes an unequal distribution of power and wealth, such that those who have these may temporarily alleviate the suffering of those who do not without radically changing the conditions under which such inequality existed in the first place.

(2) Solidarity is not altruism. Altruism is based on an identification with the needs, interests and character of a particular group or person. As such, altruism also fails to understand or change the conditions under which a particular group or person has suffered injustice.

(3) Solidarity is also not a universal principle of duty. Such a principle would undermine the singularity and contingency of multiple

conditions and subordinate them to a single abstract condition (duty) without the possibility of participatory transformation of that condition (as discussed in Chapter 3).

(4) Finally, solidarity is not a matter of allies fighting towards the same teleological objective (class struggle, socialism and so on). As we saw in Chapter 3, this is in part because contemporary revolutionary conditions undergo participatory transformations of their objectives as they proceed. Additionally, each singular-universal condition has its own objectives that would be undermined by submission to a single objective.

Negative definitions out of the way, the remainder of this chapter offers a positive account of solidarity in two stages. The first section develops a theory of how multiple singular-universal conditions can be connected together, without presupposing the representational unities discussed in Chapter 1, by drawing on Deleuze and Guattari's concept of nomadism found in *A Thousand Plateaus*. The second section then argues that the Zapatistas express this new type of political solidarity by mobilising global connections between multiple singular-universal political conditions through their *Encuentros Intercontinentales*.

SINGULAR, UNIVERSAL, INCLUSIVE

Before addressing the question of how multiple singular-universal conditions are able to connect to each other, I want to remind the reader what a singular-universal revolutionary political condition is, as it was defined in Chapter 3. The contemporary revolutionary political body, I argued, is able to unify an assemblage of heterogeneous practices of resistance without subordinating them to a form of political representation (state, party or vanguard) insofar as it makes use of a participatory politics theorised by Deleuze and Guattari as the reciprocal determination (consistency) of an abstract machine, a concrete assemblage and machinic personae. In particular, the abstract machine acts as a mutable revolutionary political condition and exemplifies the local yet absolute dimensions of the revolutionary body politic.

A revolutionary condition, or abstract machine in Deleuze and Guattari's terms, is singular insofar as it presupposes no prior identity, causality or place in the dominant matrix of political representation (territorial-state-capitalism), but it is absolute insofar as nothing is essentially excluded from participation in its infinite consequences:

it is a maximum degree of inclusion with a minimal degree of identification. It is local insofar as it has a specific proper name, site or date (Zapatista 1994, The Paris Commune, May '68 and so on), but it is absolute insofar as this proper name is open to universal participation and reinterpretation. The absolute of the abstract machine, then, should not be confused with the absolutes or universals of identity that remain the same (and pre-given) while adding on an increasing number of axioms or elements of representation (as in representational democracies, nation-states and market economies). Rather, when Deleuze and Guattari speak of a 'becoming-everybody/everything' (1987: 588/470) of revolution, this means that everybody and everything may participate in an effectuation and transformation that responds to the event. In sum, a singular-universal event accomplishes three basic operations: (1) it clarifies the distance or irreconcilability of a singularity within the dominant matrix of political representation; (2) it calls for a revolutionary decision on a specific 'undecidable' and unrepresented singularity (Deleuze and Guattari 1987: 590–1/473); (3) it then follows out the 'non-denumerably infinite' consequences of this event by constructing new concrete assemblages and machinic personae that effectuate it (1987: 588/470).

But in what sense, then, is such a condition necessarily inclusive? In *What Is Philosophy?*, Deleuze and Guattari describe this immanent condition[3] as a plane whose only regions are the elements that develop it through local operations, point by point, and within a generic relation of becoming with one another. The plane of immanence, according to Deleuze and Guattari, thus has an 'infinite' or 'absolute' movement, or 'a nonlimited locality' (1987: 474/382), 'defined by a coming and going, because it does not advance toward a destination without already turning back on itself, the needle also being the pole' (1994: 40/38) like a 'vortex' (1987: 635/509). Thus, if a revolutionary condition is defined only by those who construct it through participation in it, then it cannot be essentially exclusive (it has no essential criteria for participation, only mutable ones).[4] This is in contrast with citizenship, which is not defined by one's participation in an event or place but rather by one's representation in a legal system of rights tied to the sovereignty of a nation. The type of revolutionary political body exemplified in the contemporary return to revolution is thus singular, universal and inclusive. But this recapitulation has only heightened the problem we are trying to resolve in this chapter: if revolutionary events each have their own singular and specific conditions, elements and agencies for action, how can they possibly be said to be in solidarity with other heterogeneous conditions, elements and agencies without creating a new unity (territory, state or market)?

DELEUZE, GUATTARI AND NOMADIC SOLIDARITY

In the preceding chapters I have argued for three interpretive theses about Deleuze and Guattari's political philosophy: (1) that we should use their concept of *historical topology* as a theory of revolutionary political diagnosis; (2) that we should use their concept of *deterritorialisation* as a theory to bring about prefigurative political transformations; and (3) that we should expand their concept of *consistency* to be used as a theory of political participation. In this chapter I propose my final interpretive thesis, namely, that their concept of *nomadism* should be used as a theory of political solidarity. Defined in its most basic terms, nomadism, for Deleuze and Guattari, is a 'mode of unlimited distribution without division'. Nomadism is fundamentally a theory of political relation. It describes how singular-universal events like revolutionary political bodies relate to each other and can be distributed in a mutually inclusive way without totalisation or representation.

But why do Deleuze and Guattari call this nomadic? What is it precisely about nomadism that allows us to theorise the inclusive and mobile connection between heterogeneous political conditions? Deleuze and Guattari define the origins of the word 'nomad' following the work of French historian Emmanuel Laroche in *Histoire de la racine nem- en grec ancien* (1949). There Laroche argues that the Greek origins of the root 'νεμ' signified a 'mode of distribution' [*moyen de distribution*], not an allocation of parcelled-out or delimited land [*partage*]. 'The idea [that *nomos* meant] law is a product of fifth and sixth-century Greek thought' that breaks from the 'original Homeric root νεμω meaning "I distribute" or "I arrange"' (1949: 255 [my translation]). Even 'the [retroactively] proposed translations "cut-up earth, plot of land, piece" are not suitable in all cases to the Homeric poems and assume an ancient νεμω "I divide" that we should reject. The pasture in archaic times is generally an unlimited space [*espace illimité*]; this can be a forest, meadow, rivers, a mountain side' (1949: 116 [my translation]).

'The *nomos*', Deleuze says, thus 'designated first of all an occupied space, but one without precise limits (for example, the expanse around a town)' (1994: 54/309 n6). Rather than parcelling out a closed space delimited by roads, borders and walls, assigning to each person a share of property [*partage*] and regulating the communication between shares through a juridical apparatus, the original meaning of nomadism, according to Laroche and Deleuze and Guattari, does the opposite. Nomadism 'distributes people in an open space that is indefinite [*indéfini*] and noncommunicating' without division, borders or *polis* (Deleuze and Guattari 1987: 472/380). It is marked instead by 'traits' that are effaced and displaced within a trajectory: points of relay, water, food, shelter and so on. But just because nomadic distributions have no division or border, it does not mean that nomad space is not distributed or consistent. Rather, it is precisely because of the fact that the *nomos* defines a concretely occupied but non-limited, indefinite space that it offers us a way to think of heterogeneous political conditions as mutual and connectable without opposition. If there are no distinct divisions or delimited 'pieces' [*des morceaux*], then there can be no mutual exclusion.

If each group solidarity has its own 'specific infinity' or *distribution illimité* (Deleuze and Guattari 1994: 26/21), and there are an unlimited number of such unlimited distributions, then there is by necessity no deducible continuum between such 'non-denumerable infinite sets'. The relationship between infinite events is thus 'undecidable: the germ and locus *par excellence* of revolutionary decisions', as Deleuze and Guattari say (1987: 590–1/473). It is precisely this undecidability between infinite events that makes solidarity possible. If there were a deducible continuum between all events, then we would simply reproduce the first figure of representational (and exclusionary) universality – making solidarity both unnecessary and impossible. On the other hand, if any kind of unified continuum were absolutely impossible then solidarity would only be paradoxical and ineffective. Solidarity must lie somewhere between these two positions.

But how is solidarity actually constructed between coexistent and unlimited distributions? While it must be admitted that Deleuze and Guattari rarely mention the word 'solidarity', I want to highlight a particularly illuminating passage and a footnote from the 'Treatise on Nomadology' chapter of *A Thousand Plateaus* where they do (1987: 453–4/366). Here, they directly connect the concept of solidarity to its nomadic origins and its role in the creation of a 'collective body' [*le corps collectif*] opposed to the state, family or party body.

The nomadic origins of the concept of solidarity, according to Deleuze and Guattari, are found in Ibn Khaldun's concept of *asabiyah.*[5] In his book *The Muqaddimah: An Introduction to History* ([1377] 1958), Khaldun defines the Bedouin nomads not primarily by their ethnic, geographical, state or familial genealogy, but by their mode of life and *group solidarity* that brings various heterogeneous persons and families together. What is interesting is that, for Khaldun, solidarity is not defined by any pre-given, genealogical or even static criteria for inclusion/exclusion, but rather by contingent relationships 'between persons who . . . share a feeling of solidarity without any outside prodding' (1958: section 8). 'By taking their special place within the group [solidarity], they participate to some extent in the common descent to which that particular group [solidarity] belongs' (1958: section 13). Not only is the only condition for group solidarity, according to Khaldun, 'a commitment' to a particular group solidarity, but this mutual solidarity then creates a new common line of descent (similarly open to solidarity with other groups). Thus Khaldun can claim that 'genealogy is something that is of no use to know and that it does no harm not to know . . . [because] when common descent is no longer clear and has become a matter of scientific knowledge, it can no longer move the imagination and is denied the affection caused by [solidarity]. It has become useless' (1958: section 8). Even state political power is useless without some type of solidarity behind it (1958: section 12). The most primary form of social belonging is thus, according to Khaldun, neither sedentary (state) nor genealogical (family), but rather contingent and mobile (nomadic).

What Deleuze and Guattari find so compelling in the nomadic origins of Khaldun's theory of solidarity is that each nomadic Bedouin family acts not as a hierarchical or unidirectional condition of genealogical descent, an arranged matrimonial alliance between families, or even a state-bureaucratic descent, but rather as a contingent 'band vector or point of relay expressing the power [*puissance*] or strength [*vertu*] of the solidarity' that holds them together (Deleuze and Guattari 1987: 453/366). Families are thus assembled primarily through relations of mutual, horizontal solidarity and have nothing to do 'with the monopoly of an organic power [*pouvoir*] nor with local representation, but [with] the potential [*puissance*] of a vortical body in a nomad space' (1987: 454/366). It would thus be a mistake to understand nomadic solidarity as simply a matter of pure deterritorialisation or unlimited space: a line of flight from or internal transformation of state power. Rather, I am arguing, following Khaldun, that Deleuze and Guattari's concept of nomadism is a matter of belonging and unity among heterogeneous relays. 'Revolutionary movement', Deleuze and Guattari say, is 'the connection of flows, the composition of non-denumerable aggregates, the becoming-minoritarian of everybody/everything ... This is not a dispersion or a fragmentation' (1987: 590–1/473). Accordingly, Khaldun defines nomadic solidarity (*badiya asabiyah*) according to two axes of belonging: *the group/family* (the condition of a common descent) and *relations of solidarity* (the concrete practices of mutual support and relay between groups).

So just as a revolutionary condition immanently holds together the becoming of its heterogeneous conditioned concrete elements, so is it immanently related to other conditions like a Bedouin solidarity: without the outside prodding of territory, family or state. And since this evental condition is always a singular-universal or local-absolute, made only through local operations, there can be no event of all events. Such an event would be transcendent and outside of or excluded from events as such, as discussed in Chapter 2. But if there is an infinity of infinite events[6] whose relations are undecidable but whose conditions are decidable as universally open and egalitarian, then it is at least possible that, even though such events are non-denumerable and heterogeneous (*illimité*, for Laroche), there could be, according to Deleuze and Guattari, 'larger or smaller [infinities] according to the ... components, thresholds, and bridges' they connect (1994: 26/21). If every event is open to universal participation and transformation, then events, by definition, are not mutually exclusive. They can, however, be added, combined or mutually reinforced to certain degrees, while never becoming entirely identical. That said, since the relation between political conditions is still a fundamentally 'undecidable' one, the actual labour of following out the local consequences of the relations of solidarity requires more than just a revolutionary 'decision' that two or more revolutionary political bodies are 'in solidarity'.

Transversal Relays

Thus, if solidarity is possible, how does it work? By 'solidarity' I mean the immanent, point-by-point connection between at least two heterogeneous evental sequences (an immanent condition, its concrete elements and its forms of agency). By 'connection' I mean the degree to which a concrete element or singularity is affirmed as a consequence or singularity of both evental conditions. Since merely 'deciding on the undecidable', as I argued in Chapter 3, is insufficient for sustaining the participatory consequences and agents of such a decision, so is merely 'deciding on the undecidable' relation between two heterogeneous political *conditions*. Accordingly, it is necessary, for evental solidarity, to connect at least one consequence or element from one event to at least one consequence or element of another. The more concrete elements of an event that are connected to the elements of another event, the greater the degree of infinity in each event as well as the degree of solidarity between them. In *What Is Philosophy?* Deleuze and Guattari call this the 'external neighborhood or exoconsistency' of the event. Its transuniversal or 'transversal' relations are 'secured by the bridges thrown from one [machine] to another' (Deleuze and Guattari 1994: 87/90). This is the piece-by-piece labour of solidarity.

But since each revolutionary condition is singular, a 'connection' or 'transversality' between connections cannot mean total identification. Rather, this kind of revolution is 'constructed piece by piece, and the places, conditions, and techniques are irreducible to one another' (Deleuze and Guattari 1987: 190/157). Thus two heterogeneous conditions become more or less connected/identified through an unlimited series of concrete political practices that act as non-communicating relays. This is because 'for the nomad', according to Deleuze and Guattari,

> locality is not delimited; the absolute, then, does not appear at a particular place but becomes a non-limited locality; the coupling of the place and the absolute is achieved not in a centered, oriented globalization or universalization but in an infinite succession of local operations. (1987: 475/383)

But this infinite succession is not an indefinite delay of solidarity; it is the positive concrete articulation of increasingly greater degrees without a totality of absolute unification. As Guillaume Sibertin-Blanc puts it, the

> 'becoming-minoritarian of everyone' can be constructed ... through a universal process which involves no gushing spontaneity of 'Life' or 'History' ... but through the blocks of asymmetrical becomings where a term may become-other thanks to the becoming-other of another term itself connected to an *nth* in an open series ... No longer an extensive and quantifiable universality, but on the contrary an intensive and unquantifiable universality, in the sense that subjects become in common in a process where their identitary anchorages are dissipated, to the advan-

tage of that conception and radically constructivist practice of autonomy required by a new minoritarian internationalism. (Sibertin-Blanc 2009: 134–5)

Just as two different nomadic Bedouin families share more or less solidarity over some specific practices and thus 'participate to *some extent* in the common descent' (my italics) of each other's families, so it is possible to say that two or more heterogeneous political conditions participate to a greater or lesser degree in each other's conditions to the extent that they share a number of the same concrete consequences or relays. With this definition we are closer to the earlier political meaning of the word *nomos* as a mode of non-limited distribution than we are with the derivative fifth- or sixth-century Greek definition of *nomos* as law (*loi*), to judge (*juger*) or to govern (*gouverner*) (Laroche 1949: 256). With this definition it is also possible for one to occupy multiple heterogeneous conditions at once to the degree that a given distribution of bridges of shared commitment crosses transversally multiple political conditions. This is what Deleuze and Guattari call

> a constructivism, [or] 'diagrammatism,' operating by the determination of the conditions of the problem and by transversal links between problems: it opposes both the automation of the capitalist axioms and bureaucratic programming. From this standpoint, when we talk about 'undecidable propositions,' we are not referring to the uncertainty of the results, which is necessarily a part of every system. We are referring, on the contrary, to the coexistence and inseparability of that which the system conjugates, and that which never ceases to escape it following lines of flight that are themselves connectable. (1987: 590–1/473)

We have now been able finally to answer the question 'how can one uphold the rights of a micro-analysis (diffusion, heterogeneity, fragmentation) and still allow for some kind of principle of unification that will not turn out to be like the State or the Party, a totalization or a representation?' (Deleuze 2006: 120–1/132–3). The answer requires a revolutionary body politic to have at least four specific characteristics: singularity, universality, inclusivity and a participatory structure (defined in Chapter 3 and rephrased above). It must be local and determinate with a proper name, absolute and infinite in its consequences, and open to modification by anyone without predefined criteria. Given these four characteristics, I have shown how Deleuze and Guattari define a 'collective political body' by its nomadic solidarity following Laroche and Khaldun. Laroche defines *nomos* by its earlier Homeric roots as the open distribution or arrangement of a collective body in an unlimited and inclusive space. The forest, pasture, mountain steppe and their inhabitants all express this undivided but clearly heterogeneous kind of distributive unity. Khaldun, then, defines the connections between heterogeneous Bedouin families not by family, state or territory, but by two different axes: common descent and relations of relayed group solidarity. While groups of common descent never merge entirely, they merge to a greater or lesser degree depending on the concrete relations of group solidarity at a given time. Finally, we reached the definition of nomadic solidarity as the piece-by-piece infinite connection (bridging) of shared concrete actions by two or more heterogeneous political conditions (never merging but becoming more or less transversally identical).

III. *Zapatismo and Los Encuentros Intercontinentales*

'A World in Which Many Worlds Fit'

The concept of nomadism as a theory of political solidarity does not apply only to the historical phenomenon of nomadic peoples. As a 'mode of distribution' it can be used elsewhere and for other purposes. Thus, in this next section, I argue that the Zapatistas do precisely this with their practice of mutual global solidarity. This kind of solidarity is irreducible, not only to the practices of citizenship and difference, but to other existing models of political solidarity as well. I begin by distinguishing between four types of solidarity – internationalism, Third World solidarity, rights solidarity and material solidarity – and address Thomas Olesen's (2005) argument that they all share a one-way model of unequal solidarity. I then argue that, rather than break with these models altogether, the Zapatistas rely on and offer all these types of solidarity to some degree but ultimately rely most on a practice of global solidarity defined not by unequal relations between First and Third World, nor by north and south, but by mutual relations between singular-universals. Beyond this, I argue that their practice of creating *Encuentros Intercontinentales* (Intercontinental Gatherings) and *Puentes de Solidaridad* (Bridges of Solidarity) do more than just define a 'mutual' relation of global solidarity; they define a singular-universal practice of inclusive solidarity held together by coordinated concrete actions.

NEITHER CITIZENSHIP NOR DIFFERENCE

The singular-universal solidarity of the Zapatistas, however, does not emerge from nowhere. It emerges, along with modern citizenship and other practices of solidarity, from the development of the modernist concept of universalism: the idea of a global consciousness, a shared humanity and an aspiration to see the world as a single place. Regardless of how successful modern democracies have been at achieving this universality, the Zapatistas express a new development in its theory and practice. In contrast to the modern theory of citizenship based on the territorial nation-state that was criticised earlier in this chapter for its exclusionary character, for the Zapatistas there are no essential criteria for political inclusion/exclusion, such as what territory one was born in, what nation one is a part of, what state grants one rights and so on. 'Dignity is that nation without nationality,' they say, 'that rainbow that is also a bridge . . . that rebel irreverence that mocks borders, customs, and wars' (Marcos 2004b: 642).

Additionally, in contrast to the theory of political affinity as difference proposed by Simon Tormey (2006: 146), the Zapatistas, I argue, do not insist on the political solidarity of universal singularity or difference alone, but on a type of organised global solidarity found in the unique structure of the *Encuentros* that must be constructed through a particular network of concrete bridges against neoliberalism. Merely affirming global autonomy and difference means nothing without the discipline of building revolutionary political bodies and bridges based on participatory conditions and concrete actions. 'Shared difference' tells us nothing about the type of organisation required to assemble singularities without falling into the trap of representation. 'A world in which many worlds fit', as the Zapatistas say, thus cannot be realised by merely affirming that 'there are a multiplicity of worlds' (universal singularity) but must be constructed in such a way that many worlds fit together (through concrete bridges and encounters) without creating a representational hierarchy like a territory, nation, state or capitalist market. That way is not universal difference for the Zapatistas; that way is participatory democracy and global solidarity through networked horizontalism.

FOUR TYPES OF SOLIDARITY

The singular-universal solidarity used by the Zapatistas is different from four other kinds of solidarity: internationalism, Third World solidarity, rights solidarity, and material solidarity. Left-wing inter-nationalism, especially active in the early twentieth century, proposed socialist cosmopolitanism as an alternative to global capitalism. It was defined by two features: first, it assumed a certain homogeneity of industrial working conditions and thus a high degree of global class consciousness that was ready for revolution, as can be seen in the slogan 'workers of the world unite'. Second, it was, for the most part, vertically structured around national parties and states with socialist governments. Since the end of the Cold War, however, this type of international solidarity has virtually disappeared (Waterman 1998: 236). Third World solidarity, on the other hand, grew out of the student movement and anti-war movements of the 1960s (espe-cially in Europe and the USA) and was particularly important in sup-porting the national liberation movements of the 1970s. It was also defined by two features: first, it was concerned with economic and structural inequalities between rich and poor; and second, although it divided the world into first, second and third (or north and south), it still reflected a growing global consciousness.

Rights solidarity is concerned mainly with human rights abuses and other forms of repression by states or extra-legal forces:

> Rights solidarity work generally aims at putting pressure on human rights abusers. This may be done directly by lobbying the governments of the countries in which the violations take place, but often pressure is exerted through other governments or intergovernmental organizations expected to have a certain influence on the state in which the violations occur. (Olesen 2005: 256)

Rights solidarity is based on a strong conception of universal human rights but is often less politicised because it focuses on the violations of individual persons instead of more structural causes. Material solidarity is directed mainly towards victims of natural disasters (droughts, earthquakes and so on) or human-caused disasters (wars, refugees and so on) and to different forms of underdevelopment.

> Material solidarity reflects a global consciousness in that it constructs a world in which the fate of distant people can no longer be ignored. Like rights solidarity, material solidarity is often carried out by organizations that take a neutral position in specific conflicts. (Olesen 2005: 256)

All four of these types of solidarity, according to Olesen, display elements of inequality. These forms are all based on a predominantly one-way relationship between those who offer solidarity and those who benefit from it. The ones who offer solidarity are generally richer and have more resources to offer those who do not have them. Solidarity based on charity and altruism may have beneficial consequences, but insofar as they are not aimed at changing the structural conditions under which they currently exist, they risk perpetuating the inequality that allows them to exist. While Third World solidarity and international solidarity may be more politicised in the sense that they demand structural changes to the current global inequalities, they also rely on some of the binary historical perspectives that characterised the Cold War, where the providers of solidarity are mostly from Europe and the USA and those elsewhere receive aid on the condition they affirm the strategies of the provider.

Global solidarity, in contrast, is defined by a high degree of mutual aid between activists that blurs the distinction between the provider and the receiver of solidarity and has a larger emphasis on non-material solidarity (inspiration, education, affection and so on). All solidarity activists are understood to be affected, to varying degrees, by the same neoliberal system. Global solidarity thus emphasises similarities between socially distant people while simultaneously respecting local differences. In this way global solidarity aims to move between the singular and the universal without subordinating one to the other. This is the kind of solidarity practised by the Zapatistas.

THE *ENCUENTROS*

It would, however, be inaccurate to argue that the Zapatistas have always given or received solidarity in a purely mutual way. The Zapatistas still receive material aid from Europe and the United States to a significant degree, and human rights groups continue to be a presence in Chiapas. While the global inequality of wealth and power does pose a challenge to the aim of mutual global solidarity, this does not mean that global solidarity should not be the larger aim and practice of revolutionary movements.[7] The Zapatistas and their supporters thus aim to create the first global solidarity network based on this model of mutual aid. The network they invented to do this was called the *Encuentro Intercontinental*.

On 27 July 1996, 3,000 activists from more than forty countries converged in Zapatista territory in Chiapas, Mexico, for the First Intercontinental *Encuentro* for Humanity and against Neoliberalism. The aim of the first *Encuentro* was to gather the 'minorities of the world: the indigenous, youth, women, homosexuals, lesbians, people of color, immigrants, workers, peasants, etc.' (Marcos 2004b: 642) and create a space where they could share their struggles and create bridges of mutual global solidarity. Here, the Committees in Solidarity with the Zapatista Rebellion were created and charged with the further organisation of more *Encuentros* on the five continents – Europe, Asia, America, Africa and Oceania – in the coming years. And the closing remarks of this first *Encuentro* (Second Declaration of *La Realidad*) defined two central aims of this new network: first, to make a collective network of all singular struggles and resistances:

> This intercontinental network of resistance, recognizing differences and acknowledging similarities, will search to find itself with other resistances around the world. This intercontinental network of resistance will be the medium in which distinct resistances may support one another. This intercontinental network of resistance is not an organizing structure; it doesn't have a central head or decision maker; it has no central command or hierarchies. We are the network, all of us who resist. (Marcos 2004b: 645)

The second aim was to create an intercontinental network of alternative communication among all struggles and resistances that 'will search to weave the channels *(tejer los canales)* so that words may travel all the roads *(camine todos los caminos)* that resist . . . [and] will be the medium by which distinct resistances communicate with one another' (Marcos 2004b: 645).

In 1997 the Second *Encuentro* was held in southern Spain, drawing over 3,000 activists from over fifty countries. It was here that the plans originated for the creation of an offshoot group called Peoples' Global Action (PGA) in order to 'move beyond debate and exchange and propose action campaigns against neoliberalism, worldwide' (de Marcellus 2001). Beginning in 1998, PGA organised a series of direct actions and interventions on various global elite summits (G7, WTO and so on) that are now identified as the alter-globalisation movement. Over the years the multiplication of similar forums on global resistance – World Social Forum (2001–present), regional social forums and so on – have all emphasised the core proposals made at the First *Encuentro*: horizontal (non-hierarchical) organisation and global alternative communications without centralisation (see Khasnabish 2008: 238).

The fact that Zapatismo has profoundly influenced the last fifteen years of the largest actions and gatherings in the world against neoliberalism is by now well known and recounted in several important books on the history of the alter-globalisation movement (Notes from Nowhere 2003; Khasnabish 2008; Curran 2006; Engler 2007). But it is precisely because its historical influence is so well known that its larger strategic determination remains so obscure. Thus, beyond empirical descriptions of this history, I propose to isolate and extract two practical strategies that emerge from the Zapatista experiment that allow us both to understand the larger theory of political affinity in the present revolutionary sequence and to develop and further its practices elsewhere. These two practices are the *Encuentro* (Encounter) and the *Puente* (Bridge).

The *Encuentro* is not just a historical phenomenon or empirical gathering of various marginalised peoples against neoliberalism that takes place around the world; it is a political strategy of heterogeneous common descent and transversality. It was different from other international conferences at the time because it affirmed equally all of the heterogeneous struggles of the world (not only the class struggle, or feminism, or anti-racism and so on), and universalised these struggles as the same struggle against all forms of oppression and neoliberalism: the *Encuentros* were the first alter-globalisation gatherings. They were created as an alternative to the exclusionary affinity of citizenship based on the false universality of nations and borders, as well as to the pure affirmation of universal singularity based on shared difference alone. The *Encuentro* also invented a new kind of revolutionary solidarity historically different from others based on unequal power relations. An *Encuentro*, according to the Second Declaration, is a non-hierarchical and non-centralised space where different groups share their conflicts and agreements without the *a priori* conditions of territorial, state or economic belonging.[8] It is a space where multiple singular-universal conditions (see section II) coexist as irreducible struggles in their own right and autonomy. The *Encuentro* itself is thus not a decision-making body; it is not like the revolutionary body politic discussed in Chapter 3 (based on participatory and rotational democracy and so on). According to the Second Declaration, the *Encuentro* is a medium (*el medio*) in which distinct resistances are in the middle of something undivided, together.

But without any decision-making or criteria for inclusion/exclusion, what is the meaning of the *Encuentro*? What are they in the middle of together? According to the Second Declaration, the *Encuentro* is not an entirely neutral medium, but neither is it a new political condition to which all attending political conditions must now give themselves over. The *Encuentro* 'is not a new organization, theorization of Utopia, global program for world revolution, scheme, or enumeration of international orders ... that assures all of us a position, a task, and a title' (Marcos 2004b: 645), as the Zapatistas say. Rather, the *Encuentro* is 'for Humanity and against Neoliberalism'.

We should take care to distinguish the name of the *Encuentro*, as the transversal operation holding together many singular-universal political conditions, both from political ideology (representational or programmatic content) and from a new revolutionary body politic of all revolutionary body politics (composed of a new and larger condition, set of elements and agencies). Rather, the slogan 'For Humanity and against Neoliberalism' is a generic name or mutable referent for the descent common to two or more heterogeneous political conditions like a particular group solidarity between Bedouin families. By formulating humanity and neoliberalism in the most generic way possible, the *Encuentro* is able to achieve a maximum of inclusion and mutual support with a minimum of representation and reference.[9]

Just as Deleuze and Guattari argue, following Laroche, that the Greek root 'nem-', from which the word 'nomadism' is derived, originally implied a mode of distribution or *agencement* in an unlimited or non-divided space, so the Zapatistas have created the practice of the *Encuentro* that equally distributes heterogeneous political events (women, indigenous, teachers, environmental activists, people of all races and so on) without dividing them hierarchically or based on the exclusionary criteria invented by the state, the party or the vanguard. Perhaps another way of describing the unlimited nomadic space of the mountains, planes or forests that are without border or division is 'a world in which many worlds fit': a locality that has become unlimited alongside others. Similarly, in Khaldun's theory of solidarity, Bedouin nomad 'families' express a common descent undivided by genealogy or the state and distributed in a shared medium (*l'esprit de corps*) where several heterogeneous groups share the group solidarity of a 'collective body' (Deleuze and Guattari 1987: 453–4/366). In sum, the *Encuentro* is the name for the generic transversal relationship between multiple singular-universal political conditions without division, hierarchy or decision-making capacity. It is an open and non-divided nomadic space, but one that is clearly and unambiguously against neoliberalism and for humanity.

However, just as it was impossible to understand the concept of solidarity in Deleuze and Guattari without the concept of 'exoconsistency' (that bridged the concrete machines between different abstract machines), so it is impossible to understand the concept of solidarity in Zapatismo without also understanding the concept of the *puentes* or 'bridges' that connect the concrete actions and consequences of different political events.

Accordingly, the Second Declaration proposes a second dimension of solidarity to the first non-hierarchical, non-decision-making, collective space of the *Encuentro*: 'a network of woven channels [or bridges] so that words [and actions] may travel all the roads that resist'. Firstly, the concept of the network discussed in the Second Declaration should be distinguished topologically as an 'all channel network' (where everyone can connect horizontally with everyone else in a non-linear series: like a rhizome) in contrast to a 'chain network' (where top-to-bottom communication is mediated hierarchically: like a tree) as well as a 'star or hub network' (where actors are tied to a single central but non-hierarchical actor and must go through that node to communicate with others: like a tuber) (Ronfeldt et al. 1998: 7). Secondly, while the *Encuentro* proposes an inclusive network or mutual encounter between 'particular struggles and resistances' (singular-universal conditions), this does not guarantee that such an encounter will produce any concrete connections or coordinated actions between them. Thus, the second dimension of the *Encuentro* proposed by the Zapatistas is the creation of an alternative media network for the coordination (weaving) of concrete words and actions around the world. As Ronfeldt et al. highlight:

> More than ever before, conflicts are about 'knowledge' – about who knows (or can be kept from knowing) what, when, where, and why. Conflicts will revolve less around the use of raw power than of 'soft power,' as applied through 'information operations' and 'perception management,' that is, media-oriented measures that aim to attract rather than coerce and that affect how secure a society, a military, or other actor feels about its knowledge of itself and its adversaries. Psychosocial disruption may become more important than physical destruction . . . Mexico's Zapatista movement exemplifies [this] new approach to social conflict that we call *social netwar*. (1998: 7)

Accordingly, Marcos says, this media network is 'not about communication, but of building something' (Marcos 2001a). Media not only produces knowledge but also produces effects that transform reality. Thus, it may be 'the word which is the bridge to cross to the other' (The Zapatistas 1998: 8), but in 'extend[ing] the bridges that joined those who were the same, [it makes] them different' (Marcos 2004b: 437). The concept of the bridge, deployed often in Zapatista writings, is accordingly not a common link between two different things that brings them into a unity; it is a differentiator between two common things that keeps them apart *and* holds them together *as differentiated*. It is in this sense that the Zapatistas say that their 'goal [has been] to be a bridge on which the many rebellions in the world can walk back and forth' (Marcos and the EZLN 2008): a bridge that has connected and differentiated the mutual transformation of everyone by everyone else, communiqué by communiqué and direct action by direct action. The 'coming and going' of world rebellions across this bridge is what gives Zapatista solidarity its nomadic, ambulant and mutualistic features. But at the global level solidarity cannot be realised as a generic encounter against neoliberalism; it has to take on specific coordinated words, slogans and actions, that is, one or more bridges that connect two or more singular struggles together. The more concrete bridges or connections made through this alternative media network, the stronger and larger the network. Because the network is nothing more than the connections or bridges that effectuate it, there is no party, state or bureaucracy at the head; it is acephalic. Accordingly, it lays the largest possible conditions for a federated worldwide decision-making process.

Just as different lines of descent for Khaldun's Bedouin nomads are modified and more or less merged through concrete 'points of relay' or group solidarity (without essential determination by family or state), so the Zapatistas have inspired a global solidarity of *Encuentros* that modify and more or less merge heterogeneous struggles against neoliberalism through a concrete media and action network (without hierarchy, centralisation, territory, state or party). And just as Deleuze and Guattari say that a plane of consistency has an endoconsistency that holds its concrete machines together internally and an exoconsistency that connects it to other 'nomadic traits' or 'points of relay' on other planes of consistency outside itself, so the Zapatistas define their political plane of consistency by its participatory internal institutions (the JBGs) as well as by its external bridges to other concrete struggles elsewhere: *Puentes de Solidaridad*. Thus revolutionary events 'are defined only by their mutual solidarity' and not independently of it (Deleuze and Guattari 1987: 60/45). Opposed to static and one-way models of solidarity based on state and party bodies, the Zapatistas propose a mutual collective body defined by nomadic solidarity: walking, encountering and bridging.[10]

Conclusion

> From the global gatherings to the summit protests, the polymorphous
> spirit of Zapatismo was in the air. (Maccani 2006: 109)

At the end of the previous chapter we were confronted with the
problem of how revolutionary transformations, having become
consistently established in participatory body politics, could connect
with other such institutions to form a global alternative to state-capitalism. If there is no longer a central axis of struggle, but a multiplicity of struggles each with its own conditions, elements and agencies,
how can they be unified or organised into a global struggle without
deploying the traditional forms of state, party and representation?
This chapter's response to this problem was threefold.

Firstly, I argued that the present model of liberal citizenship based
on territorial nation-states is unable to provide a theory of universal
emancipation/solidarity because of (1) the increasing proliferation of
non- and extra-national organisations that now replace many of the
benefits offered by citizenship; (2) the increasing number of criminalised migrants that are denied citizenship; and (3) the increasing
frequency (since World War I) with which nation-states have sus-
pended the constitutional rights of citizens in modern democracies.
Additionally, territorial nation-states are necessarily exclusionary
insofar as they are limited by a particular geography, identity and
sovereign law. Conversely, I argued that the theory of universal singularity (that what everyone has universally in common is difference/
singularity-in-itself) is only able to provide an aporetic definition of
political affinity without a theory of how such singularities would be
able to assemble into specific political distributions.

Secondly, I argued that Deleuze and Guattari (following Laroche
and Khaldun) provide a conceptual alternative to these models in
their theory of nomadic solidarity based on non-divided distribution
and the federated relay between points. Given the three characteristics of a revolutionary body politic as defined in Chapter 3 (local
and determinate with a proper name, absolute and infinite in its consequences, and open to modification by anyone without predefined
criteria), Deleuze and Guattari define a 'collective political body' of
solidarity as the piece-by-piece infinite connection (bridging) of one
or more shared concrete actions between two or more heterogeneous
political conditions, never merging but becoming more or less transversally identical.

Finally, I argued that the Zapatista *Encuentros* (in combination with the JBGs) offer an alternative to both citizenship- and difference-based affinities as well as unequal forms of solidarity. I argued that just as Deleuze and Guattari's concept of nomadic solidarity was based on non-divided distribution and federated relay, so the Zapatistas' practice of mutual global solidarity is based on inclusive horizontalism and networked bridges of coordinated action. While the first provides the conditions for a generic network of mutually supported resistance against neoliberalism ('One no, many yeses'), the second weaves together (federates) these multiple relays and channels into concrete action-decisions. The Zapatista conceptual practice of the *Encuentro* aims to create a nation without nationality, a people without territory: 'a world in which many worlds fit'.

But while this chapter has been able to conceptualise the revolutionary political solidarity that characterises the present revolutionary sequence by drawing on the work of Deleuze, Guattari and the Zapatistas, it also confronts a final tension between the two dimensions internal to the functioning of mutual global solidarity: the need for an open (non-decision-making) horizontalism and the need for a coordinated network of decision-orientated action. While it may be possible for heterogeneous participatory political bodies to govern themselves, to share their methods and struggles at global *Encuentros*, and even to coordinate global actions through alternative media, this does not entirely resolve the problem of how decisions are to be made, implemented and modified at the global level without creating a global state, party or form of representation. How is it that the largest organised gathering of anti-neoliberal forces in the world, the World Social Forum, can begin to make and enforce a meaningful transition away from global capitalism? Although the question of global transition and decision-making is not answered in this chapter (or in practice by the Zapatistas or the World Social Forum), the theory of solidarity developed here does lay a fecund groundwork for answering it. In the Conclusion to this book, I end with a reconstruction and reflection upon the relative accomplishments of each chapter and the success of the argument of the book as a whole, and outline areas for further investigation.

Notes

1. 'The IOM estimates that irregular immigrants account for one-third to one-half of new entrants into developed countries, marking an increase

of 20 per cent over the past ten years' (International Organization for Migration 2008).

2. While there may be a structural exclusion and multiplicity necessary to law itself, there are certainly degrees of mobilising this combination. Modern nation-states, as Hannah Arendt feared, have succumbed to the temptation to increasingly deploy this exceptionalism.

> The clearer the proof of their inability to treat stateless people as legal persons and the greater the extension of arbitrary rule by police decree, the more difficult it is for states to resist the temptation to deprive all citizens of legal status and rule them with an omnipotent police. (Arendt 1979: 290)

3. That is, a plane of immanence; an abstract machine.
4. Although this is not to say that debate and conflicts never arise regarding the status and content of an event.
5. The Arabic word for 'socialism' is derived from *asabiyah*.
6. This is different from saying 'an infinity of events'. In Chapter 3 I argued that each participatory political body was both singular, insofar as it was a locally waged struggle, and infinite or absolute, in the sense that its consequences could be carried out anywhere by anyone and infinitely so. This is the definition of an infinite event. An infinity of infinite events is different and poses a real problem similar to one posed in set theory: 'the continuum hypothesis'. If there are multiple infinities, that is, an infinity of infinities without totality, how can we know which are larger or smaller and what their relations are? This is also the problem of solidarity between non-representational body politics.
7. Although those who currently practise rights and material solidarity would also agree that the current system of inequality is a barrier to global solidarity, the difference is that material aid solidarity does not change the conditions for the production of the material donated. The Zapatistas, on the other hand, aim to transform the conditions for material production and distribution not just in theory but also in practice. Their political philosophy is explicitly anti-capitalist and their practical creation of workers' cooperatives and use of democratic fair trade practices concretely express their rejection of private property, profit and charity. Despite their relative poverty they have done their best to provide aid to others like Cuba and Palestine.
8. The inclusive and egalitarian presupposition of the *Encuentro* immediately distinguishes it from racist or discriminatory organisations with perhaps similar structures but who discriminate *a priori* based on territorial race, nation, gender, sex and so on.
9. By defining humanity and neoliberalism so generically, the *Encuentro* not only forces a split in the contemporary situation between the current world and a new world in the making, it also defines this new world so generically that participation in it is as broad as possible. To

be clear, the positive universality is not defined by its opposition to or negation of neoliberalism, but by the constructive generic of humanity and Zapatismo itself.

10. 'Preguntando caminamos [Asking, we walk].'

Conclusion

We are witnessing today the return of a new theory and practice of revolution. In its early stages of development and far from homogeneous in character, this new theory encompasses the growing belief not only that 'another world is possible' beyond capitalism, but that it 'must be made' in such a way that the mistakes of previous revolutionary efforts are not repeated: the capture of the state, the representation of the party or the privileged knowledge of the vanguard. Philosophically, I have argued we can see this new shift in Deleuze and Guattari's concepts of historical topology, constructive deterritorialisation, political consistency and nomadic solidarity. Politically, I have argued we can see this alternative at work in the Zapatistas' use of a multi-centred diagnostic of suffering, in their creation of the *Juntas de Buen Gobierno*, in their leading by obeying and in their practice of mutual global solidarity.

But Deleuze, Guattari and the Zapatistas are neither models for how all revolutions should proceed nor representations of how they are all actually proceeding. Rather, they are only two particularly fecund sources for the emergence of four unique and influential strategies active in revolutionary politics today. What I have argued in this book is that Deleuze, Guattari and the Zapatistas have created several conceptual/practical strategies that are both indicative of and useful for the further creation of a new theory and practice of revolution that is no longer subordinated to the processes of political representation or their mere critique by a speculative leftism based on difference and potentiality. I have followed a conditional imperative: if you want to struggle, here are some strategies to do so. Accordingly, I have proposed and defended the use of four strategies extracted and reassembled from the work of Deleuze, Guattari and the Zapatistas: (1) a multi-centred diagnostic of political power; (2) a prefigurative strategy of political transformation; (3) a participatory strategy of creating a body politic; and (4) a political strategy of belonging based on mutual global solidarity. Insofar as these strategies have clarified and further developed the actual, and not merely possible, existence of a non-representational revolutionary process in Zapatismo and Deleuze and Guattari's work, this book has succeeded in this aim.

I. Method and Interpretation

These four strategies were created through a methodology of extraction and reassembly. Organised around the revolutionary themes of history, transformation, the body politic and affinity, each of the four central chapters of this book developed selected concepts and practices from Deleuze, Guattari and the Zapatistas and composed them into a new practical-theoretical strategy that responded to the question at hand. In Chapter 1, I took Deleuze and Guattari's historical topology based on the immanent processes of coding, overcoding and axiomatisation and the Zapatistas' intersectional diagnostic deployed during *La Otra Campaña* and argued that we can extract and reassemble from these what I call a multi-centred political diagnostic useful for determining the dangers and potentials for historical and revolutionary action. In Chapter 2, I showed how a prefigurative strategy of political transformation, taking place in the future anterior, could be assembled from Deleuze and Guattari's concept of deterritorialisation and the Zapatistas' *Juntas de Buen Gobierno*. In Chapter 3, I showed how a participatory strategy of revolutionary institutions could be assembled using Deleuze and Guattari's concept of consistency and the Zapatistas' practice of direct democracy used in the *Juntas*. Finally, in Chapter 4 I showed how a political strategy of belonging based on mutual global solidarity could be assembled from Deleuze and Guattari's concept of nomadism and the Zapatistas' creation of Intercontinental *Encuentros*. The aim of this extraction and reassembly was not to show how theory is derived from practice or practice from theory, but to put the two into a strategic relationship in order to respond to the problems of revolutionary praxis. Where one may have been a bit clumsy, hit a wall or left one with questions, the other breaks through and pushes forward. In this book I have tried to use theory and practice as a system of relays around four questions of revolutionary strategy.

The creation of these strategies was also accomplished through an interpretive intervention in the context of the scholarly literature on Deleuze, Guattari and the Zapatistas. For both, I made a similar intervention: to reject interpreting their work as either trying to merely tweak or fortify processes of political representation (state, party and so on) or as merely expressing the *potentiality* of another post-representational politics. Rather, I have read Deleuze, Guattari and the Zapatistas as political constructivists; that is, I have read them as making concrete contributions to the creation of a new collective political body. In the case of Deleuze and Guattari, I located this constructivist turn in *A Thousand Plateaus* and *What Is Philosophy?* and argued that we can extract from these works a positive and contemporary vision of revolutionary theory. In particular, the concept of political consistency I took from *What Is Philosophy?* in Chapter 3 relied on an extension of the definition they give to philosophy (as a constructivism) to the field of politics. This is an extension left undeveloped in *What Is Philosophy?* Thematically and conceptually, however, I have shown that such an extension is not textually unsupported and can contribute to the development of revolutionary strategy. The real motivation for this intervention is that without this constructive focus, Deleuze and Guattari's philosophy risks a variety of dangers articulated well by their critics: political ambivalence, virtual hierarchy, subjective paralysis and so on.

I chose to read the Zapatistas in a similar way that focused on their later (2003–present) writings and activities in order to highlight a similarly constructivist turn. In 2003 the Zapatistas took a step back to listen carefully to the Mexican people, to critique and improve Zapatista political processes (the place of women and the EZLN 'military') and to begin a long-term project of sustaining the autonomous Zapatista territories and their relations with other left organisations around the world. This was their constructivist turn. Beyond the 'failure' or 'success' of the Zapatista uprising to capture the state or win rights from it, I analysed the new revolutionary practices developed after the traditional ones had failed: the rejection of the vanguard, the prefigurative creation of the autonomous communes, the global network of mutual aid and so on. It is from these practices that I assembled the four strategies of a current return to revolution.

II. Difficulties and Implications

One of the difficulties of this methodology of extraction and reassembly was to articulate the heterogeneity between Deleuze and Guattari's concepts and the Zapatistas' practices without granting a privilege or explanatory power of one over the other. Instead of extracting a set of concepts and showing their implications for the history of political philosophy or extracting a set of practices and showing their implications for the history of social movements, I have chosen to assemble from Deleuze, Guattari and Zapatismo four strategies in order to show their implications for four questions in contemporary revolutionary strategy. My hope is that these strategic assemblages will in turn spawn further relays in the future. Accordingly, the strategies I developed in each of the chapters act more like circulating reference points or strange attractors for heterogeneous concepts and practices than representations of theory exemplified by practice. Each chapter has tried to maintain a real difference between theory and practice without synthesising the two. It is precisely this difference that leaves open further mutations in the strategies I have put forward. If the reader picks up on this relay style of assembly, it is entirely intentional.

The task of this book was to elaborate responses to four questions confronting the current, albeit young, revolutionary sequence: (1) What tools does it offer us to understand the current historical conjuncture of power such that political change is desirable? (2) How can this current conjuncture of power be transformed? (3) What kinds of new social bodies can be put in the place of or alongside the old ones? (4) Who can belong to or participate in this transformative social body? What I have shown by drawing on Deleuze, Guattari and the Zapatistas is that we can locate a novel and consistent set of answers to these questions. The conclusion I have aimed to draw from this effort is that we should reject the prevailing notion that 'there is no alternative to global capitalism and representational politics' and that 'another world is merely possible'. My conclusion is that another world is already under way (theoretically and practically) within and alongside the old. The task now is to develop and defend it.

The larger implication of this conclusion is that contemporary political philosophy interested in understanding the current conjuncture should offer us more than the mere conceptual conclusion that another politics is possible. Additionally, it should offer us a philosophical interrogation of actually existing strategies: what dangers they face, what kinds of changes they have made, what kinds of alternatives they propose and what the larger connections they have created are. The aim of these efforts, what Foucault called 'a history of the present', is to critically develop the theories and practices that are already in action here and now and force philosophy to become adequate with contemporary political struggle. This book has shown that such an interrogation is not only possible but also productive in offering answers to some of the basic questions often posed to post-structuralist political philosophers and contemporary revolutionaries. If not capitalism, then what else is there? This question deserves more than the affirmation that 'another world is possible'. We must be able to say that 'another world is actually under way' beneath and alongside the old, and here are some of its dimensions and features. In this way philosophy can fulfil its 'sole aim', according to Deleuze and Guattari: 'to become worthy of the event' (1994: 151/160). The future of such a research agenda will require not only an effort on the part of philosophers to create concepts that mobilise the insights gained in political struggles, but also an effort by militants themselves to deploy the insights of political philosophy where useful.

In the course of this book it may have appeared that there was an order or sequence to the strategies presented: first the diagnostic of power, then the intervention and transformation of this power, afterwards its establishment in a body politic, and finally its global or universal connection. But this is only the logical order presented in this book, not the existential coexistence in which these activities occur. Diagnosis, prefiguration, participation and solidarity often occur at the same time and to different degrees in revolutionary movements.

In addition, due to the focus of this book on non-representational revolutionary strategies, the reader may be wondering if there is any room for state politics at all in such a process. Has this book rejected wholesale the strengths and place of state politics within revolutionary struggles themselves? Absolutely not. Although I deal with this problem most directly in Chapters 1 and 2, as the second kind of political transformation (what Deleuze and Guattari call 'relative positive deterritorialisation'), it is true that many questions remain. Should revolutionary politics always and in all cases reject relative, partial or reformist transformations internal to the processes of representation (territory, state and capital)? Might even the smallest reforms, protests and desires play the role of catalysts in a larger process? Deterritorialisations are not necessarily good or bad; the question of revolution, however, is to what degree these crises, lines of flight or even reforms begin to take on an alternative and prefigurative consistency beyond the state. As such, the state itself may also play a role in this. Territory, state and capitalist processes can and do unleash potentials that should not be dismissed, but such potentials also need to take on a new consistency to become revolutionary. For example, Hugo Chavez, the current president of Venezuela, is currently trying to create a revolution by deterritorialising the state from the top down, while simultaneously creating a consistency of its fragments from the bottom up through directly democratic neighbourhood assemblies and workers' cooperatives. In Argentina unemployed workers have appropriated abandoned factories and created worker self-management within a global capitalist market. On their own these are not revolutions, but they are important processes of deterritorialisation that may contribute to and coalesce into one. As I argued in Chapter 1, there is no essentially privileged site of power or single place to begin a revolution. Thus what is required is a diversity of tactics on a diversity of fronts at the same time. This is true even if it includes the state and transitioning capitalist economies themselves.

III. Directions for Future Research

Among the four strategies proposed in this book, two are particularly fecund and require further development. The first is the strategy of creating a participatory body politic, proposed in Chapter 3. A participatory body politic is composed of three basic components: (1) the *conditions* under which it emerges and determines who counts as part of its body politic; (2) the distribution of concrete *elements* that express and constitute its body; and (3) the kinds of *subjects* who connect and transform these conditions and elements. What kind of social body are Deleuze, Guattari and the Zapatistas proposing to put in place of representational political processes? They propose the creation of a new revolutionary body politic based on the continual and mutual transformation of these three components.

What needs to be developed further in this strategy are the different dimensions under which this kind of reciprocal determination takes place. There are, for example, political relations, gender relations, economic relations, ecological relations and so on that need further elaboration appropriate to each domain. Chapter 3, however, was only able to develop this strategy in relation to the creation of a specifically political body. Further research into the concept of participation as an alternative to political representation and mere potentiality would thus require an analysis into the conditions, elements and agencies specific to these domains. For instance, the existence of a third-person form of political agency, according to Deleuze, Guattari and the Zapatistas, is not merely a human feature. This raises the question of what role ecological entities play in a directly democratic revolutionary body politic. For instance, how can ecological entities be included in political decision-making?

The second major strategy in this book that requires further development is that of global mutual solidarity. Chapter 3 argued that a post-representational revolutionary body politic is not only possible but theoretically and practically already under way. Chapter 4 argued that revolutionary body politics can share each other's struggles as their own and coordinate anti-capitalist actions on the global scale. However, this does not entirely answer the question of how decisions are to be made, implemented and modified at the global level among heterogeneous groups without creating a global state, party or process of representation. How is it that the largest organised gathering of anti-neoliberal forces in the world, the World Social Forum, can begin to make and enforce a meaningful transition away from global capitalism? Chapter 4 has laid out the philosophical and political tools for something like this to emerge, but it has not entirely been able to anticipate the next step. Further research into post-representational and anti-capitalist global governance needs to clarify and interrogate this question as it is currently happening at the World Social Forum and elsewhere. What are the theories and practices that are being proposed to turn this horizontal network into a federated decision-making body? In sum, the task of further research on the contemporary return to revolution must begin not with the mere affirmation of its potentiality, but with the concrete construction of its revolutionary actuality.

Bibliography

Agamben, Giorgio (1993), *The Coming Community*, trans. Michael Hardt, Minneapolis: University of Minnesota Press.

Agamben, Giorgio (1996), 'Unrepresentable Citizenship', in Paolo Virno and Michael Hardt (eds), *Radical Thought in Italy: A Potential Politics*, Minneapolis: University of Minnesota Press, pp. 159–66.

Agamben, Giorgio (2005), *State of Exception*, trans. Kevin Atell, Chicago: University of Chicago Press.

Ali, Tariq, Claudia Jardim and Jonah Gindin (2004), 'Naeem – Tariq Ali on Anti-neoliberalism in Latin America', *Green Left Weekly*, <http://www.16beavergroup.org/mtarchive/archives/001208print.html> (accessed 4 March 2011).

Alliez, Éric (2004), *The Signature of the World, or, What Is Deleuze and Guattari's Philosophy?*, trans. Eliot Ross Albert and Alberto Toscano, London: Continuum.

Alliez, Éric (2006), '*Anti-Oedipus* – Thirty Years On (Between Art and Politics)', trans. Alberto Toscano, in Martin Fuglsang and Bent Meier Sørensen (eds), *Deleuze and the Social*, Edinburgh: Edinburgh University Press, pp. 151–68.

Althusser, Louis (1994), *Sur la philosophie*, Paris: Gallimard.

Arendt, Hannah [1951] (1979), *The Origins of Totalitarianism*, New York: Harcourt, Brace & World.

Badiou, Alain (1985), *Peut-on penser la politique?*, Paris: Seuil.

Badiou, Alain (2000), *Deleuze: The Clamor of Being*, trans. Louise Burchill, Minneapolis: University of Minnesota Press.

Badiou, Alain (2004a), 'The Flux and the Party: In the Margins of *Anti-Oedipus*', *Polygraph: An International Journal of Culture & Politics*, 15/16, pp. 75–92.

Badiou, Alain (2004b), *Theoretical Writings*, ed. and trans. Ray Brassier and Alberto Toscano, London: Continuum.

Badiou, Alain (2005a), *Metapolitics*, London: Verso.

Badiou, Alain (2005b), *Being and Event*, trans. Oliver Feltham, London: Continuum.

Badiou, Alain (2008a), '"We Need a Popular Discipline": Contemporary Politics and the Crisis of the Negative', Interview by Filippo Del Lucchese and Jason Smith, *Critical Inquiry*, 34, pp. 645–59.

Badiou, Alain (2008b), *The Meaning of Sarkozy*, trans. David Fernbach, London: Verso.

Badiou, Alain (2009a), *Logics of Worlds: Being and Event II*, trans. Alberto Toscano, London: Continuum.

Badiou, Alain (2009b), 'Existe-t-il quelque chose comme une politique deleuzienne?', *Cités: Philosophie, Politique, Histoire*, 40, pp. 15–20.

Badiou, Alain (2010a), *The Communist Hypothesis*, trans. David Macey and Steve Corcoran, London: Verso.

Badiou, Alain (2010b), *La relation énigmatique entre philosophie et politique*, Meaux: Germina.

Badiou, Alain, and François Balmès (1976), *De l'idéologie*, Paris: F. Maspero.

Balibar, Etienne (2002), *Strangers as Enemies: Further Reflections on the Aporias of Transnational Citizenship*, MCRI Globalization and Autonomy.

Bell, Jeffrey A., and Claire Colebrook (eds) (2009), *Deleuze and History*, Edinburgh: Edinburgh University Press.

Bensaïd, Daniel (2004), 'Alain Badiou and the Miracle of the Event', in Peter Hallward (ed.), *Think Again: Alain Badiou and the Future of Philosophy*, London: Continuum, pp. 94–105.

Beressem, Hanjo (2009), 'Structural Couplings: Radical Constructivism and a Deleuzian Ecologics', in Bernd Herzogenrath (ed.), *Deleuze/Guattari and Ecology*, Basingstoke: Palgrave Macmillan, pp. 57–101.

Bonta, Mark, and John Protevi (eds) (2004), *Deleuze and Geophilosophy: A Guide and Glossary*, Edinburgh: Edinburgh University Press.

Boron, Atilio (1995), *State, Capitalism, and Democracy in Latin America*, Boulder: Rienner.

Boron, Atilio (2003), 'Poder, contra-poder y antipoder. Notas sobre un extravío teórico político en el pensamiento crítico contemporáneo', *Revista Chiapas*, 15, pp. 143–82.

Bosteels, Bruno (1998), 'From Text to Territory: Félix Guattari's Cartographies of the Unconscious', in Eleanor Kaufman and Jon Heller Kevin (eds), *Deleuze and Guattari: New Mappings in Politics, Philosophy, and Culture*, Minneapolis: University of Minnesota Press, pp. 145–74.

Bosteels, Bruno (2004), 'Logics of Antagonism: In the Margins of Alain Badiou's "The Flux and the Party"', *Polygraph: An International Journal of Culture & Politics*, 15/16, pp. 93–108.

Bosteels, Bruno (2005a), 'Post-Maoism: Badiou and Politics', *Positions: East Asia Cultures Critique*, 13 (3), pp. 575–634.

Bosteels, Bruno (2005b), 'The Speculative Left', *South Atlantic Quarterly*, 104 (4), pp. 751–67.

Boundas, Constantin V. (ed.) (2009), *Gilles Deleuze: The Intensive Reduction*, London: Continuum.

Buber, Martin (1958), *I and Thou*, trans. Ronald Gregor Smith, New York: Scribner.

Buchanan, Ian, and Nicholas Thoburn (eds) (2008), *Deleuze and Politics*, Edinburgh: Edinburgh University Press.

Burbach, Roger (1994), 'Roots of the Postmodern Rebellion in Chiapas', *New Left Review*, 205 (May/June 1994), pp. 113–24.

Burbach, Roger (1996), 'For a Zapatista Style Postmodernist Perspective', *Monthly Review*, 47 (March), pp. 4–41.

Burchill, Louise (2007), 'The Topology of Deleuze's Spatium', *Philosophy Today*, 51 (5), pp. 154–60.

Carrigan, Ana (1995), 'Chiapas: The First Post-Modern Revolution', *The Fletcher Forum*, 19 (1), pp. 71–98.

Casarino, Cesare, and Antonio Negri (2004), 'It's a Powerful Life: A Conversation on Contemporary Philosophy', *Cultural Critique*, 57, pp. 151–83.

Chatterton, Paul (2007), 'The Zapatista Caracoles and Good Governments: The Long Walk to Autonomy', *State of Nature* (Spring 2007), <http://www.stateofnature.org/theZapatistaCaracoles.html> (accessed 4 March 2011).

Curran, Giorel (2006), *21st Century Dissent: Anarchism, Anti-Globalization and Environmentalism*, Basingstoke: Palgrave Macmillan.

Deleuze, Gilles (1972), *Seminar Cours Vincennes 07/03/1972*, <http://www.webdeleuze.com/php/texte.php?cle=160&groupe=Anti%20Oedipe%20et%20Mille%20Plateaux&langue=1> (accessed 3 March 2011).

Deleuze, Gilles (1989), *Cinema-2: The Time-Image*, Minneapolis: University of Minnesota Press, trans. H. Tomlinson and R. Galeta from *Cinéma-2: L'Image-temps* (1986), Paris: Les Éditions de Minuit.

Deleuze, Gilles (1990), *The Logic of Sense*, New York: Columbia University Press, trans. M. Lester with C. Stivale from *Logique du sens* (1969), Paris: Éditions de Minuit.

Deleuze, Gilles (1994), *Difference and Repetition*, New York: Columbia University Press, trans. P. Patton from *Différence et répétition* (1968), Paris: Presses Universitaires de France.

Deleuze, Gilles (1995), *Negotiations 1972–1990*, New York: Columbia University Press, trans. M. Joughin from *Pourparlers 1972–1990* (1990), Paris: Les Éditions de Minuit.

Deleuze, Gilles (2004), *Desert Islands and Other Texts*, New York: Semiotext(e), trans. M. Taormina from *L'Île déserte et autres textes: textes et entretiens 1953–1974* (2002), Paris: Les Éditions de Minuit.

Deleuze, Gilles (2006), *Two Regimes of Madness*, New York: Semiotext(e), trans. A. Hodges and M. Taormina from *Deux régimes de fous: textes et entretiens 1975–1995* (2003), Paris: Les Éditions de Minuit.

Deleuze, Gilles, and Félix Guattari (1983), *Anti-Oedipus: Capitalism and Schizophrenia*, Minneapolis: University of Minnesota Press, trans. R.

Hurley, M. Seem and H. Lane from *Capitalisme et schizophrénie tome 1: L'Anti-Oedipe* (1972), Paris: Les Éditions de Minuit.

Deleuze, Gilles, and Félix Guattari (1987), *A Thousand Plateaus: Capitalism and Schizophrenia*, Minneapolis: University of Minnesota Press, trans. B. Massumi from *Capitalisme et schizophrénie tome 2: Mille plateaux* (1980), Paris: Les Éditions de Minuit.

Deleuze, Gilles, and Félix Guattari (1994), *What Is Philosophy?*, New York: Columbia University Press, trans. G. Burchell and H. Tomlinson from *Qu'est-ce que la philosophie?* (1991), Paris: Les Éditions de Minuit.

Deleuze, Gilles, and Claire Parnet (1987), *Dialogues*, New York: Columbia University Press, trans. H. Tomlinson and B. Habberjam from *Dialogues* (1977), Paris: Flammarion.

Derrida, Jacques (2001), *On Cosmopolitanism and Forgiveness*, trans. Mark Dooley and Michael Hughes, New York: Routledge.

Dewey, John (1906), 'Beliefs and Realities', *The Philosophical Review*, 15 (2), pp. 113–29.

Egyed, Bela (2006), 'Counter-actualisation and the Method of Intuition', in Constantin V. Boundas (ed.), *Deleuze and Philosophy*, Edinburgh: Edinburgh University Press, pp. 74–84.

Engler, Mark (2007), 'The Anti-Globalization Movement Defined', *The Encyclopedia of Activism and Social Justice*, <http://www.stwr.org/the-un-people-politics/the-anti-globalization-movement-defined.html> (accessed 4 March 2011).

Esteva, Gustavo (2001), 'The Traditions of People of Reason and the Reasons of People of Tradition: A Report on the Second Intercontinental Encuentro', in Midnight Notes Collective (ed.), *Auroras of the Zapatistas: Local and Global Struggles of the Fourth World War*, New York: Autonomedia, pp. 55–63.

Evans, Brad (2010), 'Life Resistance: Towards a Different Concept of the Political', *Deleuze Studies*, 4 (supplement), pp. 142–62.

EZLN (1994), 'Women's Revolutionary Law', in *¡Zapatistas!: Documents of the New Mexican Revolution*, New York: Autonomedia.

EZLN (2005), *Sixth Declaration of the Lacandón Jungle*, trans. irlandesa, <http://www.inmotionmagazine.com/auto/selva6.html> (accessed 4 March 2011).

Foucault, Michel (1977), *Language, Counter-Memory, Practice: Selected Essays and Interviews*, ed. Donald F. Bouchard, trans. Donald F. Bouchard and Sherry Simon, Ithaca: Cornell University Press.

Foucault, Michel (1980), *Power/Knowledge: Selected Interviews and Other Writings, 1972–1977*, ed. Colin Gordon, New York: Pantheon Books.

Foucault, Michel (1984), 'What Is Enlightenment?', in *The Foucault Reader*, ed. Paul Rabinow, New York: Pantheon Books, pp. 32–50.

Foucault, Michel (2007), *Security, Territory, Population: Lectures at the Collège de France, 1977–78*, ed. Michel Senellart, François Ewald and

Alessandro Fontana, trans. Graham Burchell, Basingstoke: Palgrave Macmillan.

Foucault, Michel (2008), *The Birth of Biopolitics: Lectures at the Collège de France, 1978–79*, ed. Michel Senellart, François Ewald and Alessandro Fontana, trans. Michel Senellart, Basingstoke: Palgrave Macmillan.

Fraser, Nancy (1989), *Unruly Practices: Power, Discourse, and Gender in Contemporary Social Theory*, Minneapolis: University of Minnesota Press.

Fuentes, Federico (2007), 'Subcomandante Marcos: Capitalism's "New War of Conquest"', *Green Left*, 705, <http://www.greenleft.org.au/node/37314> (accessed 4 March 2011).

Golden, Tim (1994), 'Rebels Determined "to Build Socialism in Mexico"', *New York Times*, 4 January 1994 (late ed.), A3.

Golden, Tim (2001), 'Revolution Rocks: Thoughts of Mexico's First Postmodern Guerrilla Commander', *New York Times Review of Books*, 8 April 2001, <http://www.nytimes.com/books/01/04/08/reviews/010408.08goldent.html> (accessed 3 March 2001).

Goodchild, Philip (1996), *Deleuze and Guattari: An Introduction to the Politics of Desire*, London: SAGE.

Graeber, David (2002), 'New Anarchists', *New Left Review*, 13 (January/February 2002), pp. 61–73.

Graeber, David (2011), 'Occupy Wall Street's Anarchist Roots', Aljazeera, 30 November 2011, <http://www.aljazeera.com/indepth/opinion/2011/11/2011112872835904508.html> (accessed 7 February 2012).

Grubacic, Andrej, and David Graeber (2004), 'Anarchism, or The Revolutionary Movement of the 21st Century', <http://makeworlds.net/node/84> (accessed 12 February 2012).

Guattari, Félix (1984), *Molecular Revolution: Psychiatry and Politics*, Harmondsworth: Penguin Books.

Guattari, Félix (1996), *Chaosophy: Soft Subversions*, ed. Sylvère Lotringer, New York: Semiotext(e).

Guattari, Félix (2008), *Molecular Revolution in Brazil*, ed. Suely Rolnik, trans. Karel Clapshow and Brian Holmes, Los Angeles: Semiotext(e).

Guattari, Félix, and Antonio Negri (1990), *Communists Like Us: New Spaces of Liberty, New Lines of Alliance*, New York: Semiotext(e).

Hallward, Peter (2003), *Badiou: A Subject to Truth*, Minneapolis: University of Minnesota Press.

Hallward, Peter (2006), *Out of This World: Deleuze and the Philosophy of Creation*, London: Verso.

Hardt, Michael, and Antonio Negri (2000), *Empire*, Cambridge, MA: Harvard University Press.

Hardt, Michael, and Antonio Negri (2004), *Multitude: War and Democracy in the Age of Empire*, New York: Penguin Books.

Hardt, Michael, and Antonio Negri (2010), *Commonwealth*, Cambridge, MA: Belknap Press of Harvard University Press.

Hardt, Michael, and Antonio Negri (2011), 'The Fight for "Real Democracy" at the Heart of Occupy Wall Street: The Encampment in Lower Manhattan Speaks to a Failure of Representation', *Foreign Affairs*, October 2011, <http://www.foreignaffairs.com/articles/136399/michael-hardt-and-antonio-negri/the-fight-for-real-democracy-at-the-heart-of-occ upy-wall-street?page=show> (accessed 4 February 2012).

Harvey, David (2010), 'Organizing for the Anti-Capitalist Transition', talk given at the World Social Forum 2010, Porto Alegre, <http://davidhar-vey.org/2009/12/organizing-for-the-anti-capitalist-transition> (accessed 4 March 2011).

Holland, Eugene (1991), 'Deterritorializing "Deterritorialization": From *Anti-Oedipus* to *A Thousand Plateaus*', *SubStance*, 20:3 (66), pp. 58–9.

Holland, Eugene (1998), 'From Schizophrenia to Social Control', in Eleanor Kaufman and Jon Heller Kevin (eds), *Deleuze and Guattari: New Mappings in Politics, Philosophy, and Culture*, Minneapolis: University of Minnesota Press, pp. 65–76.

Holland, Eugene (1999), *Deleuze and Guattari's Anti-Oedipus: Introduction to Schizoanalysis*, London: Routledge.

Holland, Eugene (2006), 'Nomad Citizenship and Global Democracy', in Martin Fuglsang and Bent Meier Sørensen (eds), *Deleuze and the Social*, Edinburgh: Edinburgh University Press, pp. 191–206.

Holloway, John (2002), *Change the World Without Taking Power: The Meaning of Revolution Today*, London: Pluto Press.

Holloway, John, and Eloína Peláez (eds) (1998), *Zapatista!: Reinventing Revolution in Mexico*, London: Pluto Press.

International Organization for Migration (2008), <http://www.iom.int/jahia/Jahia/about-migration/facts-and-figures/lang/en> (accessed 5 March 2011).

Johnston, Adrian (2007), 'The Quick and the Dead: Alain Badiou and the Split Speeds of Transformation', *International Journal of Žižek Studies*, 1 (2), pp. 56–84.

Katzenberger, Elaine (ed.) (1995), *First World, Ha Ha Ha!: The Zapatista Challenge*, San Francisco: City Lights Books.

Kersten, Axel (1997), 'Tourism and Regional Development in Mexico and Chiapas after NAFTA', *Planeta*, <http://www.planeta.com/planeta/97/0597lacandon2.html> (accessed 5 March 2011).

Khaldun, Ibn [1377] (1958), *The Muqaddimah: An Introduction to History*, trans. Franz Rosenthal, New York: Pantheon Books.

Khasnabish, Alex (2008), *Zapatismo Beyond Borders: New Imaginations of Political Possibility*, Toronto: University of Toronto Press.

Kingsnorth, Paul (2004), *One No, Many Yeses: A Journey to the Heart of the Global Resistance Movement*, London: Free Press.

Klein, Naomi (2011), 'Occupy Wall Street: The Most Important Thing in the World Now', *The Nation*, 6 October 2011, <http://www.thenation.

com/article/163844/occupy-wall-street-most-important-thing-world-now> (accessed 12 February 2012).

Lacoue-Labarthe, Philippe, and Jean-Luc Nancy (1997), *Retreating the Political*, ed. Simon Sparks, London: Routledge.

Laffey, Mark (2002), 'Retrieving the Imperial: Empire and International Relations', *Millennium*, 31 (1), p. 109.

Lampert, Jay (2006), *Deleuze and Guattari's Philosophy of History*, London: Continuum.

Land, Nick (1993), 'Making It with Death: Remarks on Thanatos and Desiring-Production', *Journal of the British Society for Phenomenology*, 24 (1), pp. 66–76.

Landa, Manuel de (2006), *A New Philosophy of Society: Assemblage Theory and Social Complexity*, New York: Continuum.

Laroche, Emmanuel (1949), *Histoire de la racine nem- en grec ancien (nem, nemesis, nomos, nomiz)*, Paris: Librairie C. Klincksieck.

Latour, Bruno (1999), *Pandora's Hope: Essays on the Reality of Science Studies*, Cambridge, MA: Harvard University Press.

Lazarus, Sylvain (1996), *Anthropologie du nom*, Paris: Seuil.

Levinas, Emmanuel (1979), *Totality and Infinity: An Essay on Exteriority*, trans. Alphonso Lingis, The Hague: M. Nijhoff Publishers.

Levinson, Sanford, and Yael Tamir (1995), 'Is Liberal Nationalism an Oxymoron? An Essay for Judith Shklar', *Ethics*, 105 (3), pp. 626–45.

Maccani, R. J. (2006), 'The Zapatistas: Enter the Intergalactic', *Upping the Anti: A Journal of Theory and Practice*, 3, pp. 105–22.

McCarthy, Thomas A. (1991), *Ideals and Illusions: On Reconstruction and Deconstruction in Contemporary Critical Theory*, Cambridge, MA: MIT Press.

Mackenzie, Iain M. (2008), 'What Is a Political Event?', *Theory & Event*, 11, p. 3.

McNaughton, Colm (2008), 'A Critique of John Holloway's *Change the World Without Taking Power*', *Capital & Class*, 32 (2), pp. 3–28.

Marcellus, Oliver de (2001), 'Peoples' Global Action: Dreaming up an Old Ghost', in Midnight Notes Collective (ed.), *Auroras of the Zapatistas: Local and Global Struggles of the Fourth World War*, New York: Autonomedia, pp. 105–17.

Marcellus, Oliver de (2003), 'Peoples' Global Action: The Grassroots Go Global', in Notes from Nowhere (ed.), *We Are Everywhere: The Irresistible Rise of Global Anti-Capitalism*, London: Verso, pp. 96–101.

Marchart, Oliver (2005), 'Nothing but a Truth: Alain Badiou's "Philosophy of Politics" and the Left Heideggerians', *Polygraph: An International Journal of Culture & Politics*, 17, pp. 119–20.

Marcos, Subcomandante (1994), 'In Our Dreams We Have Seen Another World', Zapatista Communiqué, March 1994.

Marcos, Subcomandante (1995), 'Durito: Neoliberalism the Chaotic Theory of Economic Chaos', trans. Peter Haney, <http://flag.blackened.net/revolt/mexico/ezln/marcos_durito_neolib_jul95.html> (accessed 4 March 2011).

Marcos, Subcomandante (2001a), 'Entrevista a Sub-Comandante Marcos', *El Historiador*, <http://www.elhistoriador.com.ar/entrevistas/m/marcos.php> (accessed 4 March 2011).

Marcos, Subcomandante (2001b), *Our Word Is Our Weapon: Selected Writings*, ed. Juana Ponce de Leon, New York: Seven Stories Press.

Marcos, Subcomandante (2001c), 'Punch Card and Hourglass', *New Left Review*, 9, pp. 69–80.

Marcos, Subcomandante (2004a), 'Reading a Video Part Two: Two Flaws', trans. irlandesa, <http://flag.blackened.net/revolt/mexico/ezln/2004/marcos/flawsAUG.html> (accessed 4 March 2011).

Marcos, Subcomandante (2004b), *Ya Basta!: Ten Years of the Zapatista Uprising*, ed. Žiga Vodovnik, Oakland: AK Press.

Marcos, Subcomandante (2006), *The Other Campaign/La Otra Campaña*, San Francisco: City Lights Books.

Marcos, Subcomandante (2009), quoted in 'The Dream of a Better World Is Back' by Alain Gresh, *Le Monde Diplomatique*, 8 May 2009, <http://www.middle-east-online.com/english/?id=31942> (accessed 12 February 2012).

Marcos, Subcomandante, and El Kilombo Intergalactico (2010), *Beyond Resistance: Everything – An Interview with Subcomandante Insurgente Marcos*, Cambridge, MA: South End Press.

Marcos, Subcomandante, and EZLN (2008), 'Communiqué from the Indigenous Revolutionary Clandestine Committee – General Command, of the Zapatista Army for National Liberation', 15 and 16 September 2008.

Maxwell, Kenneth, and Neil Harvey (1999), 'Review of *The Chiapas Rebellion: The Struggle for Land and Democracy*', *Foreign Affairs*, 1 March 1999, <http://www.foreignaffairs.com/articles/54737/kenneth-maxwell/the-chiapas-rebellion-the-struggle-for-land-and-democracy> (accessed 10 February 2012).

May, Todd (1997), *Reconsidering Difference: Nancy, Derrida, Levinas, and Deleuze*, University Park: Pennsylvania State University Press.

Mengue, Philippe (2003), *Deleuze et la question de la démocratie*, Paris: L'Harmattan.

Mengue, Philippe (2009), 'From First Sparks to Local Clashes: Which Politics Today?', in Constantin V. Boundas (ed.), *Gilles Deleuze: The Intensive Reduction*, London: Continuum, pp. 161–86.

Mentinis, Mihalis (2006), *Zapatistas: The Chiapas Revolt and What It Means for Radical Politics*, London: Pluto Press.

Miller, Christopher L. (1993), 'The Postidentitarian Predicament in the

Footnotes of *A Thousand Plateaus*: Nomadology, Anthropology, and Authority', *Diacritics*, 23 (3), pp. 6–35.

Mora, Mariana (1998), 'The EZLN and Indigenous Autonomous Municipalities', <http://flag.blackened.net/revolt/mexico/comment/auto_munc.html> (accessed 4 March 2011).

Neill, Monty (2001), 'Encounters in Chiapas', in Midnight Notes Collective (ed.), *Auroras of the Zapatistas: Local and Global Struggles of the Fourth World War*, New York: Autonomedia, pp. 45–53.

Notes from Nowhere (ed.) (2003), *We Are Everywhere: The Irresistible Rise of Global Anti-Capitalism*, London: Verso.

Nyers, Peter, and Kim Rygiel (eds) (2012), *Citizenship, Migrant Activism and the Politics of Movement*, London: Routledge.

O'Brien, Karen (2000), *Sacrificing the Forest: Environmental and Social Struggle in Chiapas*, New York: Westview Press.

Occupy Together (2011), <http://www.occupytogether.org> (accessed 7 February 2012).

Olesen, Thomas (2005), *International Zapatismo: The Construction of Solidarity in the Age of Globalization*, London: Zed Books.

Patton, Paul (2000), *Deleuze and the Political*, London: Routledge.

Patton, Paul (2006), 'Order, Exteriorities and Flat Multiplicities in the Social', in Martin Fuglsang and Bent Meier Sørensen (eds), *Deleuze and the Social*, Edinburgh: Edinburgh University Press, pp. 21–38.

Patton, Paul (2008), 'Becoming-Democratic', in Ian Buchanan and Nicholas Thoburn (eds), *Deleuze and Politics*, Edinburgh: Edinburgh University Press, pp. 178–95.

Patton, Paul (2009), 'Events, Becoming and History', in Jeffrey A. Bell and Claire Colebrook (eds), *Deleuze and History*, Edinburgh: Edinburgh University Press, pp. 33–53.

Pellejero, Eduardo (2010), 'Minor Marxism: An Approach to a New Political Praxis', *Deleuze Studies*, 3 (supplement), pp. 102–18.

Pleyers, Geoffrey, and Alain Touraine (2010), *Alter-Globalization: Becoming Actors in the Global Age*, Cambridge: Polity.

Prigogine, Ilya, and Isabelle Stengers (1997), *The End of Certainty: Time, Chaos, and the New Laws of Nature*, New York: Free Press.

Protevi, John (2006), Review of *Out of This World: Deleuze and the Philosophy of Creation* by Peter Hallward, *Notre Dame Philosophical Reviews*, <http://ndpr.nd.edu/review.cfm?id=10564> (accessed 7 February 2012).

Proyect, Louis (2003), 'Fetishizing the Zapatistas: A Critique of *Change the World Without Taking Power*', *Herramienta: debate y crítica marxista*, <http://www.herramienta.com.ar/debate-sobre-cambiar-el-mundo/fetishizing-zapatistas-critique-change-world-without-taking-power> (accessed 12 February 2012).

Ramírez, Gloria Muñoz (2008), *The Fire and the Word: A History of the*

Zapatista Movement, trans. Laura Carlsen and Alejandro Reyes Arias, San Francisco: City Lights Books.

Rancière, Jacques (2004), 'Who Is the Subject of the Rights of Man?', *South Atlantic Quarterly*, 103 (2/3), pp. 297–310.

Read, Jason (2008), 'The Age of Cynicism: Deleuze and Guattari on the Production of Subjectivity in Capitalism', in Ian Buchanan and Nicholas Thoburn (eds), *Deleuze and Politics*, Edinburgh: Edinburgh University Press, pp. 139–59.

Read, Jason (2009), 'The Fetish Is Always Actual, Revolution Is Always Virtual: From Noology to Noopolitics', *Deleuze Studies*, 3 (supplement), pp. 78–101.

Rodríguez, Alfredo Valadez (2011), 'The Indignados Offer Hope for Humanity: González Casanova', *La Jornada*, 17 October 2011, <http://www.jornada.unam.mx/2011/10/17/politica/014n1pol> (accessed 12 February 2012).

Ronfeldt, David F., John Arquilla, Graham Fuller and Melissa Fuller (1998), *The Zapatista 'Social Netwar' in Mexico*, Santa Monica: Rand.

Ross, John (1995), *Rebellion from the Roots: Indian Uprising in Chiapas*, Monroe: Common Courage Press.

Ross, John (2006), *¡Zapatistas!: Making Another World Possible: Chronicles of Resistance, 2000–2006*, New York: Nation Books.

Sauvagnargues, Anne (2010), *Deleuze: L'empirisme transcendantal*, Paris: Presses Universitaires de France.

Sellars, John (2007), 'Deleuze and Cosmopolitanism', *Radical Philosophy*, 142 (March/April 2007), pp. 30–7.

Sibertin-Blanc, Guillaume (2009), 'Politicising Deleuzian Thought, or, Minority's Position within Marxism', *Deleuze Studies*, 3 (supplement), pp. 119–37.

Smith, Dan (1998), 'The Place of Ethics in Deleuze's Philosophy: Three Questions of Immanence', in Eleanor Kaufman and Jon Heller Kevin (eds), *Deleuze and Guattari: New Mappings in Politics, Philosophy, and Culture*, Minneapolis: University of Minnesota Press, pp. 251–69.

Smith, Dan (2008), 'Deleuze and the Production of the New', in Simon O'Sullivan and Stephen Zepke (eds), *Deleuze, Guattari and the Production of the New*, London: Continuum, pp. 151–61.

Spivak, Gayatri Chakravorty (2010), 'Can the Subaltern Speak?', in Spivak and Rosalind C. Morris, *Can the Subaltern Speak?: Reflections on the History of an Idea*, New York: Columbia University Press.

Srnicek, Nick (2008), 'What Is to Be Done? Alain Badiou and the Pre-Evental', *Symposium: Canadian Journal of Continental Philosophy*, 12 (2), pp. 110–26.

Starr, A., M. E. Martinez-Torres and P. Rosset (2011), 'Participatory Democracy in Action: Practices of the Zapatistas and the Movimento Sem Terra', *Latin American Perspectives*, 38 (1), pp. 102–19.

Stivale, Charles J. (1998), *The Two-Fold Thought of Deleuze and Guattari: Intersections and Animations*, New York: Guilford Press.

Stivale, Charles J. (trans.) (2004), '"D" is for Desire', in *L'Abécédaire de Gilles Deleuze, avec Claire Parnet*, directed by Pierre-André Boutang in 1996, <http://www.langlab.wayne.edu/Cstivale/D-G/ABC1.html> (accessed 4 March 2011).

Thoburn, Nick (2009), 'Weatherman, the Militant Diagram, and the Problem of Political Passion', *New Formations*, 68, pp. 125–42.

Thompson, A. K. (2010), *Black Bloc, White Riot: Anti-Globalization and the Genealogy of Dissent*, Edinburgh: AK Press.

Tormey, Simon (2006), '"Not in My Name": Deleuze, Zapatismo and the Critique of Representation', *Parliamentary Affairs*, 59 (1), pp. 138–54.

Toscano, Alberto (2004), 'From the State to the World? Badiou and Anti-Capitalism', *Communication & Cognition*, 37 (3 & 4), pp. 199–224.

Toscano, Alberto (2006), *The Theatre of Production: Philosophy and Individuation between Kant and Deleuze*, Basingstoke: Palgrave Macmillan.

United Nations Department of Economic and Social Affairs (2008), 'United Nations' Trends in Total Migrant Stock', <http://esa.un.org/migration> (accessed 4 March 2011).

Virilio, Paul (1993), *L'Insécurité du territoire*, Paris: Galilée.

Virno, Paolo (2003), *A Grammar of the Multitude: For an Analysis of Contemporary Forms of Life*, Cambridge: Semiotext(e).

Walker, Simon (2005), 'Oventic Boot Cooperative Exports Boots to Canada', *Casa Collectiva*, <http://www.casacollective.org/story/news/oventic-boot-cooperative-exports-boots-canada> (accessed 4 March 2011).

Waterman, Peter (1998), *Globalization, Social Movements, and the New Internationalisms*, Washington: Mansell.

World Social Forum (2001), *Charter of Principles*, <http://www.wsfindia.org/?q=node/3> (accessed 4 March 2011).

Yakubu, Owusu (2000), 'A Commune in Chiapas? Mexico and the Zapatista Rebellion, 1994–2000', *Aufheben*, 9, <http://libcom.org/library/commune-chiapas-zapatista-mexico> (accessed 8 February 2012).

The Zapatistas (1998), *Zapatista Encuentro: Documents from the 1996 Encounter for Humanity and against Neoliberalism*, New York: Seven Stories Press.

Žižek, Slavoj (1997), 'Multiculturalism, or, The Cultural Logic of Multinational Capitalism', *New Left Review*, 225, pp. 28–51.

Žižek, Slavoj (2004), *Organs Without Bodies: Deleuze and Consequences*, New York: Routledge.

Žižek, Slavoj (2011), 'Slavoj Žižek speaks at Occupy Wall Street: Transcript', transcribed by Sarahana, *Impose*, <http://www.imposemagazine.

com/bytes/slavoj-zizek-at-occupy-wall-street-transcript> (accessed 12 February 2011).

Žižek, Slavoj, and Costas Douzinas (eds) (2010), *The Idea of Communism*, London: Verso.

Zourabichvili, François (1996), *Deleuze, une philosophie de l'événement*, Paris: Presses Universitaires de France.

Index